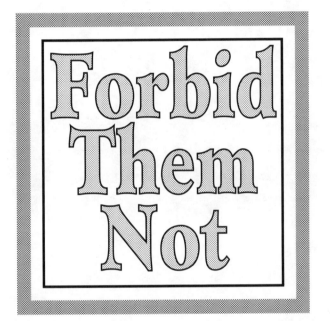

Involving Children in Sunday Worship

Based on the Revised Common Lectionary, Year A

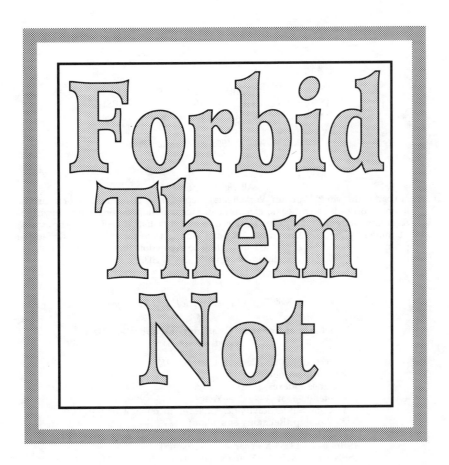

Carolyn C. Brown

Abingdon Press
Nashville

FORBID THEM NOT:
INVOLVING CHILDREN IN SUNDAY WORSHIP
Based on the Revised Common Lectionary, Year A

Copyright © 1992 by Abingdon Press

This book is printed on recycled, acid-free paper.

Library of Congress Cataloging-in-Publication Data
(Revised for vol. 1)

Brown, Carolyn C. (Carolyn Carter), 1947–
  Forbid them not.
  Includes indexes.
  Contents: Year A—   —Year C.
  1. Common lectionary. 2. Children in public worship.
  3. Worship (Religious education)
BV26.2.B76   1991   264'.0083   90-45012
ISBN 0-687-13255-X (Year A : alk. paper)
ISBN 0-687-13254-1 (Year C : alk. paper)

Scripture references from the Good News Bible—Old Testament are Copyright © American Bible Society 1976; New Testament, Copyright © American Bible Society 1966, 1971, 1976. Reprinted by permission.

Those from The New Jerusalem Bible are copyright © 1985 by Darton, Longman & Todd and Doubleday & Co., Inc. Reprinted by permission of the publishers.

Those from the New Revised Standard Version of the Bible are copyright © 1989, by the Division of Christian Education of the National Council of the Churches of Christ in the United States of America. Reprinted by permission.

MANUFACTURED IN THE UNITED STATES OF AMERICA

CONTENTS

*This is one volume in a three-volume series. Each volume contains worship material for lectionary cycle A, B, or C. Since the lections for a few special days do not change from one lectionary cycle to another, material for each of these days appears in only one of the three volumes. Appropriate cross references in the table of contents lead the reader to material in other volumes of the series.

WHAT IS IN THIS BOOK, AND HOW CAN I USE IT?

There seem to be two opposing camps when it comes to children's participation in congregational worship. On one side are those who say that worship is really for adults—that children should be taught to behave until they appreciate what is going on, or that they (and their parents) should be relieved by the provision of a children's church or other activity during the worship hour. On the other side are those who say that the congregation's worship should be reworked entirely, to make it appealing to children. Proponents of this side claim that once adults loosen up and begin to worship as children worship, they will not miss the staid old adult-oriented forms.

This book carves out a middle ground, based on the convictions that

• children *do* belong in the sanctuary, worshiping with God's people; that

• worship planners are responsible for creating worship experiences that are meaningful to all who come to the sanctuary, including children, youths, and adults (this does not require that all worshipers find all parts of worship equally meaningful, but that each worshiper has some appreciation for the whole, and special appreciation for certain parts within the whole); and that

• children can worship meaningfully, using traditional forms, *if* they are learning the meaning of those forms, and *if* the forms include content that reflects *their* lives and concerns as well as those of adults.

This book is written for worship leaders who share these views and want to be responsive to the elementary-school-aged children in worship, but who are uncertain about how to do this effectively and do not have large amounts of time to develop their skills in this area. It is written for those whose consciousness has been raised by books that advocate the inclusion of children in congregational worship, but who are at a loss for "what to do this Sunday." You will find specific suggestions for prayers, litanies, sermon illustrations, and ways to present Scripture that will include children without offending adults. Although the texts are based on the Revised Common Lectionary, those who do not follow that lectionary can use the index on page 204 to locate suggestions related to any Scripture passages.

This book can be used by the pastor who plans worship alone, by a staff team, by a liturgical team which includes both clergy and laity, or by a worship committee. It is a reference to be used with commentaries and liturgical resources in preparing a service for each Sunday. As you gain confidence and insight into what is meaningful for the children in your congregation, the ideas here should become springboards to other ideas and to home-grown prayers, litanies, and so on.

Materials for each Sunday include:

From a Child's Point of View, a commentary on each of the readings for the day. The main ideas of each passage are expressed in children's terms and connected to children's concerns. On Sundays when there is a reading that is best for children, that reading is presented first. When there is no central theme or focal reading, the texts are presented in lectionary order.

Watch Words offers vocabulary helps, warning against the use of words that are beyond the understanding of elementary children or that are easily misunderstood by them; it suggests words that speak clearly to worshipers of all ages.

Let the Children Sing suggests several hymns (chosen from church hymnals) related to the Scripture themes, and which children can sing—at least in part. The assumption here is not that every hymn sung in worship ought to be child-accessible, but that one or two each week could be. These hymns have been chosen because they have concrete language, themes to which children respond, or tunes that are easily sung. Some have been included because of the repetition of a word, phrase, or chorus which even a nonreader can sing each time it appears e.g., the Alleluias in "Christ the Lord Is Risen Today."

The Liturgical Child outlines a variety of ways to use the passages in worship to bring them alive for children (and for adults). Specific directions for dramatic readings, litanies, and congregational readings are given for some passages. Children's prayer concerns related to the theme or time of year are listed for inclusion in the congregation's prayers. In addition, possibilities are raised for relating other parts of the worship service to the day's theme for children. No worship planner will use every idea offered for every week, but can select several that will fit the worship experience planned for the congregation.

Sermon Resources are offered in the belief that children do listen to at least parts of sermons and can learn from those parts. These resources are offered to be included in the "real" sermon rather than in a segregated children's sermon. The assumption is that if we communicate to children that the sermon is for them too, they will learn to listen to more and more of it as their attention span for verbal messages grows. This section includes potential sermon illustrations and stories that will catch the attention of children and also will speak to adults, based on their childhood experiences. Occasional sermon-related assignments for children to do during the sermon also will be found here.

Finally, for each week there is a one-page **Worship Worksheet**—a sheet of games, puzzles, or questions related to the day's passages. Just as children often work on projects (even homework) while they watch TV, they are often more apt to listen to a sermon if they have something to do with their hands.

When the minister expresses interest in the worksheets as the children leave the sanctuary, posts the sheets on a bulletin board in the narthex, or refers to them during the sermon, children can see that this activity is one way they can participate in worship. Both parents and children will realize that the Worship Worksheets are not just a clever attempt to keep children quiet so that the adults can worship.

The purchase of this book gives you permission to reproduce these Worship Worksheets for your children each week. Look carefully at each worksheet before reproducing it. Some, especially those for Propers in which the readings do not share one central theme, offer two half-page activities related to separate themes. Choose the activity that goes with your worship theme and enlarge it to full-page size on a copy machine. Then reproduce that page for the children. Unless they are enlarged, the half-page activities may not provide enough space for children to work.

The Worship Worksheets can be distributed by ushers as children enter the sanctuary, left in a designated place for the children for parents to pick up, or they can be put into worship kits.

A worship kit could be a large paper envelope or sealable plastic bag containing the Sunday bulletin, the Worship Worksheet, a small pencil, and bookmarks for marking the hymns and readings for the morning. Bookmarks can be made of strips of poster board decorated with appropriate stickers. To emphasize the church year, poster board of liturgically correct colors could be used. An older children's class, a group of teenagers, or an adult may be willing to prepare such bookmarks as a contribution to the congregation's worship life. Children can be asked to leave the bookmarks and pencils in the envelopes, and the envelopes can be placed on their seats to be picked up for use the next week.

Note: In some congregations the Worship Worksheets may be difficult to reproduce. Worship leaders in such congregations may focus their efforts on other suggestions.

FIRST SUNDAY OF ADVENT

From a Child's Point of View

Old Testament: Isaiah 2:1-5. On television and in newspaper photographs, children see the gruesome results and reality of wars and struggles between ethnic groups. Though children cannot cite names and details of the conflicts, they often feel deeply for the victims in the pictures and may fear such experiences for themselves. In their own community, they may observe or even participate in ethnic conflict. At the very least, they hear racial/ethnic jokes and slurs. All this makes welcome news of Isaiah's promise that one day all nations and groups will live together peacefully.

Because children think concretely until about the age of twelve, they take Isaiah's word picture in verse 2 literally, and thus see little Mount Zion magically rise until it towers over the Himalayas. So either explain Isaiah's coded message or focus attention on the verses that follow.

Psalm: 122. A pilgrim song praising Jerusalem as the spiritual/political capital of "my people" is hard for non-Jewish Christians of any age to join in singing today. Symbolic thinkers can equate Jerusalem with the heart, or center, of God's people, wherever they may be. But children do not think symbolically, so this psalm seems strange.

Gospel: Matthew 24:36-44. Apocalyptic passages are generally difficult for children to interpret. This one, however, offers a clear, easy-to-understand warning ("Watch out, because you do not know on what day your Lord will come!"), with a familiar example of what happens when a warning is ignored (those who died in "Noah's flood").

Although the aim in the cited examples (those killed in the flood and the victim of the thief) is to avoid judgment or danger, remember that our watchfulness also enables us to be ready for good things (God's coming).

Epistle: Romans 13:11-14. Although the apocalyptic language in this passage is all but impossible for children to interpret, the message makes quick sense to children when it is linked to the Gospel lesson for the day: Because we know that God is coming among us, we should follow God's teachings. Choose your translation carefully, paying special attention to the list of sinful activities to be avoided. The Good News Bible is especially clear.

"Drunkenness" and "indecency" are no longer strictly adult sins. Fifth- and sixth-graders are especially vulnerable. Many drug and alcohol abusers tell about first experiences at the age of eleven or twelve. General "immorality" needs to be made specific by reference to the Ten Commandments. "Fighting" and "jealousy" are chronic at all ages; examples from family and neighborhood life abound.

Watch Words

Plowshares, pruning hooks, and *sickles* are not familiar tools today. You will need to describe them before children can understand Isaiah's prophecy.

Tell the children that *Son of man* in Matthew is simply another name for *Jesus.*

Avoid words such as *debauchery, licentiousness,* and *reveling.* Instead, talk about drug and alcohol abuse, fighting, greed, jealousy, and breaking rules to get your own way.

Let the Children Sing

"O Come, O Come, Emmanuel" is an Advent hymn with abstract language unfamiliar to children, but with music that offers sad verses, followed by a happy promise in the chorus. The verse that begins "O come, Desire of nations bind all peoples" is a prayer for world peace. Point this out before the congregation sings the hymn. Paraphrase the prayer in the verse and the promise in the chorus in simple, concrete words. Encourage children to sing that verse, even if they cannot sing the others.

With urging, even nonreading children can join in on the repeated opening lines of the verses in "Christ for the World We Sing." Much of the poetic language of the rest of the hymn is hard for children to read and interpret.

Older children can follow the music and message of "In Christ There Is No East or West," especially if it is sung frequently in your congregation.

The Liturgical Child

1. To emphasize God's presence with us both in worship and in our daily life, sing, or have a choir or older children's class, sing "Let All Mortal Flesh Keep Silence" both before the call to worship and before the benediction.

Call to Worship: God comes to be with us when we worship. Let us sing, and listen, and pray in God's presence.

Charge and Benediction: God is coming into our world. Pay attention! Be ready! Live as God's people! And God's peace will be with you, and it will spread out until it includes the whole world! Amen.

2. Many children learn "Dona Nobis Pacem," a prayer for peace, at church school or camp. To use it in worship today:

● Invite a children's class or choir to sing the round as the first candle of the Advent wreath is lighted. Introduce the candle as the candle of God's promised peace.

● Invite the congregation to sing the basic melody as a response to each of a series of short prayers for peace in our families, our community, and the world.

Note: The candles of the Advent wreath do not have any set meanings; this opens up the possibility of linking them to the texts of the day. This year's texts suggest a series of God's promises, beginning with God's peace.

3. After reading the implications of Paul's instructions in Romans 13:11-14, reread it as the Charge, reminding the worshipers that Paul was speaking to each of us.

Sermon Resources

1. Create modern paraphrases of Isaiah's weapons-to-tools prophecy. For example, tanks could be turned into tractors, and aircraft carriers could be refitted as floating sport camps or cruise ships. What are the possibilities for missiles, machine guns, hand grenades and so forth? (The Worship Worksheet challenges children to draw these conversions.)

2. To explore the importance of watching and being ready, tell stories:

● Tell three parallel stories about what children, youths, and adults did the day before the flood; the day Jesus was born in Bethlehem; and a "normal" day today. Include in each story examples of people who are being watchful, as Paul instructed, and others who are not.

● Tell a story about a child who stayed at a friend's house long past time to return home and missed sharing a treat brought by a neighbor. (This story sets up a situation in which we are urged to do right—not to avoid punishment, but to avoid missing out on something desirable. Paul was not as concerned that the Romans would be punished if not prepared as that they would miss out on sharing in the joy of God's presence and peace.)

● Describe preparations for the visit of a much-loved out-of-town relative. Mention house cleaning, planning meals and activities that person would enjoy, thinking of things you want to share with them and ask them. Then talk about preparing for God's presence. Describe "cleaning" the jealousy and quarreling out of our families and "cleaning" racial jokes and names out of our mouths, because God has promised to bring peace to all the people of the world. Explore some of Paul's other instructions in a similar way.

Listen carefully when **Isaiah 2 :1-5** is read.

Isaiah promised that one day God will bring peace for the whole world.

People will be able to bend their swords into ploughs for farming.

In this box, draw a weapon.

In this box, turn the weapon into a tool. (A tank could become a bulldozer.)

First Sunday of Advent/ © 1992 by Abingdon Press.

SECOND SUNDAY OF ADVENT

From a Child's Point of View

Old Testament: Isaiah 11:1-10. Because they are so dependent on their leaders, children are very appreciative of those who are fair. A teacher who grades fairly, a coach who gives everyone a chance, or a Scout leader who does not play favorites is highly valued. Having had experience with leaders who are less than fair, children appreciate the fair ones and claim God's promise of a totally fair leader.

A sprout growing out of a stump is not common enough in nature to assume that children (or urban adults) will be familiar with the phenomenon. It will need to be scientifically explained before children will understand Isaiah's message. Older children, once they understand the Jesse tree, often find great hope in it for all the seemingly hopeless situations in their lives and world.

Psalm: 72:1-7, 18-19. This psalm praises two leaders: Solomon (and his son); and God's messiah. Children begin to understand the psalm when they hear it as a public prayer for King Solomon, and they can add their prayers for their own leaders. Then they are primed to think about God's promised leader, who is more fair than even the most just human leaders.

Epistle: Romans 15:4-13. One example of God's justice is that God kept the promise that Jesus would come to the Jewish people. (Keeping promises is part of God's justice.) But Jesus kept the promise for everyone else. God's justice is for everyone, so God wants us to work on getting along with all people. For Paul, that meant spending his life introducing the Christian faith to non-Jews and trying to help Jews and Gentiles get along. For children today, it means treating everyone—people of other ethnic, economic, or neighborhood groups; and even people they do not like—with love and respect.

Because this is a complex passage, few children will make any sense of the text as it is read. Plan to present its message to children through the sermon.

Gospel: Matthew 3:1-12. Children are fascinated by the colorful aspects of John the Baptist. They need to hear that John wore animal skins and ate locusts (grasshoppers) and honey because they were easy to find. John was too busy telling people about God's justice to spend time cooking or finding neat clothes. Compare his dedication to that of athletes preparing for the Olympics, or a person who is so busy making a gift for a friend that she forgets to eat.

John's poetic images (Abraham's children, axes laid to trees, sandals to be carried, winnowing forks, chaff burning in unquenchable fires) are too much to explain in one worship service. So simply present John's message in words children understand—that God does not care whether your families are rich or poor, whether your brothers and sisters are smart and attractive or embarrassing, whether your friends are the "in" group or "nerds," or which church you go to. God cares about what *you* do. God expects *you* to live by God's rules or to repent (change your ways).

12

Watch Words

Children use *fairness* instead of justice. *Fairness* is often applied to everyday situations, while *justice* seems removed from everyday concerns. Use the terms interchangeably and often, to help children recognize their connection.

Define *repent* if you use it. John does not want us to be sorry for the unjust things we do. He wants us to stop treating people "unfairly" or "unjustly."

Avoid *Gentile*. Speak instead of God's justice, which includes all people. Name specific, familiar groups that are treated today as Gentiles were treated in Paul's day.

Let the Children Sing

"Hail to the Lord's Anointed" is based on Psalm 72. Older children can match the verses in the psalm with those in the hymn, but the vocabulary of the hymn is challenging, even for twelve-year-olds.

"Lord, I Want to Be a Christian" is the easiest hymn with which children can sing their repentance.

The Liturgical Child

1. In the worship center, display a Jesse tree. Ask a creative person to make an arrangement in which an evergreen branch is drilled into a small stump, or a pot covered with burlap to look like a stump. Or wrap a sand-filled bucket with brown craft paper to look like a stump, and "plant" a small tree or evergreen branch in the bucket.

2. While lighting the candle of God's promised justice as the second candle of the Advent wreath, read Isaiah's prophecy, or some statement such as this:

> We all want to be treated fairly. God has promised that one day we will be. Last week we lighted the first candle of Advent, for God's promised peace. Today we light the second candle, for God's promised justice. We light it for all the little kids who are picked on, for those whose poverty means they never get a fair chance at anything, and for those who live in countries ruled by unfair people and laws. God promises that day there will be justice for us all.

3. Invite the congregation to read Psalm 72 as if they were in a crowd, shouting to a king they hope will be a just leader. Divide the congregation in half and ask the people to read the verses alternately, loudly and enthusiastically.

4. If you pray for just leaders, include children's leaders—teachers, coaches, and club leaders.

5. Create a litany prayer of petitions, to each of which the congregational response is, "Thy Kingdom come. Thy will be done on earth as it is in heaven."

Sermon Resources

1. Explore Old Testament stories about our longing for, and failure to attain, justice. As each story is told, add a poster board ornament to your Jesse tree (Or ask a child to add the ornament). Consider the following ornaments/stories:

● Adam and Eve begin the human failure to live by God's rules (an apple with a bite out of it).
● Through Moses, God gave us a clear set of rules for just living. But God's people immediately and repeatedly proved that knowing the rules does not give us the power to create a just world (Ten Commandment tablets).
● David and Solomon tried to build a just nation. Though they did well, neither was perfectly just, and the kings who ruled after them were often miserable failures. No human can establish God's justice (star of David, or crown).
● Knowing that we could neither follow just rules nor build a just world on our own, God promised to establish the justice. God would send a Messiah. Describe how Jesus inaugurated this justice in his ministry, death, and resurrection (cross and crown).

2. Invite children and other worshipers to create new pairings of animals who will get along. Such pairings lead to joining usually uncooperative human groups.

3. Paraphrase Paul's encouragement to Jews and Gentiles to get along. Address it to different groups that do not treat one another well today. Consider including older and younger brothers and sisters, rival school groups, even "the boys" and "the girls." Such a paraphrase might be repeated as the Charge and Benediction.

4. Open a sermon on justice with the cry, "But it's not fair!" followed by examples ranging from a child whose friends are going to a movie while she must visit a sick aunt with her family, to a poor athlete who tries hard but never gets the good results of a gifted athlete who hardly seems to try at all, to people who live under oppressive governments and social systems.

In the box below, draw a picture of something that is not fair.

IT'S NOT FAIR !

Draw the picture again in this box, so that it *is* fair.

THAT IS BETTER !

Write a prayer about the people in your pictures.

THIRD SUNDAY OF ADVENT

From a Child's Point of View

Old Testament: Isaiah 35:1-10. This poetic prophecy makes most sense to children when set in its historic context. They need to know that the people who first heard this had been led in chains across a hot, dry desert, to live as conquered people in a foreign land. Isaiah is telling them that God will one day rescue them and lead them home. The poem is the answer to their request, "Tell us what it will be like when God rescues us." The answer is that even the weak and those with handicaps will walk, singing and dancing and in complete safety, across a blooming desert to God's city. Older children can begin to understand that just as God promised to rescue those people, God promises that one day all of us who have handicaps will be healed, the desert will bloom, and we will all live safely and happily together.

Psalm: 146:5-10 or Luke 1:47-55. Both these texts are happy lists of things God does. The psalm tells us what kinds of things God is interested in and working on. The activities are concrete and everyday, and children will understand most of them as they are read. Do explain unfamiliar phrases: "execute justice" means to provide justice; all "those who have fallen," "those who are bowed down," and "the bent" are lame; "sojourners" are not just any travelers, but the outsiders who live among us.

The Magnificat is Mary's list of the wonderful things God is doing in Jesus. It is readily understood by children, particularly when read from the Good News Bible. Children accept and appreciate Mary's delight at being chosen by God,

but are as disconcerted as their elders by her celebration of the downfall of the "haves." That may make the psalm the better choice today. See the Fourth Sunday of Advent (Year C) for further explanation and ideas for using the Magnificat.

Gospel: Matthew 11:2-11. When John the Baptist wanted to know if Jesus was God's promised leader, Jesus listed what he was doing. His activities matched God's promises. When this answer is read with the Old Testament texts of the day, children quickly see the comparison and realize that Jesus was saying to John, "I am what I do. And I am doing the work of the Messiah."

The details of Jesus' great compliment to John in verses 7-11 make it hard for children to understand. Since children gain little from understanding the compliment, it is not worth the effort to explain the details. Until they are older, it is enough to know that Jesus said that John was the greatest prophet ever.

Epistle: James 5:7-10. This passage about patience is mainly for adults and those children who have personal, direct need of God's healing and rescue. Most other children do not have the sense of urgency that God should keep the promises about healing which makes patience necessary.

Warning against possible misinterpretation: As children grow increasingly impatient for Christmas, this passage, taken out of context of the other readings, can be misunderstood by children as yet another insistence on patience and good behavior. "The Judge who waits at the door" sounds a lot like Santa Claus.

Watch Words

If you use the term *Magnificat*, explain its source and meaning.

Let the Children Sing

"Come, Thou Long-expected Jesus" describes the activities of Jesus in ways that parallel today's texts, but the language is foreign to children. To help them learn this hymn and to call adult worshipers' attention to its meaning, put one or two verses into familiar words and illustrate their meaning with local examples.

Sing the Canadian Indian version of the Christmas story, " 'Twas in the Moon of Wintertime," to highlight the story from the perspective of those who often are unwelcome even in their own land. If the congregation does not respond to new hymns, ask a choir or children's class to share this as an anthem.

The Liturgical Child

1. Light the third candle of the Advent wreath for God's promise of healing and happiness. Read Isaiah 35, or the following:

> We lighted the first candle of the Advent wreath for God's promise of peace. We lighted the second candle for God's promise of justice. Today we light the third candle, for God's promise of healing and happiness. All people everywhere want to be healthy, safe, and happy. As we light it, we remember those who are sick and need God's physical healing; those who are unwelcome where they must live, and work, and go to school; and those for whom life is filled with danger. God has promised that one day, all of us will dance and sing happily together.

2. Invite five readers (perhaps older children or youths) to read Isaiah 35 in topical sections, as if they were Isaiah, announcing God's promises to captured people. Practice with readers for clear, enthusiastic readings.

Reader 1:	verses 1-2	(Nature will bloom.)
Reader 2:	verses 3-4	(Tell the weak and frightened that God is coming.)
Reader 3:	verses 5-6*a*	(Those with handicaps will be healed.)
Reader 4:	verses 6*b*-7	(The desert will bloom.)
Reader 5:	verses 8-10	(On God's Way—no hurt at all.)

The congregation responds to these promises by reading Psalm 146:5-10 in unison. The New Revised Standard Version offers an inclusive translation in which many lines begin: "The Lord." Young readers will be able to follow along if these lines are printed one below the other, emphasizing the shared first words.

3. Use Psalm 146:7-10 as an outline for prayer. Read each description of what the Lord does, then pray for people in need of that help, and/or the work of the church in that area. For example:

The Lord lifts those who are bowed down.

> O Lord, we remember this morning those who cannot walk. We remember those who have suffered diseases and accidents that left them in wheelchairs. We remember the children in war zones whose legs have been blown off by land mines. And we remember those whose bones no longer support them in their old age. Help us find ways to join you in lifting them up. Be with the doctors who seek cures and rehabilitation. Be with those who support the lame in living full lives in spite of handicaps. Be with those who wait patiently for your promise that one day we will all dance together in your kingdom.

One person can lead this prayer; or two people can lead, one reading the lines of the psalm, the other responding with related prayers.

Sermon Resources

1. When John's disciples asked Jesus who he was, he told them to look at what he did. Challenge worshipers of all ages to consider how what they do says who they are. To spur their thinking, describe a day in the life of a household of people of different ages, doing as Jesus did: children befriend the lonely, teens and adults are involved in volunteer work, and all look out for one another. A similar story could be told about a week in the life of your congregation. Stress the possibilities for working with God to make the Advent promises come true.

2. Point out the serpent on a Tau Cross chrismon ornament. Briefly, tell the story of God's healing people bitten by snakes. Compare this symbol to the medical symbol. (Have a poster or plaque with the medical symbol on it. A physician in the congregation may have one to loan.) Explore the church's healing ministry as sharing in God's Advent work.

17

Listen carefully when **Matthew 11 :2-11** is read.

John the Baptist asked Jesus if he was the Messiah. Jesus told John to look at what he did to see if he was acting like the Messiah.

Draw or write about things you do that show that you are a follower of Jesus.

(*your name*) _____ is a follower of Jesus.

FOURTH SUNDAY OF ADVENT

From a Child's Point of View

Gospel: Matthew 1:18-25. Today's soap-opera-watching, worldly wise children can appreciate Joseph's dilemma, if the language about conception is rephrased into plain talk about pregnancy (i.e., after they were engaged, Joseph found out that Mary was pregnant; this was a problem because you are not supposed to be pregnant before you are married). Details about Jewish betrothal practices will interest older children and will add both to their understanding of the corner Joseph was in, and to their appreciation for his brave response to the angel's message. Boys, especially, benefit from exploring Joseph's important supportive role in the Christmas stories.

Elementary-school-age children are not mentally ready to enter the debates about the virgin birth. For them, it is amazing, but acceptable, that God chose to "be with us" by being born as a baby and living among us. Only after they develop the ability for abstract thought will the questions about the virgin birth make sense.

Epistle: Romans 1:1-7. Children will not understand this passage as it is read. It helps to introduce the literary form—that is, the greeting from the letter of introduction which announces Paul's visit to the Roman Christians. The complex sentences and ideas in this passage should be paraphrased. For example:

> From Paul to the Christians in Rome: Let me introduce myself. I am a slave of Jesus Christ. God loves me, even though I do not deserve it. And God has given me a job to do. I am to tell the good news about Jesus to people everywhere and help them live as disciples. I plan to come to Rome to share God's good news with you soon. So in advance, I send you God's loving grace and peace.

Like Joseph, Paul knew that God was with him, loved him, and had given him important work to do. The "Emmanuel promise" is that God is also with us and working through us.

Old Testament: Isaiah 7:10-16. This passage presents images and vocabulary problems which scholars debate, so it is not surprising that children can make little sense of the passage as it is read. It does, however, offer children two important truths that will need to be dug out of the text during the sermon.

First, children can hear, with the frightened King Ahaz, that God is with us always—even when two strong kings (or neighborhood bullies or older siblings) are plotting against us. God will be with us when we are facing all sorts of difficult situations, and God will still be with us after even the worst situations have been resolved.

Second, they can hear the promise of a special Son whose name will be Emmanuel, because he will indeed be "God with us," and they can add the word *Emmanuel* to their vocabulary.

Psalm: 80:1-7, 17-19. This prayer for deliverance is included among today's readings because of its reference to Joseph. Unfortunately, that reference, and most of the other images of this psalm, assume detailed knowledge of the Temple and Jewish tribes. Children, therefore, will make little sense of it. This one is for biblical scholars.

19

Watch Words

Use *Emmanuel* and *God with us* frequently and interchangeably. Avoid *incarnation*, a long, strange theological word which means the same thing.

Avoid *conception*, "that which was conceived in her," and Mary's *virginity*. Instead, talk about the fact that Mary was *pregnant*, and God was the father of her baby.

Let the Children Sing

"O Come, O Come, Emmanuel" is a natural choice for this Sunday. While its vocabulary and images are difficult for children, they respond quickly to the change of mood between the verses and the chorus. Simply alert the congregation to the problems mentioned in the verses and the happy "Emmanuel promise" recalled in the chorus. Encourage children to sing the chorus, even if they cannot read all the words in the verses.

"Once in Royal David's City" speaks of God's presence with us in Jesus, in simple words that children can read and understand. The third verse of "Away in a Manger" also recalls the "Emmanuel promise."

If you focus on the work of Joseph and Paul, invite the children's choir or a children's class to sing "The Friendly Beasts," which notes the work each animal did when Jesus was born.

The Liturgical Child

1. Light the fourth candle of the Advent wreath for God's Emmanuel promise, "I will be with you":

> God promised that one day a son would be born who would be named God With Us. Jesus' last words before he went back into heaven were, "Remember, I will be with you always." God promises that we will never be alone. Just as God was with us in Jesus, God is with us every day. So today, we light a candle for God's Emmanuel promise. God is with us.

2. "Kum Ba Yah," which means "come by here" is known by many children. Ask a children's class or choir to sing it as a response to the congregation's prayers of petition and intercession. Or invite the whole congregation to sing the chorus, in response to each of a series of petition prayers. Be sure to point out its meaning before it is sung.

3. Children's Christmas excitement is probably at fever pitch this Sunday. Remember in the church's prayer their hopes for wonderful gifts, anticipation of visits with grandparents and cousins, and delight in other Christmas traditions. Also pray for kindness and patience in the days between now and Christmas.

Sermon Resources

1. Abandonment is one of the deepest fears of childhood. So tell stories about the feeling of being lost in a grocery or department store (remember that young children assume that it is the parent and not the child that has wandered off or gotten lost); of wondering whether your parents have forgotten you when you are the last to be picked up after some activity; of fearing, while waiting with a babysitter or staying alone for the first time, that your parents will never return. You may want to speak of the special fear of children whose parents have divorced—that the parent with whom they live will move out, as did the other parent. Use these stories to set the stage for exploring the value of God's promise to be with us.

2. Feature Joseph exploring his part in Jesus' birth and early childhood. Point out the importance of his quiet, behind-the-scenes role.

3. Explore Joseph's big decision about Mary and Jesus. Note Paul's self-introduction as a person God loves, and for whom God has a task. Point out the similarities in Paul's situation and Joseph's. Then challenge worshipers of all ages to see themselves as persons God loves, and for whom God has tasks.

Shade each space with a ＊ in it to find a word and a phrase that mean the same thing. Listen for them in worship.

The word is _____.

The phrase is _____.

Fourth Sunday of Advent/ © 1992 by Abingdon Press.

CHRISTMAS EVE/DAY
(SECOND PROPER)

Note: The Revised Common Lectionary offers three sets of readings for Christmas Eve/Day. The readings are identical in each of the three cycles. In this series, Year A offers the second Christmas Proper (texts from the Roman Shepherd's Mass held at dawn on Christmas Day); Year B offers the third Christmas Proper (texts for later in the day or on the Sunday following Christmas); Year C offers the first Christmas Proper (the traditional texts for Christmas Eve and midnight). Any of the three is appropriate for use at any Christmas worship service.

From a Child's Point of View

Gospel: Luke 2:(1-7) 8-20. The emphasis here is on the story of the shepherds. This story is familiar, but it is heard for only one month a year. While it is easy for children to follow the drift of the story, many words and phrases baffle them. Put "glory to God in the highest!" into everyday words: "Everyone and everything in all the universe praise God!" Illustrate God's intention for "peace on earth, goodwill among men" with specific examples of peace—within our families, among children at school, among the nations of the world. Imagine, with the children, what it looked like when "the glory of God shone round about them."

Epistle: Titus 3:4-7. The language of this passage makes it impossible for children to understand as it is read. The message must be presented in the sermon, songs, and prayers.

Paul's message is that God loves us and comes to live among us—not because we deserve it, but because God loves us so much. When linked to the Gospel lesson, the message is that God (unlike Santa Claus, who comes only to "the nice") comes to everyone—even poor, dirty shepherds.

Old Testament: Isaiah 62:6-12. This passage is filled with too many poetic images to explain to children on Christmas. Read it for adults as a message of promise and hope, addressed to such people as the Christmas shepherds.

Psalm: 97. This psalm, praising God who rules over the whole world, also is difficult for children. Verses 1-6, 9, and 11 are filled with language and images that are confusing when taken literally, the only way children can take them. The Good News Bible or The Jerusalem Bible offers the best translation for children.

Consider replacing this with Psalm 96, suggested in Proper One for Christmas Eve/Day (Year C resources). Though it also is filled with abstract language, the mental pictures Psalm 96 creates make more sense to children.

Watch Words

Wrap Jesus in *soft cloths* rather than *swaddling clothes* and explain that a *manger* is a feed trough, not a special bed for Baby Jesus. Paraphrase Mary's *pondering* into *thinking* or *wondering about*.

Remember, *grace* is loving those who do not love you back; *mercy* is forgiving people who do not deserve your forgiveness; and *righteousness* is obeying God's rules.

Let the Children Sing

"Angels We Have Heard on High," with its chorus of Glorias, and "The First Noel" (verses 1-2) are the most familiar and easiest of the shepherd carols for children. The language of "Hark! The Herald Angels Sing" is harder for children to understand. "Infant Holy, Infant Lowly," while less familiar, has easier words and can be read by young readers. "Go, Tell It on the Mountain," which many children know, has three verses about the shepherds.

" 'Twas in the Moon of Wintertime," which appears in many new hymnals, sets the Christmas event in the context of some modern shepherds, Canadian Indians. Children enjoy this version of the story. If your congregation is uncomfortable with unfamiliar hymns, ask a choir to sing it.

The Liturgical Child

1. Instead of, or as part of, the prelude music, invite the gathering congregation to sing carols (especially shepherd carols). This gives "hyped-up" children something to do as they settle in for the service, and it gives everyone a chance to sing favorite carols. Simply print the titles and hymn numbers in the worship bulletin, in the sequence in which they will be sung. In informal congregations, children might be asked to play one carol each on their musical instruments.

2. If Communion is served, present it as the banquet table (Christmas dinner table) of God's people. Imagine and name all the people, even the "shepherdy" people, whom God welcomes to the table. Think both locally and globally. Celebrate the fact that God also asks each of us, no matter how good or bad we may have been, to come to the table.

3. Pray for all the "shepherdy" people in the world and for all people who may feel "shepherdy." To make it a litany prayer, ask the congregation to respond to each petition with: "Good News! God loves us."

Sermon Resources

1. On Christmas Eve, children are overstimulated and excited. To get their attention, worship must involve as many senses as possible. A service of lessons and carols accompanied by a simple pageant, with parts taken by youths or adults rather than by children, is often most effective:

Away in a Manger

(Mary, Joseph, and baby take places.)
Meditation on who the shepherds were and who they are today
(shepherds sit around campfire)
Luke 2:8-14
(angel comes to shepherds)
"Angels We Have Heard on High"
Luke 2:9-16
(shepherds kneel at manger)
"Silent Night"
Luke 2:17-20; Titus 3:4-7
Meditation on God's love for the shepherds and for us
Christmas prayer for shepherds everywhere
"Go Tell It on the Mountain"
(shepherds leave)

2. Idea to Develop for a Sermon: In casting parts for a Christmas pageant, there are always volunteers for the Holy Family (the "stars"), the wise men (the exotic ones), the angels (they get to wear halos), and even the animals. But those who end up as shepherds usually feel stuck. Shepherds are nothing special. In Bethlehem, they were the most uninteresting and ordinary of people. People who were shepherds and had to stay up and out with the sheep all night during the winter were the unluckiest of the unlucky. They were really stuck.

One of the biggest surprises of Christmas is that God told a bunch of shepherds about Jesus first. We carefully choose the people we tell big news to or share important secrets with. We tell our best friends or our family. But when God had the biggest announcement of all time and wanted to share the best secret ever, God told the shepherds. Telling shepherds was like sending an important message to an elementary school by telling first-graders instead of the principal, the teachers, or some fifth-graders. Telling the shepherds was like telling the kids who never have their homework done and are always chosen last for team games. God was letting us know that God loves and cares for ordinary people like shepherds, and like us (even on our dirtiest, unluckiest days).

3. There is no Worship Worksheet for Christmas Eve. The service should be so dramatic that paper and pencils would just get in the way.

FIRST SUNDAY AFTER CHRISTMAS

From a Child's Point of View

Gospel: Matthew 2:13-23. The story of the flight into Egypt is the key text for children today. It offers in a story what the other texts explore in poetry and theological discourse. In presenting this story, however, remember that it may be unfamiliar. Few Christmas pageants or storybooks include these events. You will need to set them in context following the visit of the wise men.

Because many children know refugee children or have seen refugees on television, they are responsive to the plight of Mary, Joseph, and Jesus. While repulsed by Herod's murder of the children, they are aware that such terrible deeds are done. They also know a little about the hardships involved in escaping to and living in a foreign country.

When the story is read in light of the other texts for the day, especially the Epistle, it tells us that God is with us in the worst of situations. Indeed, God in Jesus has "lived through" many awful things, so we can trust God to understand our problems and sufferings.

Epistle: Hebrews 2:10-18. No translation makes this passage child-accessible. The New Jerusalem Bible does offer a useful phrase in "we are all of the same stock." With help, children recognize different kinds of farm stock (cows, pigs, chickens, etc.) and can appreciate Jesus as being of the same stock we are. In other words, Jesus is like us and understands what our lives are like.

The expiation and sacrifice ideas that undergird this passage and are the basis of much of Hebrews are beyond the understanding of children. Chil-

dren will need to wait until they are mentally able to stand in the shoes of those for whom animal sacrifice was meaningful, before they can make sense of a loving God who requires that Jesus be just like us, in order to be killed in our place so that we may be forgiven.

Psalm: 148. Children read this psalm most readily as a response to God's Christmas love in the birth of Jesus and the happiness they have just experienced in the celebration of Christmas. Younger children especiallly enjoy the calls for specific animals, the weather, and other parts of creation to praise God. Older children realize that inanimate objects cannot praise God in the same way humans do, but they do not yet quite grasp the poetry of mountains or winds praising God. They are more comfortable with adding new calls for praise from different groups of people. The simple words and familiar vocabulary enable middle-elementary children to read it with the congregation.

Old Testament: Isaiah 63:7-9. This is the beginning of another poem that praises God's great deeds among the people of Israel. Its content is too general and requires too much background knowledge to make much sense to children. But if it is introduced as a message for people who have been conquered and carried off to a foreign land, children can catch a few of the hopeful phrases.

They especially appreciate the idea in verse 9 that God personally cares about us and is with us. God does not send substitutes or assistants. God comes in person.

Watch Words

Avoid such terms as *slaughter of the innocents.* Instead, speak concretely of Herod's order that all little boys under the age of two be killed.

Today's texts are filled with general theological terms that children and many adults will not understand. So cite examples, rather than use such generalities as *steadfast love, mercy, graciousness, salvation, sanctification,* or *consecration.*

Let the Children Sing

"What Child Is This?" and "Once in Royal David's City" are hymns that stress the lowliness of Jesus' birth in simple language older children can read easily.

"All Creatures of Our God and King" parallels the psalmist's calls to specific parts of creation for praise. The repeated Alleluias are easy for young readers. If "The Friendly Beasts" was sung before Christmas, link the care of the animals it describes with the animals' praise called for in this hymn.

"From All That Dwell Below the Skies," with its more general praise but the same tune and repeated Alleluias, is a good second choice.

The Liturgical Child

1. Invite the congregation to join you in reading Psalm 148, following the pattern below. (The words can be printed in the bulletin.) This could be an effective call to worship. Groups 1 and 2 may be either the choir and the congregation or two halves of the congregation. Before the reading, point out that Group 1 calls on everything *above* the earth to praise God; then Group 2 calls on everything *upon* the earth to praise God.

All:	**verse 1a**
Group 1:	verses 1b-4
All:	**verses 5-6**
Group 2:	verses 7-12
All:	**verses 13-14**

2. To set the Gospel story in context, precede the reading by reviewing the events of the visit of the wise men and posing two questions: What did Herod think and do when the wise men did not return? What did Mary and Jesus do after Jesus was born? Challenge worshipers to find the answers to those questions as the text is read.

3. Pray for refugees. Pray for specific groups. Mention the difficulties of learning new languages, eating different food, learning new manners, getting along in new schools and jobs, and being homesick.

4. Include in prayers of confession and petition the week-after-Christmas concerns of children: being bored with no school and nothing to look forward to; broken toys; disappointments about gifts—not getting what we wanted or finding out that what we wanted is not as special as we thought it would be; weather that keeps children cooped up indoors.

5. To explore the great deeds of God that are referred to generally in the texts, create a litany in which the leader describes specific deeds of God, with the congregation responding, "God did that! Praise God!" to each one. Include such deeds as God creating the world, rescuing Hebrew slaves from Egypt, giving us ten good rules to live by, being born in a barn to live among us as Jesus, sending the Spirit to give power to the church, working through your church to . . . , and so on.

Sermon Resources

1. Tell stories about modern refugee families. Describe what happened in terms of God's presence with and care of the refugees. If your congregation has sponsored such families, and it would not be an unwelcome intrusion of their privacy, tell their story.

2. Many of the stories about Saint Francis of Assisi relate to the season and to today's theme. He gave up his comfortable life to serve the poor. He created the first creche, or live nativity, to bring the Christmas story alive to his illiterate congregation. He was so in touch with nature that he preached to a wolf and to birds. This awareness is reflected in his hymn "All Creatures of Our God and King."

Listen to **Psalm 148**. Then turn this picture of the earth
into a praise psalm.

Write ⟩ on the earth words that call animals or different

people to praise God.

Draw ⟩ around the earth things that may praise God.

(I started with a family and some trees.)

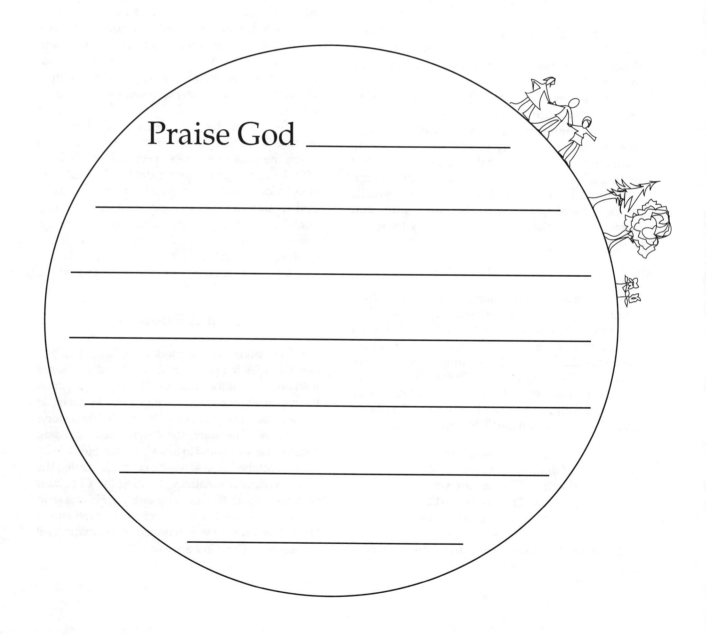

Praise God _____

_____

_____

_____

_____

_____

SECOND SUNDAY AFTER CHRISTMAS

Note: The readings for this Sunday are the same for all three years of the New Revised Common Lectionary. They are provided for use on those occasions when Epiphany (January 6) is celebrated on a weekday following the Second Sunday After Christmas.

From a Child's Point of View

Gospel: John 1:1-18. Though "the Word," "the light," and "the life" in this poem are too abstract for children, the poem has the answer to questions they often ask: "What is the difference between God and Jesus?" and "How are God and Jesus related?" John's answer is that God and Jesus are one. Jesus was part of God when the world was created. God became a person in Jesus of Nazareth. No one has seen God, but anyone who has seen or read about Jesus has seen or read about God, and therefore knows all there is to know about God.

If you explore "the Word" (Logos), introduce it to children as a code word for God. Though this oversimplifies the term, it allows older children to hear John's message—that God and Jesus are one throughout history, even before Creation.

Children also can appreciate that God's presence with us as a person, Jesus, is the most important of the many ways God has loved us and cared for us. John mentions God's gift to Moses of the Law (the Ten Commandments). Other texts for the day mention God's other gifts in creation and in the history of Israel.

Epistle: Ephesians 1:3-14. Paul begins his letter to the Ephesians by listing God's gifts to us. Paul's list is filled with abstract theological terms that mean nothing to children as they are read. In children's terms, these are the gifts:

● God chose us before the creation of the world. To children, this says that God's love for us is so big that it stretches back before the creation of the world. Such love gives children both security and a sense of identity as members of God's people.

● God gives us forgiveness.

● God promises that one day God will bring the whole world together in peace.

These gifts will need to be named and illustrated with everyday examples in the sermon.

Old Testament: Jeremiah 31:7-14 or Sirach 24:1-12. Jeremiah 31:7-14 is a specific example of God's saving care. When the people of Israel were in exile in Babylon, Jeremiah promised them that God would rescue them, and he described what life would be like when that happened. With this background information, children can catch some of the phrases and respond to the hopeful feeling of Jeremiah's promises.

Sirach 24:1-12 celebrates the fact that Wisdom (Old Testament precursor to "the Word" in John's prologue) is in residence in the Jewish nation for all time. Because there is no way to explain Wisdom/Word that does not make it seem to children like a fourth person of the Trinity, either select Jeremiah's text or present Wisdom as another code word for God (like Word) and read this passage as a celebration of God's presence with people of faith.

Psalm: 147:12-20 or Wisdom of Solomon 10:15-19, 20b-21. Both these poems list several examples of God's loving activities in our behalf. Because the psalm identifies familiar natural gifts as the gifts of God, while the Wisdom poem refers to historical deeds which few children will recognize as gifts of Wisdom, the psalm is the better choice for children. If the weather is wintry, children will especially enjoy the references to God's winter gifts of snow and frost and ice (sleet or hail).

Watch Words

Be careful about "God" vocabulary, especially Trinitarian language. God is called Father, Son, and Holy Spirit. God is also called Creator, Redeemer (Rescuer), Friend, and much more. It is easier for children to understand *Word* or *Wisdom* when they are presented as part of the second list, than if they are related to the Trinitarian list.

Either avoid *incarnation* or make it the word of the day, defining it and using it frequently to build familiarity.

Let the Children Sing

To praise Christ, sing either "Rejoice, Ye Pure in Heart," with its repeated chorus, or "When Morning Gilds the Skies," with its repeated phrase, "May Jesus Christ be praised!"

The easiest incarnation hymn for children is "That Boy-child of Mary," which uses simple vocabulary.

The link between the creator God and Jesus in today's texts makes it a perfect time to sing the familiar "Fairest Lord Jesus." "All Things Bright and Beautiful" is another good hymn to God the creator.

The Liturgical Child

1. Read John's prologue during the lighting of the Advent wreath candles and Christ candle. An acolyte stands at the center of the sanctuary with a candle, or the candle lighter, raised high while verses 1-5 are read, lights the four candles of the wreath during verses 6-13, and finally lights the Christ candle as verse 14 is read. The acolyte and reader (perhaps a parent/older child team) need to practice a time or two to get the timing right.

2. Before reading the Jeremiah passage, explain the situation of the people for whom it was originally written. Invite listeners to imagine they are living among the captives in Babylon; urge them to imagine how the captives felt when they heard these words.

3. In a bidding prayer, name the many gifts God gives us: family; people who are our heroes, heroines, and guides; special friends; congregational life; the natural order, particularly the pleasures of winter weather; events in the world in which you sense God at work; and most especially, Jesus. Pause after describing each general gift to allow worshipers to pray about specific gifts they recognize in their own experience.

Sermon Resources

1. Preach about God's gifts to us: God created a beautiful world for us to enjoy, explore, and care for. (Focus on the joys of winter weather.) God has given us directions for happy living—for example, the Ten Commandments. God has come to help us when we get into trouble. God's best gift is coming to live among us and to save us, gift-wrapped in the person of Jesus of Nazareth.

The title of the sermon might be "Whad Ya Get from God?" Open with the question children frequently ask as they meet friends—especially on the first day of school after Christmas—"Whad ya get?" Tell about one gift you were given, then move on to what God gives all of us every day.

The Worship Worksheet challenges children to think about gifts from God in their own lives. Encourage them to listen to the sermon as they draw or write about their gifts. Be ready to respond to their work as they leave the sanctuary.

2. To help children understand John 1:10-13, point out examples from the Christmas stories of people who did not know who Jesus was. For example, the innkeepers of Bethlehem did not know it was Jesus who would be born when they sent Mary and Joseph away. The shepherds, on the other hand, listened to the angels and knew who Baby Jesus was.

Draw or write about some of God's gifts to you.

A Special
Person

A Talent
God Gave
Me

My
Favorite
Weather

Draw a picture of a story about
God's best gift-- JESUS.

FIRST SUNDAY AFTER THE EPIPHANY /BAPTISM OF THE LORD

From a Child's Point of View

Gospel: Matthew 3:13-17. Children easily follow the action in this story as it is read. When they are reminded that one purpose of baptism is naming, or claiming identity as one of God's people, children are primed to explore Matthew's use of the story of Jesus' baptism to tell us who Jesus is. Matthew tells us that Jesus is both the Messiah ("This is my Son," from Psalm 2:9) and the suffering servant ("my servant, with whom I am well pleased," from Isaiah's "suffering-servant" song). That combination was unusual for Jewish readers and is unusual for today's children, who seldom see a king as a servant, but usually as one to be served.

If it is pointed out, older children will follow with interest Matthew's strategy (repeated throughout his Gospel) of quoting Old Testament verses that would be familiar to his Jewish readers, to explain the importance of who Jesus is and what Jesus did.

Epistle: Acts 10:34-43. Peter's sermon at the home of Cornelius is a summary of Jesus' ministry and passion. Unfortunately, no translation presents it in words and sentences children can understand. If it is introduced as a very short story about the whole life of Jesus, from his baptism to his death and resurrection, older children can trace the sequence of those events as they are read.

The main value of reading this passage to children shortly after Christmas is that it helps them connect the stories of Jesus the baby, with those of Jesus the man.

Old Testament: Isaiah 42:1-9. There are two distinctive ways to deal with this text.

1. The text can be read as an explanatory footnote to God's statement at Jesus' baptism. Thus God is giving Jesus his "servant" job description. Jesus is described as one whose whole life is to be dedicated to working for justice and caring for those who need help. Just as we receive a name and become one of God's people at our baptisms, Jesus received a name, "My Son," and a job description, "my (Suffering) Servant," at his baptism. (It helps to point out before the reading that all the "hes" and "yous" refer to Jesus.)

2. Or the text can be read in its Old Testament context, in which the servant is the nation, or the faithful. Read thus, it becomes a mission-oriented job description for the church. In this case, children should be instructed to imagine that God is speaking directly to them and their church. If worshipers follow in pew Bibles as Scripture is read, point out before the reading that verse 5 is just a very lengthy "God said." This will help older children to follow God's interrupted message.

Psalm: 29. This psalm traces the path of a thunderstorm coming in from the Mediterranean Sea, crossing the mountains, and moving out into the desert. With help, children can hear the thunder out over the water (vss. 3-4), watch the lightning break cedar trees and make the hills seem to skip in the flashing strobe-light (vss. 5-7), and see the damage caused by hail (vs. 9). The final verses speak to the frightened child in all of us, reminding us that God is Lord of even the wildest storms, and praying that God will give us both strength to survive the storm, and peace in spite of the storm.

Watch Words

Do not assume that children know that *Messiah* means God's king, or that *suffering servant* was a term that referred to a person or group of persons who would suffer in order to rescue God's people. Speak of Jesus as the *Serving King* for clarity with children.

Translate Isaiah's *bruised reeds* and *dimly burning wicks* into *people who have serious problems.*

Explain that Peter *hanging on a tree* is another way to say that he was *crucified.*

Let the Children Sing

Sing "Tell Me the Stories of Jesus" or "O Sing a Song of Bethlehem," to review Jesus' life.

Praise Christ with "Come, Christians, Join to Sing," with its chorus of repeated Alleluias.

Pair "Fairest Lord Jesus" with Psalm 29, to celebrate God's lordship over nature.

The Liturgical Child

1. Psalm 29 is a text for Baptism of the Lord also in Year C of this series. "The Liturgical Child" for that day gives directions for a congregational reading of this psalm, complete with stormy sound effects.

2. If baptisms are part of today's worship, introduce them with emphasis on the fact that baptism gives one a new identity as a child of God, a member of God's family, a disciple, and so on. Invite children to sit or stand near the baptismal font to hear this explanation and to observe the sacrament where they can see well.

3. Select as an affirmation of faith for the day a creed that tells the story of Jesus in simple language. The Apostles' Creed is one that many children know and that can be read easily by older children who do not know it. In the invitation to recite the creed, urge worshipers to pay particular attention to what it says about Jesus.

4. Provide illustrations of Jesus' activities as the Serving King. Point out any examples in stained-glass windows, paintings, or symbols in the sanctuary. Consider posting around the sanctuary large pictures of Jesus at work (from the church school picture files).

5. If you focus on the Isaiah text in its Old Testament perspective, paraphrase it to address the congregation in the Charge and Benediction:

> God says, Behold, you are my servants, whom I uphold. You are my chosen, in whom I delight. I have put my Spirit upon you, to bring forth justice in all the world. Do not be discouraged or accept failure. Justice will be done. Remember, I am the Lord. I have called you. I have taken you by the hand and led you. You will be a light to the nations.

Sermon Resources

1. Open the sermon by talking about the significance of names. Tell your full name and explain what the parts of that name say about you (i.e., you are a member of a given family, and you may have been given a significant first or middle name). You may or may not want to pay attention to the titles such as Miss, Ms., Mrs., Mr., Reverend, or Doctor, added to names to tell more about who a person is.

Next, speak about names given at baptism. Point out that a person's given name is always stated. Then note any other names that are given in your congregation's rite. For example, in the Presbyterian ritual, the words are, "(Given name), Child of God." Explain what it means to accept those new names.

Finally, explore the new names Jesus received at his baptism: My Son and Suffering Servant.

2. Introduce and explore the title Serving King to describe Jesus. Compare that vision of a king with the kings in fairytales or a winner in the game King of the Hill. Cite familiar stories about Jesus to show how Jesus lived up to that title. Describe life for his subjects in the kingdom of Jesus, the Serving King.

Listen carefully when **Matthew 3:13-17** is read.   Then draw pictures of . . .

. . . what happened in this story.

. . . Jesus being the Serving King.

. . . you serving others.

. . . one way your church serves others.

SECOND SUNDAY AFTER THE EPIPHANY

From a Child's Point of View

Old Testament: Isaiah 49:1-7. Within this complicated "servant song" are several themes that are important to children but which children will not recognize as the passage is read.

First, children need to explore the possibility that they (or their congregation) are the servants to whom God is speaking. They were chosen and named by God, who has a plan for them. Seeing themselves as well-polished weapons (or tools), cared for and hidden away by God until the right moment, builds children's self-esteem and contributes to their sense of identity and purpose, based on belonging to God and doing God's will.

When it is singled out for rereading and explanation, the conversation between God and the servant in verses 4-6 reassures children that though they, like the servant, often feel they are not doing anything great, God is using them. So often their daily activities and frustrations seem very insignificant. It seems that they will be forever "just kids." In the middle of winter, after Christmas and with a long way to go until Easter, it seems as if nothing exciting or important will ever happen. To them, as to the servant, God insists that they are important; they are light—not just for the neighborhood or school, but for the world!

Children begin to understand what it means to be the light of the world with their feelings, rather than their minds. Even the youngest can describe the difference between fearful, hard-to-get-around-in dark, and comfortable, easy light. Middle-elementary children can identify "dark" versus "light" feelings and experiences. Based on

this, they can begin to understand that some actions and words bring dark, while others bring light. Many fifth- and sixth-graders can finally articulate what it means to bring light to the world and be light for the world.

Psalm: 40:1-11. This psalm is so rich with poetic images and references to the sacrificial worship of the Temple that it is all but incomprehensible to children. If it is introduced as the thanksgiving poem of a person who has been in deep trouble and gotten out, children will catch meaningful phrases here and there. Older children, if challenged, may be able to pick out the psalmist's promises to use his mouth to tell about God's love and power.

Epistle: I Corinthians 1:1-9. If you plan to emphasize the First Corinthians readings during the coming weeks, children will be interested in the letter format, especially in the greeting in verses 1-3. Knowing who wrote, and the church to whom the person wrote will bring the passages to life.

The prayer of thanksgiving in verses 4-9, however, is voiced in such abstract language that children cannot follow it in any translation. Its talk of gifts and waiting for the day of the Lord need such extensive explanation that children cannot get through the explanations to the message. Read this text for those with more mature minds.

Gospel: John 1:29-42. This text offers two examples of witnesses. John the Baptist was the kind of witness Isaiah's servant was called to be and that the psalmist promised to be. He simply and bravely told the crowds what he had seen and knew to be true. God had promised that John

33

would see the Holy Spirit in the form of a dove descend on the One God was sending. When John saw the dove, he told everyone what had happened and pointed out who Jesus was. Andrew heard what John said, he followed Jesus, and he later took his brother to meet Jesus. Children are challenged to tell what they know, as John did. They are especially encouraged to be witnesses to their friends, as Andrew was to his brother.

Watch Words

Refer to courtrooms and news reports to describe what it means to be a *witness*. If local TV stations carry programs titled "Eye Witness News," use this as a familiar example of our use of *witness*.

Do not use the symbolic term *light of the world* without speaking in children's terms about what it means.

Let the Children Sing

Sing about witnessing to what happened at Christmas with "Go, Tell It on the Mountain." Children can sing the opening line of each verse and enjoy the spreading light in the chorus of "We've a Story to Tell to the Nations." If children know "Pass It On," they can sing it with the congregation, or as a choir, to commit themselves to be witnesses.

The Liturgical Child

1. Light candles in the worship center as part of the Call to Worship. As the candles are lighted, have a worship leader read John 8:12 or a call to worship such as the following:

> Isaiah said, "The people who walk in darkness have seen a great light." Jesus said, "I am the light of the world." We light this candle (these candles) to remind us of the light of God's love and presence with us. Let us worship God.

At the conclusion of worship, carry the light of the candles to the rear of the sanctuary as a charge is given. An acolyte may light the taper of a long-handled candlelighter, snuff the candles, then recess with the lighted taper held high. Or in a less formal setting, an appointed worship leader may simply rise and carry out a still-lighted worship-center candle.

> *Charge:* Jesus said, "You are the light of the world. . . . Let your light shine before others, so that they may see your good works and give glory to your Father in heaven."

2. Explain the setting of, and the movement within, Psalm 40:1-11. Then offer a brief time in which worshipers may silently identify times when they were in deep trouble and were rescued. Finally, invite them to join the psalmist in thanksgiving. In the worship bulletin, print the words of the psalm in the following format:

> People: (The psalmist speaks to the congregation.) verses 1-3
> Leader: (The priest replies to the psalmist.) verse 4
> People: (The psalmist speaks to God.) verses 5-11

Sermon Resources

1. Describe the functions of several kinds of light, then challenge worshipers to take on the function of one or more of these lights as they light up the world:
   ● airport searchlights that point the way home;
   ● lighthouse beacons that alert people to danger;
   ● fireplace or campfire lights where people laugh and tell stories and enjoy an evening together;
   ● detectives' flashlights used to find the truth of serious problems;
   ● night-lights that comfort people with troubles.

2. There are many references to tongues in today's texts. Tongues can get people of all ages into trouble. So preach about what we do with our tongues. Topics of interest to children include telling lies, twisting the truth to our advantage, tattling (telling "the truth" in order to get other people in trouble), blurting out things that hurt others (either in anger or on purpose), saying things we know will stir up trouble, and being quiet when we know we should speak.

Listen carefully when **Isaiah 49: 1-11** is read. Unscramble 3 ways Isaiah describes the work of God's people.

God said, "You are . . ."

1. y m   e v n s r t a

    _ _   _ _ _ _ _ _ _

2. d e h s i l o p   r o w a r

    _ _ _ _ _ _ _ _   _ _ _ _ _

3. t h l i g   o t   h e t

    o n i a n t s

    _ _ _ _ _   _ _   _ _ _

    _ _ _ _ _ _ _

Circle the description you like most. Draw or write one way you can be like that during the week.

Ask God to help you with this work.

THIRD SUNDAY AFTER THE EPIPHANY

From a Child's Point of View

Gospel: Matthew 4:12-23. For children, this is the key text of the day. Though few will be drawn into Matthew's concerns about where Jesus lived (vss. 12-16), many will recognize and enjoy the story of the calling of the four fishermen. Though the story is clear and easy to follow, it offers two *puzzles.*

The first is this: Why did these people, who had never met Jesus before, according to Matthew, respond to such a brief invitation? There are several possibilities. They could have been so bored with fishing that any distraction was welcome. But today's children are carefully warned about accepting interesting invitations from strangers. Or they might have been fascinated by the possibility of dealing with people instead of with slippery, wriggling fish. But most children see fishing as an active, interesting job and therefore discount this possibility.

The second puzzler is this: Why would Jesus ask James and John to desert their father in the middle of their work? Didn't Jesus care about Zebedee, who depended upon their help with the family fishing business?

There are no acceptable answers to either of these puzzlers. Children, however, appreciate hearing them recognized, pondered briefly, and perhaps consigned to the list of interesting questions to ask "when we meet the disciples in heaven."

The crux of this passage is that being a disciple involves making decisions. Just as the fishermen needed to decide whether to stay at their boats or to follow Jesus, so disciples today must make decisions about what they will and will not do. Just as the fishermen were brave enough to try something new, so disciples today must have the courage to try new things—things like peacemaking, learning to pray, and working for justice.

Old Testament: Isaiah 9:1-4. This text is read today because Matthew quotes it to make a point about Jesus. Children will miss both Matthew's point and Isaiah's prophecy as presented here. Some may recognize the phrase "the people who have walked" as one they have heard before.

Psalm: 27:1, 4-9. This song of confidence in God's care expresses a feeling children appreciate, but uses difficult vocabulary. The New Jerusalem Bible has the clearest translation of these terms. The references to taking refuge at the Temple require knowledge of Old Testament sanctuary laws which children do not have. In spite of these difficulties, older children can follow this psalm when it is introduced as a good prayer for disciples who are making brave decisions.

Epistle: I Corinthians 1:10-18. Many of the problems at Corinth are familiar to children. The problem addressed here is that people are forming little groups, each thinking it is better than the others and letting the others know that. Among middle-elementary children, such petty rivalry may explode between groups gathered around popular leaders: "I'm on Mr. Brown's team. He's the best, and we're the best! It's too bad you can't be on our team!" In its extreme, the pleasure of the game is lost in bickering between teams, both on and off the field.

Among fifth- and sixth-graders, small, tight friendship groups often become the standard on which children base their self-esteem. Being able to claim so-and-so as "best friend" and jockeying for position at tables can develop into vicious, divisive, group dynamics. To all people trying to prove their own importance by putting others down, Paul says, "Get along with one another!"

Watch Words

There are no major vocabulary traps in these texts.

Let the Children Sing

"Tu Has Venido a la Orilla" (Lord, You Have Come to the Lakeshore) is the one hymn totally based on the call of the fishermen.

To help children sing "Jesus Calls Us," with its difficult vocabulary, point out before singing that verse 2 is about the fishermen Jesus called, and the other verses are about Jesus calling us.

Other discipleship hymns for children include "I Sing a Song of the Saints of God" and "Lord, I Want to Be a Christian."

If you focus on the Epistle, sing "Let There Be Peace on Earth" and "I Come with Joy" (if you celebrate Communion).

The Liturgical Child

1. Read verses 1 and 4 of Psalm 27 with dramatic exuberance as the Call to Worship. Pause between the rhetorical questions in verse 1. Raise a finger at the beginning of verse 4 to emphasize the "one thing" to be asked. Follow the Call to Worship with a hymn of praise.

2. In prayer, confess failures in decision making:

> Lord, Peter and Andrew and James and John made bold decisions to leave their boats to follow you. We wish we were as brave in making the decisions we face. But we are not. We confess that even when we know exactly what you would have us do, we often choose to do the opposite. We fear the laughter and anger of others. We lack the courage to try new ways of discipleship. We are slower still in making decisions that offer no

clearly right solution. We think and worry and put off deciding. Sometimes we wait so long that we miss out completely on chances to be your disciples. Forgive us. Be with us when we face disciples' decisions. For we pray in Jesus' name. Amen.

Assurance of Pardon: Remember that Peter, Andrew, James, and John did not always make brave and right decisions. Sometimes they made angry decisions, frightened decisions, or plain stupid decisions. But Jesus kept loving them and forgiving them and putting them to work. We are promised the same. God loves us and forgives us and calls us to be disciples—in spite of ourselves. Thanks be to God! Amen.

3. In a bidding prayer, give worshipers short silent moments to pray for those with whom they have trouble getting along in their families, at school or work, in their neighborhood, at church, and so forth.

Sermon Resources

1. There are several popular series of children's adventure books which ask the reader to make decisions in the course of the story. The reader is then directed to turn to the page which continues the story based on that decision. Children enjoy and benefit from rereading these books and trying out the results of different decisions.

Use this format to explore the decision that faced the fishermen when Jesus called them to leave their boats and follow him. Briefly tell what would have happened if they had simply said, "No thank you," or if they had said, "We'll think about it," or if they followed. Then present a variety of modern discipleship decisions, ranging from whether to attend church school to policy decisions that face church boards (such as stands on the death penalty). Informal congregations might enjoy voting on the options by show of hands and hearing the results of their decisions. More formal congregations could simply hear the decisions and the results of some of the options outlined. Listeners of all ages are thus reminded that we exercise our discipleship when we make decisions.

2. Groups of children whose bickering parallels that of the groups at Corinth include: "the boys

against the girls," at everything from who gets better grades to backyard one-sex-only clubhouses; the "big kids" against "the babies"; me and my two friends against everyone else; and in some communities, my group against other racial or ethnic groups.

Most winters produce a crop of carefully folded paper "cootie catchers" which younger elementary children use to catch invisible "cooties" off other children, generally outsiders. Ask an older child to make one so that you can demonstrate its destructive use during the sermon. (Many adults recall the pain inflicted by cootie catchers in their childhood.)

Answer: Matthew 4: 19

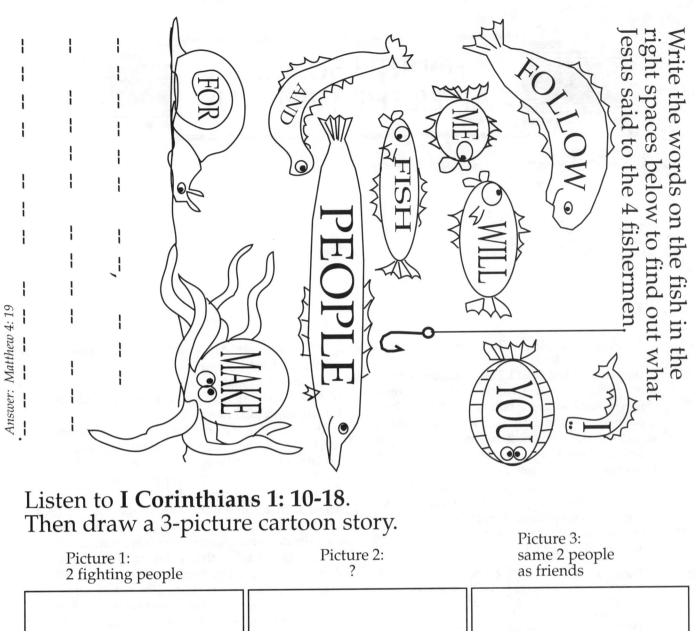

Write the words on the fish in the right spaces below to find out what Jesus said to the 4 fishermen.

FOLLOW ME, AND I WILL MAKE YOU FISH FOR PEOPLE.

Listen to **I Corinthians 1: 10-18**.
Then draw a 3-picture cartoon story.

Picture 1:
2 fighting people

Picture 2:
?

Picture 3:
same 2 people
as friends

What could happen in Picture 2 to help fighters become friends?

FOURTH SUNDAY AFTER THE EPIPHANY

From a Child's Point of View

Gospel: Matthew 5:1-12. The Beatitudes is one of those familiar passages which adults often think children ought to learn, but which children have little chance of understanding without significant adult help. First they must explore the meaning of *blessed*. If "blessed" is paraphrased as "happy," that happiness must be defined and differentiated from short-term, shallow satisfaction. Then they need help wading through each verse, many of which are abstract descriptions of human activity followed by somewhat vague promises. Here is one paraphrase suitable for children:

> Happy are those who are gentle,
>   for they are in charge in God's kingdom.
> Happy are those who grieve,
>   for God will comfort them.
> Happy are those who obey God,
>   for God will make them leaders.
> Happy are those who wish for fairness for
>   everyone,
>   for their wish will come true.
> Happy are those who forgive others,
>   for they shall be forgiven.
> Happy are those who put being a disciple first in
>   their lives,
>   for they will know God personally.
> Happy are the peacemakers,
>   for they will be called the children of God.
> Happy are those who are mistreated when they
>   do what God wants,
>   for the kingdom of heaven is theirs.
> You will find happiness and peace deep within
>   you when you are teased or mistreated,
>   or when others tell lies about you,
>   because you are my disciple.
> You will be happy because you will know
>   that you are one of God's people,
>   and God's people have often suffered.

Old Testament: Micah 6:1-8. The courtroom scene in verses 1-5 requires knowledge of covenant theology and events in Old Testament history that children do not yet possess. Read this for the adult biblical scholars.

The question and answer in verses 6-8 offer more to children, but need an introduction to explain the practice of offering animals, farm products (the oil is olive oil, not petroleum), and even children as sacrifices. Because children hear about such sacrifice from the vantage point of a child rather than that of an adult, children often are offended and frightened by these references. They can't imagine that a loving God would demand such a thing, but they worry that God might ask their parents to demonstrate their loyalty by killing them. They need to be reassured that the writer shares their views and that God has never and will never suggest such a show of loyalty. In fact, Micah's point here is that God is not interested in gestures like animal or human sacrifice. What God wants is for us to treat each other fairly and with love.

Epistle: I Corinthians 1:18-31. Few children will follow the reading of the text with its references to Greek wisdom and Jewish love of signs. But the point the passage makes about what is strong and weak—or what is wise and foolish—is critical to their response to the teachings in the Old Testament and Gospel passages. All children are encouraged to be wise and strong. Paul reminds them, along with the people at Corinth, that though God's rules may seem like foolish rules for sissies, they really are for the strong people.

He illustrates his point by pointing to Jesus'

crucifixion. Tied up, whipped, and crucified, Jesus—and God—looked weak, while the Roman soldiers and the religious leaders who wanted Jesus dead looked strong. But it turned out that Jesus was stronger. Similarly, though it looks as if demanding and getting your own way is stronger and wiser than giving up what is rightfully yours in order to take care of others, it turns out that the latter makes our life together happier.

Psalm: 15. While children do not catch the exact meaning of the psalmist's questions about God's hill and tent, they do catch his meaning: "Who is qualified to come near to God in worship?" A child's paraphrase of the answer:
> Those who obey God,
> who do what is right,
> who tell the truth,
> who say no mean words about others,
> who do nothing mean to their friends,
> who refuse to tell bad stories about other people,
> who cannot be tempted by wicked people,
> who respect God's people,
> who do what they say they will—no matter what,
> who do not share just hoping to get something back, and
> who will not hurt others in order to get a gift;
> People who do these things will always be safe with God.

Watch Words

Do not use the word *Beatitude* or speak of *the Beatitudes* without explaining what they are. Also explore the meaning of *blessed*. Many children use "bless" only in reference to a prayer before eating or in response to a friend's sneezes.

Let the Children Sing

The third verse about right and wrong makes "This Is My Father's World" a good general praise hymn for the day.

"What Does the Lord Require?" with its repeated chorus, which even the youngest can sing, is based on Micah 6:8. Other choices include "Lord, I Want to Be a Christian" (to which you could make up new verses related to today's theme), and "We Are Climbing Jacob's Ladder."

The Liturgical Child

1. Use Psalm 15 as the Call to Worship: The leader asks the questions (vs. 1); the congregation reads the answer (vss. 2–5a); and all read the conclusion (vs. 5b). The New Revised Standard Version provides the most child-accessible translation.

2. Create a responsive prayer of confession based on the Beatitudes. The worship leader states the beginning of each Beatitude ("Blessed are the . . ."), then describes how we fail to live in that way ("but we prefer to . . . ."). The congregation's response to each confession: "God, forgive us" (or sing the first line of the Kyrie).

3. Invite the children to come and sit with you at the front for the reading of the Gospel. Once they have arrived, point out that Jesus often gathered his disciples around him just like this, to tell them how they were to live. Briefly introduce the format of the Beatitudes before reading the lesson; after the reading, thank the children and send them back to their seats.

4. In prayers of petition, pray for God's foolishness for whatever situations, groups, and individuals have specific need of it. Include family situations, such as sharing a room with a baby sister or doing all the chores no one wants to do, as well as community and global situations.

5. Address Psalm 15 to the congregation as the Charge just before the Benediction.

Sermon Resources

1. Create beatitudes which reflect the secular values in our culture, and compare them to those of Jesus. For example:

> Blessed are the winners, for they are the only ones who count. (This is especially good at Super Bowl time and during local sport championships.)
> Blessed are the well-dressed; for everyone will envy their style.
> Blessed are those with the best toys, for they will always have fun.

Listen carefully when **Matthew 5: 1-12** is read. Pick your favorite Beatitude and print it inside the frame. Draw pictures about that Beatitude. When you get home, cut out and tape your framed verse where you will see it every day this week.

Blessed are . . .

FIFTH SUNDAY AFTER THE EPIPHANY

From a Child's Point of View

Old Testament: Isaiah 58:1-9a (9b-12). Isaiah's basic message is that God is more interested in the way we treat other people than in religious observances such as fasting. Before children can understand the passage, they need a thorough explanation of *fasting,* as it was intended to be practiced and as it was misused. Children are generally interested in the idea of not eating and of wearing sackcloth and ashes in order to focus attention on God. They understand how easy it would be to become "crabby" while fasting and how fasting could be used to draw attention to "what a neat person I am."

Older children need to explore the difference between religious fasts, which focus attention on God, and hunger strikes, which people use to try to force governments or other groups to meet their demands. Because fasting is not part of the Christian experience of many children today, it is easy for them to see the point Isaiah was making to those who were misusing the practice. The challenge is to help children see that we can misuse worship attendance and our other religious activities in the same way.

When exploring the list of activities in verses 6-7, be sure to include some in which children participate.

Psalm: 112:1-9 (10). Psalm 112 is an acrostic which describes the righteous. The lines are a somewhat disjointed series of statements which include abstract vocabulary (*gracious, merciful*) and unfamiliar phrases (*conduct their affairs, deal generously, will never be moved*). Older children, if encouraged, can understand a line here and there as the verses are read. In general, children will learn most as the ideas in the psalm are discussed in more familiar terms.

Epistle: I Corinthians 2:1-12 (13-16). Children will make little sense of this passage as it is read, but within it are two points about wisdom ("being smart") that they need to hear. To children, "wisdom" is being able to understand what is going on around them and knowing what to do in all situations—"street smarts" for their particular streets is the wisdom they crave.

Paul's point in verses 6-11 is that there is a specifically Christian "wisdom" that is different from what many people today think is wise. Others may suggest that it is wise to cheat, be nice only to people who can help you, grab the things you want and need, and even steal when necessary. But Paul says that wise Christians tell the truth, share, and treat everyone lovingly—especially those who have nothing to give.

In children's words, Paul's message in verses 1-5 is, "I am not a smart person who figured out all this about God on my own. Everything I have told you comes from God. God's wisdom is better than any ideas people have ever come up with."

Gospel: Matthew 5:13-20. This passage uses everyday things—salt and light—to encourage people to be disciples and to describe the world's need of disciples. But do not assume that children on their own will be able to list the characteristics of salt or follow what is said about lighting a home at night. They will need to hear these things reviewed in detail.

The discussion of keeping the Law in verses 17-20 requires knowledge of "the righteousness of the Pharisees" that is beyond the understanding of children.

Once they recall the functions of salt and light, children will be ready to compare them with the functions of disciples. They can also appreciate the picture of a world without salt or light and recognize that their discipleship makes a big difference.

Watch Words

Righteous does not have positive connotations among children. They are most likely to have heard it as *self-righteous* and associate it with unnecessarily strict and prudish approaches to life. They would prefer to be among "disciples" or "people of God" than to be "the righteous."

Wisdom is not a word children use on their own. Do not use it without exploring its meaning in terms of practical, common-sense ability to get along in any situation.

Do not use *fasting* without explaining the practice. Clarence Jordan, in *Sermon on the Mount* (Judson, 1970), defined true fasting as working so hard or being so committed to something that we forget to eat. In this view, *fasting* is a verb form of the adverb *fast* and means to move so quickly and intently toward a goal that all else is forgotten. Children enjoy identifying times they have *fasted* in this sense.

Let the Children Sing

Most hymns about light focus on Jesus as the light and include very difficult vocabulary and concepts for children. Probably the best choice of a discipleship hymn is "Lord, I Want to Be a Christian."

If it is familiar, sing "Be Thou My Vision." Consider using the hymn as an outline for a sermon that compares God's wisdom with that of the world.

The Liturgical Child

1. Before reading Isaiah 58:1-12, introduce both the intended practice of fasting and the way people were abusing it. Briefly point out the question/answer format in the passage. Then have the passage read by two readers, one taking the prophet's part, reading accusingly verses 1-2 and 3b-12; the second reader interrupts in the role of the surprised people, to pose the question in verse 3a. Both readers should use voice inflection and facial expression to emphasize both the format and the meaning of the exchange. Practice reading so that the rhetorical questions in verses 5-7 imply their answers.

2. *Prayer of Confession:* Lord, we can taste the difference salt makes on food, and we can see the difference light makes. We also know that you call us to make a difference in our world, but we confess that much of the time, we would rather not make a difference. We are not brave enough to take a stand for what we know is right. We prefer to stay with our own friends rather than make friends with the friendless. We would rather do what we want to do than take care of others. We want to be one of the crowd and safe. Forgive us. Give us the power to light up the world with your love and to season it with your justice. Amen.

Sermon Resources

1. To explore the significance of Isaiah's message to nonfasting Christians, describe the actions and feelings of a family as the members get ready for, go to, and return from church on Sunday, without ever experiencing or sharing God's love. Include griping about having to go, arguing about what will be worn; children bickering in the car; children calling other children in their class cruel names; adults making negative comments about the sermon; and so forth.

2. Compare the uses of salt with the functions of disciples. Just as salt is used to clean and heal (e.g., gargling with warm salt water), so Christians are to work on healing people who are hurting. Just as salt is spread on sidewalks to melt ice and snow, Christians can work on "melting" the hatred and similar attitudes which make the world dangerous. Just as salt makes popcorn and fries tastier, Christians can make life happier by doing little kindnesses and saying friendly words. Just as salt works with the ice to make unnecessary but delicious ice cream, Christians, out of love, work to provide some of the things people need in order to enjoy life. Christians know that God

wants everyone to enjoy some of the good things of this world.

3. Advertise a new product—saltless salt. It looks like salt but does not taste like salt. It shakes and pours like salt, but it does not melt ice or make food tastier. It burns like salt burns on a cut or sore throat, but it does not heal. Compare this useless product with people who claim to be Christian but do nothing to help those who are hurting; who spread bitter feelings instead of happy ones; and so forth. Suggest that such Christians are as useless as saltless salt.

Shade each space with a dot in it to find a word we use in worship today.

Listen to **I Corinthians 2: 1-12** and to what the preacher says. Then write your definition of this word.

Unscramble each group of letters to find out what Jesus told us.

1. You are the __ __ __ __ __   __ __   __ __ __ __   __ __ __ __ __ __.

2. You are the __ __ __ __ __   __ __   __ __ __   __ __ __ __ __ __ __.

SIXTH SUNDAY AFTER THE EPIPHANY
(PROPER 1)

From a Child's Point of View

Old Testament: Deuteronomy 30:15-20 or Sirach 15:15-20. Elementary-school children learn slowly, through experience, that the choices they make every day have consequences. At this age—as in weak moments later in life—they blame others for the consequences of their decisions. But as they grow, children take more and more responsibility for their actions. Both these passages speak to children who are learning to make choices and to accept the consequences.

In the Deuteronomy text, Moses tells Jews on the edge of the Promised Land that they will need to make choices in their new home. If the children are reminded of all that happened during the Exodus, they will realize that God had clearly shown these people how to make choices. They knew what God promised and what God expected. "Standing in the sandals" of these Jews, older children can begin to identify the choices they faced and what God had shown them about what they were to do.

It is important to point out that Moses did not say that God would punish the people if they made the wrong choices. Rather, Moses insisted that following God's ways leads naturally to good results, while following selfish, wicked ways leads to bad results.

The Sirach text presents the same message in more general terms. While children need help to identify both the freedom of choice and the inescapable consequences offered in verse 16, the fire and water are familiar enough to make their point with even the youngest children.

Psalm: 119:1-8. The vocabulary of this psalm makes it almost impossible for children to follow. However, when they know that this is an acrostic made up of short statements about the benefits of following God's ways, children may understand one or two statements. Older children are helped if they are alerted before the reading to the eight words that are used for God's rules in these eight verses: *Law, testimonies, ways, precepts, statutes, commandments, ordinances,* and *statutes* (repeated).

Gospel: Matthew 5:21-37. Only the most mature children can grasp Jesus' point about living by the Spirit rather than by the letter of the Law. Their understanding begins with recognizing the close connection between strong feelings and actions. Younger children, however, are still learning to understand and live by the rules. For both, it may be more helpful to focus on one of Jesus' three examples.

The first example is the easiest because it deals with a familiar problem: anger. Jesus insists, and children know, that calling brothers and sisters names or being furious with friends (no matter how much the names and fury are deserved) leads to trouble. When we carry angry feelings around with us, eventually they explode into name calling, kicking, punching, and even killing. Because of that, Jesus says it is important to get rid of angry feelings. It is so important that even going to church to worship God should be put off until we work out angry problems with others.

Note: Jesus never says that being angry is bad, only that it is dangerous. Children need to be assured that everyone becomes angry and that angry feelings are an important sign that something is terribly wrong. Challenge children to recognize this sign—angry feelings—and find ways to resolve the problem to which it points.

Jesus' second example is adultery—or family loyalty. He presents God's intention that people should live together in marriages and families, and that they should love and trust each other in all things at all times. In today's culture, that is not the norm, so children need to hear Jesus' vision affirmed, while they also need to hear that failed marriages, especially those of their parents, are forgivable. (Just as God forgives us when we fail to be kind or to be peacemakers, God forgives husbands and wives who fail to make their marriages last a lifetime.) But they do need to know that God expects us all to work hard to make our families lifetime commitments, and they need encouragement to dream of lifetime marriages for themselves. Though Jesus speaks of husbands and wives, children also are expected to be loyal to their families. This includes babysitting with younger siblings (or grandparents), paying attention to and really listening to each other, working to get along together, and so forth.

Though they need adult help to decipher Jesus' third example, children, with their love of elaborate secret club oaths and "cross my fingers, hope to die," understand Jesus' insistence that we simply do what we say we will do. We should be so dependable that oaths are not necessary.

Epistle: I Corinthians 3:1-9. The problem in the Corinthian church and the language with which Paul addresses it are beyond the understanding and experience of children. Paul's message about the immaturity of arguing and jealousy, however, does speak clearly to them. Children, often warned not to act like babies, enjoy Paul's telling the adults that they are acting like babies when they fuss and argue. That chuckle opens the door to discussion of our tendency, at all ages, to such behavior, and the challenge to grow beyond it.

Watch Words

Avoid abstract terms such as *good and evil* or *life and death* in describing the choices people face.

Instead, speak of *obeying God's rules* or *following God's ways.*

Instead of speaking of *adultery* or *lust,* talk about family and marriage *loyalty.*

Let the Children Sing

Commit yourselves to making good choices with "Seek Ye First" and "Open My Eyes, That I May See." Though it is not familiar to most children and some of its concepts are abstract, the vocabulary of "God of Our Life Through All the Circling Years" is simple enough for older elementary children to read and sing.

Sing about the resolution of angry feelings and bickering with "Let There Be Peace on Earth."

Praise God for the blessings of family and church in the concrete words of "For the Beauty of the Earth."

The Liturgical Child

1. Before reading the Deuteronomy text, set it in context by recounting events from Exodus in which Jews learned what God wants and promises. Invite worshipers to imagine themselves among the crowd gathered near the border of the Promised Land. Then assume the role of Moses, addressing his followers with great passion and dramatic flair. Use your hands to indicate the two options being offered. Point at the crowd as you warn them in verse 17; point to heaven as you call for witnesses in verse 19.

2. Ask eight readers (perhaps an older children's class) to read this psalm, each reader reading one verse. Before the reading, explain that in this acrostic (alphabet poem), each verse is a separate statement about obeying God's rules. In Hebrew, each line begins with the letter Aleph.

3. Build a prayer of confession on our failures to choose God's ways as they are expressed in the Ten Commandments. One leader could read the Commandments, pausing after each one for another leader to offer a brief prayer related to it.

Or a single leader could offer ten prayers, following the same structure: "You have called us to . . . [cite one command], but we have chosen to . . . . Forgive us."

4. Use the Ten Commandments in a responsive affirmation of faith. The congregational response to the reading of each command: "God, we want to choose your ways."

5. If you focus on family loyalty, provide an opportunity for couples to renew their marriage vows, or for members of families to make promises to one another. Informal congregations may enjoy gathering in family groups to hold hands as they make the promises. Be sure to urge those whose families are not present to imagine the other members around them. Then line out promises for family members to repeat.

Just because we live together, that does not mean that we are a family. Loving one another, taking care of one another, and sharing good and bad experiences makes us a family. So now, in the presence of God, who creates all families, I invite you to make these promises to the members of your family:

You are my family. Because I love you, I promise to . . .

- really listen when you talk to me;
- tell you about both the good and the bad things that happen to me;
- make time for us to do things together;
- put up with you when you are crabby and moody; and
- pray for you every day.

Let us pray. Lord, these are not easy promises to keep. Be with us. Help us to keep our promises on happy days when they are easy, and on miserable days when they are hard to keep. Help us remember our promises when what is happening to us seems so much more important than what is happening at home. Help us to share your love with one another until it spills over to people beyond our family. Amen.

Sermon Resources

1. Many parenting books speak about disciplining children with the "logical, natural consequences" of their activities. Tell stories about such discipline—perhaps from your own childhood—and compare it to the way God disciplines us.

2. This three-step method of dealing with anger helps people of all ages:

Step One: Work off the angry feelings. Everyone needs to know some safe, satisfactory ways to work off the steam of anger. Children often find that shooting baskets by themselves or some other physical exercise does the job.

Step Two: Think it through. After the angry feelings have been reduced, ask yourself the following questions:

What *really* happened?

Why did he/she/they do that?

Why did I do that?

What needs fixing?

What can I do to help fix it?

Step Three: Go to work. Decide what you need to do and get any help you need to do it. It often helps for a family member or friend to work with you, especially if you need to talk with the others involved.

3. A story about family loyalty in spite of problems, *Beezus and Ramona* by Beverly Cleary describes nine-year-old Beezus' difficulties with a very pesky preschool sister. The last chapter tells how Ramona ruined *two* birthday cakes on Beezus' birthday, and how their mother and her sister told of the problems they had getting along when they were little girls.

CHOOSE GOD'S WAYS AT HOME?

CAN WE

AT SCHOOL?

WHAT TO DO? HOW

SHALL I FOLLOW GOD'S RULES

Today we are thinking about making choices. Draw or write one choice you will make this week.

Will you choose to follow God's ways?

Turn each letter in ANGRY into a picture of something that makes you feel angry.

I was here first!

A N G R Y

Write a prayer about your feelings.

Amen.

Sixth Sunday After the Epiphany/ © 1992 by Abingdon Press.

SEVENTH SUNDAY AFTER THE EPIPHANY
(PROPER 2)

All of today's texts are about getting along with other people.

From a Child's Point of View

Old Testament: Leviticus 19:1-2, 9-18. For children, these are God's directions for getting along with others. The first two verses make it plain that to be one of God's people, one must follow these directions. The Good News Bible offers the clearest translation, but even some of its details require explanation. Children need to be told about the old practice of leaving some of the grain and fruit in the field for the poor. Older children will be interested in the responsibility of serving on a jury or as a witness in a trial. The rules that affect children most are those in verses 11 (do not steal, cheat, or lie); 14 (do not make fun of anyone with a handicap or weakness); 16 (do not tell lies about people); 17 (do not bear grudges); and 18 (do not try to get even with those who hurt you).

The summary of the rules in verse 19 is familiar to many children. The teaching point here is that love does not refer to how we feel about our neighbors, but about how we treat them. God expects us to treat all people with the same fairness and kindness with which we want to be treated.

Psalm: 119:33-40. All the lines in this section of the acrostic about God's Torah begin with the Hebrew letter He (ה). They also use the same eight synonyms for *Torah* that were found in the verses read on the Sixth Sunday After the Epiphany. Of these, only *Law, Commandments,* and *ways* make immediate sense to children.

Older children who are learning to recognize synonyms at school enjoy using that term in worship. Children will make sense of one or two of the verses as they are read.

Gospel: Matthew 5:38-48. This is one of the "hard sayings" for Christians of all ages. Jesus' point is that following God's directions for getting along with others is easy when we are among friends. The real challenge comes when we are dealing with people who not only will not love us back but probably will take advantage of us and bully us. Jesus insists that as God's people, we are to continue to treat those people well, no matter how they treat us.

For children, "You have heard it said" often refers to the encouragement of adults to learn to stand up for themselves against aggressive children. The challenge to Christian children and their adult guides is (1) not to sink to the level of meanness of those who make life difficult; and (2) to find creative, loving ways to get along with people who hurt you. Children need to know both that this challenge is not easy for Christians of any age and that God expects each of us to work hard at it.

Epistle: I Corinthians 3:10-11, 16-23. The Corinthian squabble between the followers of Apollos and the followers of Paul is beyond the comprehension of children. But they can explore Paul's insistence that a congregation (both in Corinth and today) is God's temple and that we are to take good care of that temple. Detailing that care by saying we should treat one another with lovingkindness, do the work needed to keep the church going, contribute money to pay church expenses, do the work of the church in the neighborhood and world, and so forth, helps children understand and apply Paul's message.

Watch Words

If you use the term *holiness code*, take time to explore what it means to be *holy*. Remember that *holy* is used today only at church and in cursing.

Avoid uncommon terms such as *deal falsely*, *defraud*, *revile*, *slander*, and *render justice*, used in many translations of Leviticus. Instead, speak about *lying, cheating, cursing*, and *being fair*.

Vengeance or *revenge* and *retaliation* are *getting even*, in children's words.

Because they perceive *enemies* as bad, many children will claim to have none. So if you use the term, define it in terms of people who make our lives difficult. Point out that all of us have some enemies, and challenge worshipers to identify theirs. Then proceed to Jesus' teachings about getting along with these folks.

Let the Children Sing

"Lord, I Want to Be a Christian" is the most familiar and best understood hymn for this theme. You may want to improvise new verses based on points of the sermon. "Let There Be Peace on Earth" is another good choice.

Praise God for the blessings of family and friends in the concrete words of "For the Beauty of the Earth."

Sing "We Are the Church" by Avery and Marsh to celebrate God's Temple.

The Liturgical Child

1. Bid worshipers to pray for people with whom they live, work, and play every day. Pray for members of our families, wonderful friends we see every day, friends who live in other cities or states, people at work or school with whom we must get along, people with whom it is hard to get along, groups of people with whom our community/nation has trouble getting along. After identifying each person or group for whom worshipers are to pray, pause to allow individuals to pray for specific people they know.

Example: Lord, we know that you create every person and love each one. But each of us knows at least one or two people who are very hard to love. They seem to be out to hurt us and make us look bad. They make us want to strike back, or at least protect ourselves. But you expect us to love them. That is not easy. Be with us and hear our prayers for people who hurt us. (*silence*)

2. Ask eight older children to read the eight verses of Psalm 119:33-40. Individuals may memorize or read their verse. If this is a class project, suggest that the students discuss the meaning of these verses as part of their preparation.

3. Read in unison Psalm 119:33-40 as an affirmation of faith in response to a sermon exploring God's directions for getting along with others. (The Good News Bible offers the simplest translation for children.)

4. Remind worshipers that I Corinthians is a letter from Paul to a church he had helped start and where now the people were fussing among themselves and criticizing what Paul had done. Read the text imagining that you are Paul, walking the floor as you dictate this letter. Shrug your shoulders and turn your hands palms up as you read verse 3. Stroke your chin or make another thoughtful gesture as you read verse 4*a*. Raise a finger and come to attention to make the emphatic point of 4*b*, then on verse 5, point toward the congregation to direct them not to judge.

5. If you celebrate Communion, note that God dreams and works toward a day when all people everywhere will gather around the table. Invite worshipers to imagine gathered at this table both people with whom they get along well and those with whom it is difficult to get along. Recall that God loves and forgives all of us.

Sermon Resource

In *Henry and the Clubhouse* by Beverly Cleary, ten-year-old Henry confronts several problems with an after-school paper route. One of them is an embarrassing four-year-old girl named Ramona, who tries to follow and help him every day. He tries several ways to discourage her, but never resorts to mean tricks. He is, however, persistent and creative. He is successful when he writes to Sheriff Bob, her TV hero, and asks him to tell her on television not to follow him around. Sheriff Bob does. Find this book in most children's libraries and bookstores.

Decode this message. In the space below each letter, write the letter that comes before it in the alphabet.

Z P V   T I B M M   M P W F   Z P V S

___ ___ ___   ___ ___ ___ ___ ___   ___ ___ ___ ___   ___ ___ ___ ___

O F J H I C P S   B T   Z P V S T M F G

___ ___ ___ ___ ___ ___ ___ ___   ___ ___   ___ ___ ___ ___ ___ ___ ___ ___

Turn each head into a drawing of a person you know. Draw at least one

● good friend
● adult
● younger child
● person with whom it is hard to get along.

Talk to God about each person you draw.

Seventh Sunday After the Epiphany/ © 1992 by Abingdon Press.

EIGHTH SUNDAY AFTER THE EPIPHANY
(PROPER 3)

From a Child's Point of View

Basic to our lives is the sense that the world is either trustworthy or dangerous. Psychologists tell us that this sense of trust or mistrust is set in infancy by early experiences of having our needs for food, comfort, and love either met or ignored. We, however, continue to shape and reshape our trust or mistrust of the world throughout childhood and adulthood. Today's texts contribute to that process by insisting that we can trust the world because God is in control. For children whose needs have been met, this is confirmation of what they experience. For children whose experiences have led them to distrust, this is a new way of looking at the world and offers much-needed hope.

Old Testament: Isaiah 49:8-13. This prophecy assumes knowledge of the story of the Exile and speaks of what God is going to do in the past tense. Its poetic comparisons of God's people to a covenant, prisoners, sheep, and travelers on a variety of roads confuse literal thinkers. The only translation children can decipher, even with adult help, is that in The Good News Bible.

The message behind the prophecy (that God has both the will and the power to rescue us from our biggest messes—even from Exile), however, offers children important security. The world may be dangerous, but the powerful God who loves them is watching over them and will protect and rescue them.

Psalm: 131. This psalm also speaks of trusting God's power. Unfortunately, it focuses on an image of childhood that is not particularly meaningful to children. Because children do not yet have much experience with trying to "make it on their own" or "being self-made," they cannot appreciate the difference in that kind of striving and the trust of a child napping in a parent's arms. Explore trusting God, rather than this poetic image of trust.

Gospel: Matthew 6:24-34. Worrying is the opposite of trusting. Like adults, children worry, and some worry more than others. Jesus' list of things people worry about makes sense to children. Most children spend time every day thinking about dinner. Some worry about whether there will be enough to go around. Others worry about whether they will get foods they like.

Many worry about what they wear. Clothes consciousness starts early! Even first- and second-graders know which designer labels are in. And those who do not worry about what they wear worry about how they look. If an inch could be added to height by worry, all children who dream of becoming professional basketball players would be taller!

Children also worry about the possibility of war and being a victim of violent crime. A chief childhood worry is that of being abandoned or left behind. Even in the safest situations, children can get caught up in imagining frightening "what ifs."

It is easy for children to misunderstand that Jesus is saying they do not need to worry, because God will provide everything they wish for—like magic. What Jesus does say is that if we will use the time and energy we spend on worrying about

54

ourselves on doing the work of God's kingdom, we will find that we have enough food, satisfactory clothes, and the ability to do what we need and want to do. That is hard for children, as well as for adults, to understand and try.

Epistle: I Corinthians 4:1-5. Children will have difficulty following Paul's message as it is read. But in the context of today's other readings, it has an important point for them—that they, like Paul, are neither to worry about what other people say or think about them, nor to judge what others do. God is the only one whose opinion matters, and God has given us clear instructions. So our task is to do what we know is right as God's people.

Watch Words

Trusting God is depending on God. *Worry* is the opposite, the result of depending only on ourselves and on people around us. Children learn more from examples of people who *trust* than from statements about *trusting*.

Avoid speaking of *weaned children* to bypass the giggles among the knowing. Follow the lead of the Good News Bible and speak simply of a *young child*.

Let the Children Sing

Praise the God who cares for the birds, the flowers, and us with "All Things Bright and Beautiful," "God of the Sparrow," or "This Is My Father's World."

Children can hear the trust in the feeling with which many congrgations sing "How Great Thou Art," even before they understand all the words. The repeated phrase and simple chorus of "God Will Take Care of You" make it a hymn of trust which young readers can sing with understanding.

The progression of ages in "Lord of Our Growing Years" keeps the attention of children.

Commit yourselves to not worrying by singing "Be Thou My Vision," if it is familiar to your children.

The Liturgical Child

1. If possible, feature in the worship center native wildflowers or boughs that bloom or bud in your community during this season. Choose plants that do not depend on a human gardener. For example, few bulbs are native, but forsythia or redbud trees are.

2. To create a litany about trusting God, describe briefly several biblical examples of God's saving activity (e.g., bringing the exiles home); then describe several situations today in which God's saving activity is needed. After each description, the congregation responds: "God is our help."

3. Invite worshipers to pray silently as the worship leader prays aloud this prayer of confession:

God, we know that you love us and care for us. So we are ashamed to admit that we are worriers. We worry about what we eat, what we wear, where we live, and who we know. We worry about how we look. We worry that we are too short or tall, too fat or thin, too bald or hairy, too young-looking or too old. We worry about whether we are smart enough, successful enough, or even funny enough. We worry about whether we have enough money. We worry about whether people like us. We worry about what might happen to us. We worry about the future. We wring our hands, tie our stomachs up in knots, and give ourselves headaches. Forgive us. Teach us to relax our hands and minds and hearts. Remind us of your promise that you will be with us and will care for us always. Teach us to trust you, for we pray in Jesus' name. Amen.

Assurance of Pardon: (Open your hands palms up and out.) Hear the good news. God is in charge. Everything does not depend on us. God takes care of the birds of the air, the flowers in the field, and us. God not only created us and cares for us, but God forgives us. Jesus died so that we might be forgiven and freed from our worries to lead abundant lives. Thanks be to God!

Sermon Resource

List all the things you do or could worry about as you prepare to preach a sermon (e.g., you could get a catch in your throat, forget what you planned to say, someone could walk out on you, etc.). Make similar lists of what a child could worry about on the way to school and what one celebrity (maybe a movie star or the President) could worry about on the way to work.

Hidden in the crowd are 2 words we will use in worship today. Shade in the spaces that have this face ☺ .

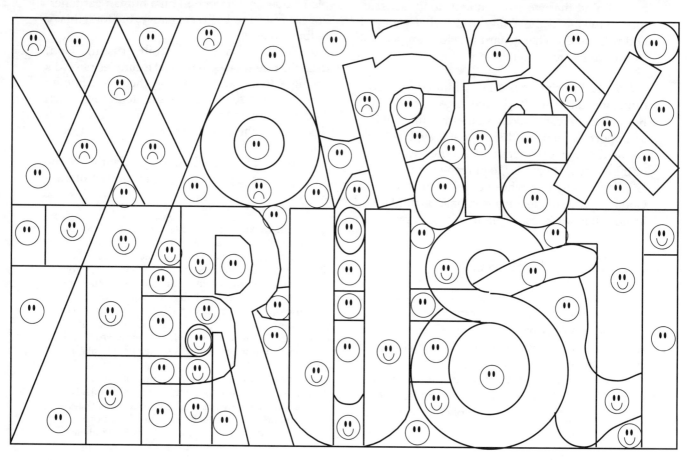

The words are ☹ _ _ _ _ _ and ☺ _ _ _ _ _ .

Write a prayer telling God one thing you worry about.

☹ _____
_____
_____

Write another prayer. Ask God to help you worry less about this. Or tell God one way you will work on worrying less about it.

☺ _____
_____
_____

Eighth Sunday After the Epiphany/ © 1992 by Abingdon Press.

LAST SUNDAY AFTER THE EPIPHANY
TRANSFIGURATION SUNDAY

From a Child's Point of View

Gospel: Matthew 17:1-9. Children can follow the events of this story fairly easily, but they need help in interpreting them. Perhaps the simplest interpretation is that God was telling the disciples something they should already have figured out, that Jesus was God's Son. But God was taking no chances. To make sure they got the message, God let them see Jesus in powerful new light; God sent Moses and Elijah (two famous Old Testament leaders) to show their support for Jesus; then God told the disciples, flat out, that Jesus is the Son of God.

Epistle: II Peter 1:16-21. On one level, this passage is proof that God's efforts at the transfiguration worked. Now the disciples knew who Jesus was. Peter (or his followers) did not need to make up any stories to explain who Jesus was. They only needed to tell what they had seen and heard. Few children can move beyond this interpretation to consider possible references to the Second Coming, or the writer's concerns about how prophecy is to be interpreted.

Psalm: 2 or 99. Psalm 2 celebrates God's choice of a Messiah, or Son. In a certain sense, it is a great joke at the expense of all the kings and princes, the political leaders who thought they were running things. God began by laughing at their foolishness (vss. 1-4) and announcing the enthronement of the ruler God had chosen (vss. 5-6). The new king then warned the others that they had better respect God (vss. 7-11).

If it is pointed out to them, older children will recognize the phrase, "This is my beloved Son," as an indication that this psalmist, hundreds of years before Jesus was born, already knew God's secret about the coming Son and was looking forward to the day that Son would come.

Psalm 99 assumes familiarity with Old Testament vocabulary and stories that few children possess, so Psalm 2 is a much better choice for children.

Old Testament: Exodus 24:12-18. Adults appreciate the similarities between this story and that of Jesus' transfiguration on the mountain, but children find no particular meaning in those similarities. Instead, they are impressed by all the fire and clouds that come with God's presence. For some, this is proof of God's great power. For others, it raises questions about why such displays are not seen today. There are no satisfying answers to such questions when posed by literal thinkers.

Watch Words

The word *transfiguration* is so obsolete that the only dictionary definition is a reference to this event in Jesus' life. Consider exploring the story without using the word at all. If *Transfiguration Sunday* is part of your tradition, use the word only as the name of the day, rather than as a description of what happened.

Let the Children Sing

"O Wondrous Sight! O Vision Fair!" retells the story of the transfiguration in words that most fifth- and sixth-graders will be able to read and sing.

To praise Jesus the Christ, sing a song many young people know, "Alleluia, Alleluia," or a traditional hymn, "When Morning Gilds the Skies." Nonreaders, when encouraged, can join in on the repeated "May Jesus Christ be praised!" and older readers will slowly pick up some of the other phrases.

Sing "Fairest Lord Jesus" only if children have learned it and sing it often in choir or church school.

Do not overlook the gospel hymn "I Love to Tell the Story." Its simple language makes it easy for children to read and understand.

The Liturgical Child

1. Before reading the account of the transfiguration, instruct all worshipers to close their eyes and see in their imagination the events described in Matthew.

2. The New Jerusalem Bible titles Psalm 2 "A Messianic Drama." Following that idea, ask three readers to present the psalm as a simple play. The three readers stand at the center of the worship area, with the narrator off to one side and God a bit behind or perhaps on a step above the Messiah:

Verses 1-5   Narrator reads.
Verse 6   God gestures toward the Messiah while speaking.
Verses 7-11   Messiah reads. Beginning with verse 10, he points finger at the congregation to warn the kings.

If possible, have all presenters memorize their lines, and practice together so that everyone is comfortable. Work for expressions that communicate the humorous put-down of the would-be rulers. This would be most effective with teenage or adult presenters.

3. Create a responsive Affirmation of Faith. A worship leader reads the phrases about Jesus in the Apostles' Creed, and after each phrase, the congregation responds: "God said, 'This is my beloved Son in whom I am pleased.' We will listen to him."

Sermon Resources

1. One way to explore the transfiguration is to present it as God telling us a very special secret: "This is my beloved Son, with whom I am pleased." Point out that God told the secret more than once. God told it first when Jesus was baptized, but only John heard. God told it again at the transfiguration, when Peter, James, and John heard. Following Jesus' instructions, the three disciples kept God's secret until Easter. Then they told everyone. Our task is to tell God's secret until everyone in the world has heard it.

Listen carefully as **Matthew 17: 1-9** is read.

Then draw a picture of what you think the disciples saw on the mountain.

Cross out every fourth letter in this trail of letters.
Write the remaining letters in the spaces below.

START ➭ T H I X S I S I N W R H O M E Y A S
M E D.
M Y B K E L O
O M V E D R S O N Y I N
A M R W E L L L P L R E A S

GOD'S SECRET:

"_ _ _ _ _   _ _   _ _   _ _ _ _ _ _ _   _ _ _   _ _   _

_ _ _ _ _   _ _   _ _   _ _ _ _   _ _ _ _ _ _ _."

ASH WEDNESDAY

Note: The readings for Ash Wednesday and Good Friday are repeated in each of the three cycles of the Revised Common Lectionary. In this series, Year A includes resources for Ash Wednesday; Year B includes resources for Holy Thursday; Year C includes those for Good Friday.

From a Child's Point of View

Old Testament: Joel 2:1-2, 12-17 or Isaiah 58:1-12. If presented as an eschatological event at which God will swoop down to judge us, Joel's "day of the Lord" frightens children and tends to make them feel doomed and hopeless. However, if the focus is on the fact that God cares about the way we act as individuals and as groups, and will judge us accordingly, the "day of the Lord" calls children to reflect upon their current activities and reform them as needed. Indeed, Joel's promise is that if we do reflect and change what needs changing, God will forgive and accept us. Thus, the "day of the Lord" calls us to take responsibility for our actions, rather than threatening us with destruction for our failures.

Choose the Isaiah text only if your congregation practices fasting. Verses 3a-6 speak most clearly to children.

Psalm: 51:1-17. This psalm is filled with abstract words about sin and forgiveness, but it also overflows with feelings of repentance. Children respond to these feelings if they are told that this is David's prayer after the prophet Nathan had publicly accused him of murdering a man in order to steal his wife. They understand how awful David felt when he saw his actions for what they

were and realized that, in child's language, "This is not the only awful thing I've done. I've been doing and saying bad things since I was born, no matter how hard I try to do better."

Once they explore the spirits of greed, selfishness, lovingkindness, and so forth, children understand David's plea for a "right spirit" in verse 10. But the "clean heart" will be interpreted literally, unless specific help is given to translate it into a "fresh start," and the "broken spirit" of verse 17 will sound very undesirable.

Epistle: II Corinthians 5:20b–6:10. The verses from 5:20b through 6:2 are the heart of the Ash Wednesday call to Lenten repentance. Unfortunately, the language is not child-accessible. The message is that God has been trying to make friends with us and is waiting for us to respond. Today is a good day to do so. Children will need specific directions on how to be God's friend.

In verses 3-10, Paul defends his ministry. Exploring his defense distracts children from the focus of the day.

Gospel: Matthew 6:1-6, 16-21. The bottom line of these teachings from the Sermon on the Mount: Don't be a show-off about being a Christian. God is not impressed by how often we go to church, how many church school awards we win, or how much we put into the offering plate, *if* we are doing those things just to impress other people and God. God can see through what we do to what we feel. God is looking for loving concern for other people and love of God.

The teaching about storing up treasures where they cannot be destroyed is one that children will not understand until they have more experience with treasures that turn out to be worthless. For now, it is an interesting lesson for them to hear and start living with.

Watch Words

Pay attention to your "confession" vocabulary. Use *sin* and *wrongs*, rather than obsolete words such as *transgressions* and *iniquity*. Remember that to many children, *offense* is the team with the ball. Speak of God's *love* and *forgiveness*, rather than *mercy*, *grace*, or *pardon*. Define *repenting* as changing our ways. To get past literal pictures of *cleansing* and *purging*, talk about God's call to clean up our act or a decision to clean up our language. Speak of a *humble*, rather than a *broken* spirit, as in The Good News Bible.

Let the Children Sing

Repentance hymns are filled with atonement language that makes little sense to children. Though they may sing along on the familiar ones, like "Amazing Grace," children seldom understand these hymns at any depth.

Consider making up verses to "Kum Ba Yah," to trace the flow of worship: "Someone's crying . . .; praying . . . ; forgiven . . .; happy . . . ."

To commit yourselves to Lenten disciplines, sing "Lord, I Want to Be a Christian," "Open My Eyes, That I May See," or "I'm Goin'a Sing When the Spirit Says Sing."

The Liturgical Child

1. If your congregation has a regular spoken or sung response to the prayer of confession, use it as the congregational response to a litany of confessions. Before using it, state the Kyrie response in children's language (e.g., "God forgive me; Jesus forgive me"). Repeating the response after a series of confessions is meaningful on Ash Wednesday and deepens the understanding of the confessional section of regular Sunday worship.

If your congregation does not use a regular response, create a similar litany prayer, using "Create in me a clean heart, O God, and put a new and right spirit within me" as the response.

2. Give each worshiper a slip of paper on which to write attitudes, relationships, and activities about which the person needs to confess. Provide time for this during worship. Collect the papers in offering baskets and burn them with some palm branches in a basin. These ashes will be very dark and can be used to mark the foreheads of worshipers.

3. The ashes for Ash Wednesday are traditionally made by burning last year's Palm Sunday palms as a sign that our best intentions (like the Hosannas of Palm Sunday) often end in failure (like the "crucify him" shouts of Good Friday). With this explanation, children can wear the ashes as an admission that no matter how hard they try, they always make sinful mistakes.

4. Silence for personal prayer is an important part of Ash Wednesday worship. Children benefit most if such silences are brief and are preceded by instructions, such as, "Let us each confess our failures in treating our families well." Such silences invite children's participation. Longer silences (e.g., the silence during the imposition of ashes) become times to sit still enough not to bother neighbors. For the sake of the children, fill longer silences with music.

5. If you celebrate Communion, remember that children do not understand atonement theology or language. For them, Communion says simply that God forgives them and takes care of them in spite of their sins. A time of confession, followed by the celebration of Communion (God's forgiveness), and finally by commitment to Lenten disciplines, make a meaningful worship sequence for children.

Sermon Resources

1. Keep the sermon brief. The heart of Ash Wednesday worship is the liturgy.

2. Use the sermon to point out specific Lenten disciplines for church members. Some for children include: (1) Set aside a time each day for individual or family prayer. *Pockets* is an excellent children's magazine which includes a monthly devotional reading guide for elementary children. (Order from *Pockets*, 1908 Grand Avenue, P.O. Box 189,

Nashville TN 37202-9929); (2) try a new church activity such as a weekday club or choir; (3) work on one particular attitude or relationship, to make it more like one Jesus would want; and (4) participate in a church mission collection.

Note: There is no Worship Worksheet today. This service should be so participatory that paper and pencil would be in a child's way.

FIRST SUNDAY
IN LENT

Note: The first Sunday in Lent of each year focuses on the temptation of Jesus. Check other books in this series for additional resources for this Sunday.

From a Child's Point of View

Old Testament: Genesis 2:15-17, 3:1-7. Recent studies indicate that all people move through predictable stages or tasks as they develop moral reasoning. The stage of a worshiper's moral development greatly influences the understanding of this Old Testament story.

In the earliest stage, children accept rules as irrefutable. By the age of four or five, they realize that those who are biggest and most powerful set the rules. Decisions to obey or disobey rules are made in order to receive rewards or escape punishment from the powerful. To people who reason this way, this story says that God is the biggest and most powerful being in the world. Indeed, God created the world, and therefore God's rules are to be obeyed. There are serious consequences when one breaks the rules.

Most young elementary children begin to realize that a person's motivations for breaking or obeying rules are important. They struggle with the difference between meaning well and simply being defiant. They experience situations in which the right and loving thing to do requires breaking the rules. From that perspective, the defiance of Adam and Eve is the key to the Fall. Adam and Eve knew what was wrong to do, but they did it anyway, simply for their own satisfaction.

That defiance is further defined by older elementary children, who generally see the world as a conglomerate of groups and individuals, each with an assigned role. It is important to these children to be a "good girl," a "good scout," and so forth. Therefore, when Adam and Eve defied the rule and ate the forbidden apple because they wanted to be "like God," they were stepping beyond their place and role. They were not being "good" people. By stepping out of their role, they broke the trust and peace with each other and between themselves and God. Shame and division resulted.

The challenge to children at each level is that they not do as Adam and Eve did. The *truth* is that people of all ages often do.

Gospel: Matthew 4:1-11. The temptations Jesus faced in the wilderness are very similar to those children face today. The first temptation was to be selfish, to take care of his own wants and needs. This temptation confronts children in the drive to get the biggest piece of pizza, the best basketball, the prettiest clothes, the most video games, and so forth. Jesus insisted that there are better things to do than worry about how much we gather for ourselves.

Jesus' second temptation was to use his powers for attention—to show off. Children today must decide whether to use their talents and abilities to gain praise and attention, or to help others. Jesus refused to be a show-off.

The third temptation was to be king of the world. Kings make all the decisions. Everyone else does what the king says. Children often wish they could be king or queen and, for once, be in charge. Jesus, though he would have made the very best king ever, refused to take such power. Instead, he chose to obey God.

Matthew presents Jesus' response as a decision to live within the role of a "good" person, as God intended. He planned to obey God.

Epistle: Romans 5:12-19. Paul's highly abstract theology is beyond the mental abilities of children. To their literal minds, it is neither sensible nor fair that either Adam's disobedience or Jesus' obedience should affect them. Read this passage for the adults. The children will find more meaning in comparing the actions of Adam and Jesus.

Psalm: 32. A child's summary of this psalm:

Happy are those who are forgiven by God. When the psalmist tried to cover up his sins, he felt guilty and awful. When he finally admitted what he had done and apologized, God forgave him. He says that a God who forgives you can be counted on to take care of you in any situation. And you would be smart to listen to that God and do as that God teaches.

The sin vocabulary and poetic images make this psalm difficult for children to follow as it is read.

Watch Words

The Fall, to children, is simply a title for the story of Adam and Eve's disobedience. The theological significance of a fall from grace is beyond their literal thinking.

Temptation is a familiar word. Review the Ash Wednesday Watch Words related to *sin.*

Let the Children Sing

To sing about resisting temptation, choose "O Jesus, I Have Promised" or "Take Time to Be Holy."

The connection between God's creation of the world and the battle against sin makes "This Is My Father's World" a good choice. Explore the meaning of verse 3 before it is sung.

Most children also know the creation hymns, "All Things Bright and Beautiful" and "For the Beauty of the Earth."

The Liturgical Child

1. Place an apple or an apple with a bite out of it in a greenery display in the worship center.

2. Matthew's account of the temptation is primarily a conversation between Jesus and Satan. As you read, take the two roles. Let the tone of Satan's sly superiority and Jesus' positive commitments be heard in your voice. Turn slightly toward one side while reading Satan's propositions, and toward the other side while reading Jesus' replies. Use your hands to point to the sweep of lands being offered, and to emphasize the suggested leap from the top of the Temple.

3. Focus confession on our tendency to be like Adam and Eve, rather than like Jesus:

Lord God, who created us, we confess that we are a lot like Adam and Eve. We too want to be "like God." We want to be in charge of everything, to know everything, to do everything our way. We are willing to break the rules and hurt one another to have our way. Forgive us.

Help us instead to learn from Jesus. Remind us that having what we want and need is not so very important. Tame our wild desires to be the center of attention, the star, the winner *every time.* Teach us to know your will and to obey. For we pray in Jesus' name, Amen.

Sermon Resources

1. Before the sermon, or before reading the Genesis text, give each worshiper a piece of wrapped hard candy, but instruct everyone not to eat the candy. During the sermon, describe different reasons for eating the candy as a springboard to exploring our responses to other temptations. At the end of the sermon, invite worshipers to eat the "teaching aid" if they wish.

2. *Obey* is a key word in the Genesis and Matthew stories. It marks the difference between Adam and Jesus. It is also something most of us do not like to do. Children do not like to obey, and they long for the day they will not need to obey anyone. Most brides no longer promise in their wedding vows to obey their husbands. In business, management techniques often stress group decision-making, rather than obedience to directives from the boss. Children appreciate having their feelings about obedience recognized and hearing about adult problems with obedience.

3. Tell stories about sinners whose experiences follow that of the psalmist (e.g., a child who called a sister a name that hurt badly—first trying to ignore what had happened, then feeling guilty before the sister and before God, finally apologizing to both and accepting forgiveness).

Note: If you use the "Lent detective" section of the Worship Worksheet, be sure to include all the needed information during worship.

Today is the first Sunday of Lent.
Be a detective. Listen and watch
for clues in worship to complete
your mission report.

Adam and Eve were tempted to disobey God.
Jesus was tempted to be a selfish
show-off.

Draw or write about what tempts you.

Mission: Fill in the missing
information.

Today is the first Sunday
of ___ ___.

Lent is a time to get
ready for ___ ___.

Lent lasts ___ days.

The church color for Lent
is ___ ___. The
color of ___ ___ is
the same.

Answers: Lent, Easter, 40, purple, Advent

First Sunday in Lent/ © *1992 by Abingdon Press.*

SECOND SUNDAY IN LENT

From a Child's Point of View

Old Testament: Genesis 12:1-4a. Children can follow this story easily. God asked Abram to move to an unknown land where he would become the father of a nation. Abram went, but the difficulty involved in his going is recognized only when the details of the move are explored. Children who have moved especially appreciate the risk involved in packing up everything, to move to an unannounced destination. They also can wonder, with Abram, how a childless old man was to be father of a country, in a land where other people already lived and ruled. The point is that for Abram, faith was believing God's promise and trusting God to make that promise come true, in God's own time and own way.

Epistle: Romans 4:1-5, 13-17. The vocabulary and theology of this passage are so abstract that this text will mean nothing to children as it is read. Behind it, however, is a simple two-part message children can understand.
1. Abraham had not done or said anything special to make God choose him. God loved him. And it's the same with us. We can do nothing to make God love and choose us. God just does.
2. The mark of being one of Abraham's people or Abraham's family is to trust God as Abraham did.

Psalm: 121. This psalm celebrates the faith in God which we share with Abraham and Paul. If it is read with feeling, some of its meaning will come through to children. To help them understand it more fully, introduce it as a song sung by Jews as they walked up the steep, hot road to Jerusalem to celebrate religious holidays at the Temple. The hill they looked to was the hill on which the Temple was perched.

They celebrated God's unsleeping care of them through the nights (when robbers might attack) and during the heat of the day. Children can then imagine themselves among the travelers, singing this psalm as they walk. Older children can be challenged to write similar psalms to celebrate God's constant care, to be recited while going to school or staying home alone at night.

Gospel: John 3:1-17 or Matthew 17:1-9. Most children and many adults empathize with Nicodemus in this situation. They simply never quite understand Jesus' abstract, symbolic talk. They feel as put down as Nicodemus did by Jesus' surprise that such a great leader couldn't follow this simple discussion.

There are two ways to present this passage that make sense to children. The first is to focus on Jesus' comment about the reality and power of the invisible wind, and explore the reality of other invisible powers, such as God's love and power. Jesus calls Nicodemus and us to depend on these invisible realities, rather than on things we can see. The second is to focus on Jesus' insistence, in John 3:16, that we can trust God to love us and to save us. There is no need to depend upon ourselves.

The transfiguration story (Matt. 17:1-9) makes more sense to children in the context of the last Sunday after the Epiphany (Transfiguration Sunday) than in the context of today's Lenten texts about trusting God. Should you elect to use it, find resources in "Last Sunday After the Epiphany."

Watch Words

Faith is trusting God. In today's texts, it refers more to a way to live every day than to a set of mental affirmations. Faith is acting as if you can depend on God's love, whether on the playground or when sharing a bedroom with a younger brother or sister. It is acting as if following God's directions is the way to a happy life.

Beware of the vocabulary of Romans. *Justification* and *righteousness* are indefinable for children. *Grace* is a girl's name or a prayer before meals. The *Law* stands for the police, not for earning favor with God by following the rules.

Let the Children Sing

Invite worshipers of all ages to recall their own baptisms by singing "Child of Blessing, Child of Promise." Suggest that they imagine that the whole church is singing it directly to them.

Sing about living by faith with "He Leadeth Me, O Blessed Thought" (children will join in mainly on the chorus), "Be Thou My Vision" (if it is sung by children in other church activities), and "I Sing a Song of the Saints of God" (to celebrate faith heroes and heroines like Abraham).

The Liturgical Child

1. Invite worshipers to declare their membership in the children of Abraham in an Affirmation of Faith. The congregation's response to each affirmation: *We are the children of God.*

Children of Abraham know that God created them and loves them, and chooses them to be among God's people. (RESPONSE)
Children of Abraham know that even if they tried there is nothing they can do that would be good enough to impress God. They also know that they do not have to earn God's love or be good enough for God. God loves them anyway. (RESPONSE)
Children of Abraham know that God is in charge. They trust that if they follow God's directions, all of God's promises to the children of Abraham will come true for them. (RESPONSE)
Children of Abraham know that God is in charge. They do not act like they are in charge.

And, they do not let any person or power be more important than God. (RESPONSE)
Children of Abraham know that God loves all people. They know that everyone they meet could be a child of Abraham and so treat them as brothers and sisters. And, they know that God will not rest until every person in the world is part of the family. (RESPONSE)

Sermon Resources

1. *The Velveteen Rabbit* by Margery Williams (Doubleday, 1969) is a familiar story. Basically, it is a discussion about what makes a stuffed animal "real" (or what makes a person "real"). The conclusion is that one is real when all your buttons have been loved off, your fur (or hair) played into a frayed mess, and so forth. In the context of Jesus' words about the wind, this story tells us that invisible love is more important than a visibly beautiful, intact exterior.

2. Describe some of the ways Abraham might have tried to make himself the "father of a great nation" (e.g., raise an army to drive out the Canaanites; write a constitution and laws to enforce; buy a crown for himself). Instead of doing these things, he trusted God to do what God had promised. Abraham followed God's directions and lived quietly in the country ruled by other people.

God has promised us good lives. It is tempting to take control, respond violently to people who tease and bully us, and make sure we get as much of what we want as we can. Instead, we should follow God's rules, even when it seems that will not be to our advantage, and trust God's plan.

3. Elementary-age children are very interested in clubs, teams, and other groups. When asked to introduce themselves, many older elementary children reply by naming groups to which they belong. They take their membership requirements, group oaths, and rules quite seriously.

Pick up on their keen interest by inviting worshipers to be one of the "children of Abraham." Describe the benefits in terms of God's promise in Genesis 12. Outline members' discipline in terms of trusting God every day. And note the inclusive entrance requirements. Challenge worshipers to join this group and then live as the children of Abraham.

Find the hidden word in each drawing below.

1. _ _ _ _ _   2. _ _ _ _ _   3. _ _ _ _ _   4. _ _ _ _

Listen for these words in our songs and prayers.

Write a definition of each word.

or

Write a sentence using each word.

1. _____
_____

2. _____
_____

3. _____
_____

4. _____
_____

THIRD SUNDAY IN LENT

From a Child's Point of View

Old Testament: Exodus 17:1-7. Do not assume that children know the context of this story. Before reading it, explain that the people Moses led across the desert had been slaves in Egypt. God had sent ten horrible plagues to convince the king of Egypt to let them go, and then had rescued them when they seemed hopelessly trapped between the king's army and the Sea of Reeds.

Though the children will follow the action of the story, they will need help to recognize the amazing lack of trust on the part of the people whom God had cared for so well. Older children enjoy exploring the meaning of the names: Massah, which means *trying* (as in "You are trying my patience!) and Meribah, which means *fault-finding* or *complaining*. The significance of the names helps them to recognize the sin of the people.

Psalm: 95. The praise hymn in verses 1-7a is easy for children, but before they can understand the warning in verses 7b-11, they must hear the Exodus text with enough attention paid to the names Massah and Meribah that they will recognize the reference to that story. To children, the warning is not to try God's patience with constant complaints about what they want and need, but to trust God to love and care for them. Verse 10 in The New Jerusalem Bible speaks clearly to older children. God is speaking:

For forty years that generation sickened me,
and I said, "Always fickle hearts;
they cannot grasp my ways."

Grumbling and otherwise trying the patience of parents can be used as an example of what it means to *test* someone and *try their patience*. But do not use this psalm as a warning against complaining in general. Focus on trusting or not trusting God.

Epistle: Romans 5:1-11. This passage states the point of the Old Testament texts in a Christian setting, and in theological language that is beyond children. Read it for the adults.

Its message in relation to the other texts is that though the travelers in the desert had ample proof of God's love and care, we have even more striking proof in Jesus. If this is pointed out in concrete terms, it can remind the children that they should not follow the example of the exslaves in the desert.

Gospel: John 4:5-42. This complicated passage includes a word play on *water*, a tricky conversation about an old Jewish-Samaritan dispute, the use of water as a symbol for all that is life-giving and refreshing, and a collection of harvest images. To avoid totally overwhelming children, consider reading only verses 5-26.

Even older children have trouble appreciating Jesus' word play on living or running water. They respond more quickly to the general need for water. Though symbolism is difficult for children, the symbol here is a good one for beginners. John's point is that God's Word and loving care are as important as water to our survival and to our refreshed happiness. Exploring the function of water, and then comparing it to the function of knowing God and God's Word leads children to John's message.

Watch Words

In today's texts, *faith* is trusting God to continue loving and caring for us as God has done in our past.

Avoid all forms of *justified* and *reconciled* in Romans 5. Instead of explaining these complex, abstract terms, move directly to Paul's insistence that we need not worry about anything because God continues to care for us.

Rather than speaking of God's *providence* (most recognized by children as the capital of Rhode Island), cite specific examples of that loving care.

Let the Children Sing

Praise God, who loves and cares for us in so many ways, with "Now Thank We All Our God" or "For the Beauty of the Earth." Both cite everyday examples of God's love in simple words.

For yourselves and for the slaves in the desert, sing "God Will Take Care of You." Nonreaders can join in on the much repeated title phrase.

The Liturgical Child

1. Present today's texts dramatically:

● Let the frustration of all parties show in your voice and your posture as you read the exchanges in Exodus 17. Use the tones and the inflections that thirsty, tired people would use at the end of another hot, dry day.

● Present the Gospel text as a play, with the worship leader reading John 4:5-7a from the lectern as a costumed Jesus takes his place by a well (or sits on a stool). A woman enters carrying a water jug, and she and Jesus engage in conversation with parts memorized (if possible). Ask older youths or adults to take these parts, and work with them on facial expression, posture, and voice inflections. Their presentations will be essential in bringing an intricate conversation to life. The narrator could read verses 39-42 to complete the story.

● Preserve the division in Psalm 95 by having the congregation read verses 1-7a in unison or responsively, with a worship leader reading verses 7b-11 in the role of the warning priest.

2. Go all-out to appeal to the sense of hearing. Fill the sanctuary with the sound of bubbling water; borrow or rent a champagne fountain and fill it with water. Then challenge a parishioner to create a worship center by placing greens and flowers around the fountain. The display could be on the chancel table or off to one side, perhaps near the baptismal font.

Sermon Resources

1. Imagine with the congregation that it is a hot summer day. Describe the heat of the burning sun, sticky sweat, a dry thirsty mouth. Remember together how it feels to jump into a cool swimming pool or stand in a cool late-afternoon rainstorm. Think about cold drinks you enjoy in summer and imagine drinking an icy cold glass of water. Then review what Jesus was telling the woman at the well and us. (During late winter in cold climates, worshipers of all ages are quite willing to try this, though they may claim they cannot remember ever being hot, or even warm.)

2. Create a modern-day version of the complaining travelers in Exodus 17. Describe a family on the second day of a long drive to Disney World (or some other distant place children love to go). Describe the late afternoon grumbling: "Aren't we there *yet*?"; "He's on my side, Daddy! He's picking on me"; "Nobody ever pays any attention to me!"; "What do you mean, there isn't a motel for the next hundred miles! I thought you had this planned!"; "How come we can't fly? The Joneses did!"; and so forth. Compare this grumpy group with the thirsty slaves freed from Egypt.

3. After exploring the lack of trust among the Hebrews at *Massah* and *Meribah*, give worshipers individual packets of M & Ms. Suggest that as they enjoy this treat later today, they name one way God loves and cares for them for each piece of candy eaten. Families might enjoy eating the candies together and sharing their ideas.

Listen to the story in **Exodus 17: 1-7** about the complaining people. Draw or write about something that makes you complain.

This drives me nuts!

Why should this happen to me?

I don't know what to do!

Write a prayer about this problem.

_____
_____
_____
_____
_____
_____
_____
_____

Remember that God loves you and promises to take care of you.

FOURTH SUNDAY IN LENT

From a Child's Point of View

Old Testament: I Samuel 16:1-13. This story of Samuel anointing David king gives children hope. God did not select the oldest or most grown-up, but the one his family considered too young to come to the sacrificial feast. Children who eat in the kitchen while adults eat in the dining room, or who are left at home with a baby-sitter while parents go to interesting-sounding parties and movies, appreciate God's choice of someone like them.

God's message to Samuel about how God "sees" or judges a person offers children both security and a challenge. The security is that God sees them as they really are. Teachers, coaches, other kids, and even parents may misjudge their behavior. But God knows who they really are, appreciates good intentions that come out all wrong, and empathizes with their internal struggles with problems that others discount. The challenge is to use God's standards in judging others. God sees beyond what a person looks like and does, to what a person thinks and feels. We are to try to do the same.

Psalm: 23. This psalm of trust in God's care and protection is based on two images—the shepherd and the banquet table. Children who attend church school throughout childhood collect the details of shepherd life (pastures, still waters, rods, staffs) and explore the figure of the shepherd as one who is devoted to the sheep and can be depended upon to care for them. These children recognize at an early age that in the Bible sheep often stand for God's people in the same way the American eagle stands for Americans. The un-churched urban child, however, is likely to identify a shepherd as a fierce guard dog, and thus be baffled by the psalm.

Among the banquet images, the overflowing cup needs to be introduced as a continually refilled cup. There are children for whom an overflowing cup at the dinner table rates a scolding for clumsiness. And the only sensible response to having oil poured on your head is gratitude that you do not live in the day when that was considered a treat.

Epistle: Ephesians 5:8-14. Light and darkness are rich images, based in experiences shared by people of all ages. When children are in bed, they are afraid of what they think they may see in the dark. They also worry about bumping into things or falling down if they try to move about in the dark. Based on such experiences, they prefer to be children of light rather than children of the dark. Younger children accept the designation of God's people as the children of light in the same way they accept the name and symbol of their sport team. Older children can begin to identify ways that God's people are like light for the world: We light up the world by loving instead of hating and by caring for those who need help.

Those children who hide in the darkness under the covers, in the closet, or in a clubhouse, to do things they know they should not be doing, understand Paul's instructions to do only those things that can be done without shame in full daylight.

Gospel: John 9:1-41. This story is long and complicated. After hearing it read, few children

73

will be able to retell it in any detail. They will depend on the preacher to raise a few key points and retell the related parts of the story.

Chief among those points is that Jesus loved the blind man enough to do what he could (in Jesus' case, to heal him!). Everyone else was sitting around feeling sad about the man's blindness and wondering why he was blind. We can expect God to respond to our problems with action, just as we are to follow Jesus' example in responding to the needs of others.

Older children enjoy exploring the comparison of the physical blindness of the man with the blindness of the religious leaders (their refusal to see who Jesus was and what God was doing). With help, they can identify other attitudes as blindness: racial or ethnic prejudice (refusal to see certain groups as children of God); hatred of individuals (refusal to see even disagreeable people as God's children); and greedy self-centeredness (refusal to see anyone's needs but our own).

Watch Words

Be careful about "shepherd" vocabulary. *Rods* and *staffs*, in particular, may need explanation.

Let the Children Sing

Choose a hymn version of Psalm 23 that is familiar to your congregation and follows the biblical text closely.

Beware of the confusing light images and difficult light language of many hymns focused on light. To sing about our mission to the world, try "God of Grace and God of Glory." Younger children will pick up the repeated phrases.

If your children are familiar with "What a Friend We Have in Jesus," sing it to celebrate Jesus' loving action.

If you focus on David's character, sing of other faith heroes with "I Sing a Song of the Saints of God."

The Liturgical Child

1. If you use candles in your Sunday morning worship, take time to point out their significance in relation to today's texts about light.

2. To help children keep up with the story in John 9, ask a group to pantomime the story as it is read. Since this requires at least ten players (2 disciples, 2 neighbors, 2 Pharisees, the blind man, his 2 parents, and Jesus), it may be a good project for a youth class. Because there is so much movement, plan for at least one good rehearsal. Costumes would be nice but are not essential.

3. Offer a Confession of Sin based on light and dark:

Lord, you have called us to be children of light, but we live more like children of darkness. We allow dark, unhappy feelings to run our lives. We do, in secret, things we want to hide from everyone—especially from you. And we openly say and do things that make people's lives dark and miserable. Forgive us. Help us to soak up so much of your light and love that we cannot help shining for others. We pray in the name of Jesus, who is the light of the whole world. Amen.

Assurance of Pardon: Jesus said, "I am the light of the world," and he said to his disciples, "You are the light of the world." The Bible promises us that "the light shines in the darkness and the darkness has not put it out." So we are forgiven and are called to be the children of light.

Sermon Resources

1. David is often referred to as "a man after God's own heart." Explore Psalm 23 to learn what God might have liked about the person who wrote it, and what God might want to see in us:

Verses 1-2: David did not worry about what he would eat or wear. He trusted God's loving care.

Verse 3b: David expected God to tell him what to do. He knew that God would help him know right from wrong. Note his response when Nathan pointed out his murder of Uriah.

Verse 4: David was brave. Nothing frightened him when he was doing God's work. Cite as an example his killing of Goliath.

Verse 5: David was willing to live with some enemies around, and he expected that life would be good in spite of them.

Verse 6a: David enjoyed life as God's good gift and expected it to be good and happy.

Verse 6b: David wanted to be near God every day, especially in worship. Point to his writing of psalms and the abandon with which he danced before the Ark of the Covenant.

Listen carefully to the stories about David and to Psalm 23, which David wrote.

Draw a picture of something David did *or* write words that describe David. Circle the words that also describe you.

Paul warned us to be children of light, not children of dark. Write the words that describe children of light in the blanks beside the word LIGHT. Write the words that describe children of dark in the blanks beside the word DARK.

haters bickering cruel

kind loving gentle

greedy strong sharing

L__ __ __ __ __
__I__ __
G__ __ __ __ __
__H__ __ __ __ __
__T__ __ __ __

__ __ __ __D__
__A__ __ __ __
__R__ __ __
__ __ __K__ __ __ __ __

Answers:
Light: loving, kind, gentle, sharing, strong
Dark: greedy, haters, cruel, bickering

FIFTH SUNDAY IN LENT

From a Child's Point of View

Commentaries from an adult point of view stress the comparisons of life and death in these passages. Undergirding those comparisons is the reality of God's amazing power. God could bring dry bones back to life, a defeated nation back into existence, even the dead Lazarus back to life. Focusing on God's power prepares the way for experiencing God's power in the events of Easter.

Old Testament: Ezekiel 37:1-14. The details of Ezekiel's vision make a great mental picture. Children enjoy visualizing the bones coming together into skeletons, being covered with muscles and skin, then being brought to life by God's breath. On their own, most children interpret the vision rightly—that God is powerful enough to bring dead bones back to life as living people. Few children can, or need to, get beyond the literal vision or its basic message. They enjoy and find security in God's great power.

Children have great difficulty with the opening graves and promises of verses 11-14. Some older children can follow an explanation of what God was telling a group of defeated, hopeless people who had been deported to a foreign land. For these children, Ezekiel's message is that there is no situation so hopeless that God cannot turn it around.

Gospel: John 11:1-45. This is a long and complicated but interesting story which parallels Ezekiel's vision. Both Martha and Mary believed that Jesus had the power to heal the sick, and they all but accused him of allowing Lazarus to die because he had not come more quickly. Martha even suggested the possibility that Jesus could still act on Lazarus' behalf—but she did not fully believe it. Then, surprise! By raising Lazarus, Jesus demonstrated that he (and God) were even more powerful than death. Jesus' power was greater than even his best friends and supporters dared to dream.

In verses 5-16, another power confrontation is introduced. The disciples did not want Jesus to go back to Judea for fear of the powerful Jewish authorities who wanted to kill him. That, of course, points to the ultimate power confrontation that will come during Holy Week. Children, however, will have trouble following the conversation in these verses, so it may be wise to omit the verses in order for them to hear the rest of the story.

Two trivial details in this story interest children—Mary's concern about the smell of Lazarus' dead body, and the fact that verse 35, "And Jesus wept," is the shortest verse in the Bible.

Epistle: Romans 8:6-11. This passage is a theologian's summary of, and response to, the truths found in Ezekiel's vivid vision and the story of Jesus' raising of Lazarus. Children understand more of the vision and the story than of this discourse. Their thinking abilities are not developed enough to deal with the symbolism of life in the flesh, in the Spirit, or in Christ. Consequently, they will make little sense of the passage as it is read. Its message to children will need to be presented in the sermon in terms of the importance of "being on the side of" or "belonging to"

76

God, whose power is described and celebrated in the other texts of the day.

Psalm: 130. The feelings of this penitential psalm speak more clearly to children than do its abstract words. They hear mainly the pain of "out of the depths I cry to you, O Lord," and the trust of the repeated references to "waiting for the Lord."

Watch Words

The *sinews* in Ezekiel's vision are muscles and tendons.

Let the Children Sing

To sing about God's great power, try "I Sing the Almighty Power of God," which points out the familiar evidence of God's power in simple language, or "When Morning Gilds the Skies," with its repeated phrase. Avoid hymns filled with long abstract words, Such as "Immortal, Invisible, God Only Wise." If spring is beginning, sing "Fairest Lord Jesus."

Imagine yourselves among Ezekiel's reconstituted dry bones before singing "Breathe on Me, Breath of God." Older worshipers will sing from the hopeless "bone dry" situations in their lives. Young children will imagine themselves among the bones being given new life by God. Both can be true worship.

The Liturgical Child

1. Before reading the Ezekiel text, urge children to pay attention to what happens to all the bones. Then present the passage with all the dramatic flair of the poet/prophet Ezekiel, speaking to a room full of exiles.

2. For the sake of children who cannot follow the discussion between the disciples and Jesus, begin reading the story about the raising of Lazarus with verse 17. Before reading, identify the characters and the situation. Remind listeners about Jesus' special friendship with Mary, Martha, and Lazarus—two sisters and a brother who lived together.

If you include the first 16 verses, consider moving to different points in the chancel, tracing Jesus' movements in the story. Carrying your Bible, read verses 1-16 at one side of the chancel, move to the other side to read verses 17-34, then step or turn toward the center of the chancel to read the final scene at the tomb.

Prepare this reading carefully. It is long and complicated. If it is read without dramatic flair, children will soon be lost. But it is so intensely emotional that it can be melodramatic. Practice reading the conversations so that they reflect the emotional situation, but point beyond the feelings to what is happening.

3. Use Psalm 130 as the base for prayers of confession. The worship leader describes a series of sinful "depths" into which we sink. The congregation's response to each one: *"Out of the depths, we cry to you, O Lord. Lord, hear our voice!"* For example:

> Lord, you have given us families as good gifts, but we turn them into big problems. We fuss over who must do what work; we treat one another with less kindness than we treat strangers on the street; we remember the wrongs we endure at home, but we forget the loving care we find there. (RESPONSE)
>
> Lord, you have placed us on a planet blessed with food and water and air . . . . (RESPONSE)

Base the Assurance of Pardon on verses 3 and 4. (The New Jerusalem Bible offers a good translation for children.)

Sermon Resources

1. The vision of dry bones brings Halloween to the minds of children. Capitalize on that connection by telling about the origins of Halloween (All Hallow's Eve). Bonfires were burned that night to chase away evil spirits and powers, and on the following day, All Saints Day, the people celebrated the good spirits and powers. Together, these days were a celebration of God's power over all other powers of the world. Today's texts celebrate God's power over invaders (Ezekiel) and death (Matthew). There is no power that can defeat God.

2. Devote the whole sermon to telling stories of God's surprising power. Select stories from the Bible, literature, and everyday experience in

which people find themselves in hopeless situations and are surprised by God's power. Include the stories in today's readings, some stories about times when it seemed impossible that brothers and sisters could ever get along, dry-bones-to- new-life stories from the history of your congregation or community, and others. Conclude each account with a refrain such as, "It would have been hopeless, but God is powerful."

Listen carefully when **Ezekiel 37: 1-14** is read. Draw pictures of what happened to all those bones.

There was a valley full of bones.

The bones came together.

There was flesh and skin on them.

Breath came into them and they stood.

Listen carefully to the story about Jesus raising Lazarus from death. Then correct the mistakes in the story below.

When a messenger told Jesus that Ben was sick, Jesus went to see him immediately. Ben died before Jesus got there. Mary and Jane said that Jesus could have healed their father if Jesus had come in time. Jesus went to the tomb with them. At the tomb, Jesus laughed. Then he told them to unlock the door. When the door was opened, Jesus said, "Live again, Ben!" And Ben lived.

Answer: Read John 11: 1-45.

Fifth Sunday in Lent/ © *1992 by Abingdon Press.*

PALM/PASSION SUNDAY

Note: Only the Gospel texts (the three Synoptic narratives) differ from year to year for Passion/ Palm Sunday. Check other cycles of this series for additional commentary and suggestions. Year C offers help in structuring liturgy; years A and B offer additional specific resources.

From a Child's Point of View

Consider the children when deciding whether to celebrate Palm or Passion Sunday. If they will not worship with or around the Passion stories on Holy Thursday or Good Friday, celebrate Passion rather than Palm Sunday. No worshiper of any age can fully understand or share in Easter joy without experiencing the betrayals and crucifixion.

Gospel: Matthew 21:1-11 (Palm). In Matthew's account of this event, all the people of Jerusalem turned out to welcome Jesus. Children know that a king should enter town on a spirited white charger and ride over a plush carpet or a carpet of flowers. Jesus rode on a donkey on a path of tree branches and coats. His choice of a mount shows what kind of king Jesus intended to be. The pathway of coats demonstrates the people's devotion. (Imagine explaining your soiled coat to your mother that evening!)

In Matthew's Gospel, Jesus was welcomed as the Son of David. If you explored David's character on the fourth Sunday of Lent, children will be ready to compare David and Jesus. Both were God's chosen kings, though neither was born as a wealthy prince and both were overlooked at first. David was known as "a man after

God's own heart," while Jesus was "God's own Son." Jesus, however, was "God with us," and is therefore far greater than David—or any other king.

The challenge of this Palm Sunday account for children is to welcome Jesus as king of their own lives, with as much enthusiasm as the crowds in Jerusalem showed.

Psalm: 118:1-2, 19-29 (Palm). This psalm is a liturgy for welcoming a victorious king to the Temple. Children enjoy acting it out as it is read and learn from the process that even kings are subject to God. Though they have trouble identifying Matthew's quotes because the English translations of the psalm do not use the word Hosanna! children quickly identify the similarity of Jesus' entrance to that of the king.

Gospel: Matthew 26:14–27:66 or 27:11-54 (Passion). Children respond strongly to the pain of Jesus' betrayal by Judas, his denial by Peter, and the desertion of the others. They know from experience how it hurts when friends fail us.

Children need to hear a clear physical description of the crucifixion in order to understand its pain. They need to know that Roman whips were tipped with metal and glass, and people sometimes died from the whippings. Unless they comprehend that Jesus died as painful and terrible a death as ever was invented, they cannot fully appreciate the wonder that God still allowed it and forgave the human race for doing it. So we do them no favor when we downplay the gore and violence.

Psalm: 31:9-16 (Passion). If it is presented as a prayer Jesus could have prayed on the cross, children will hear in this psalm a number of short phrases which they can imagine Jesus praying.

Epistle: Philippians 2:5-11 This great hymn of the early church describes in cosmic terms the things that the passion story describes in earthy realities. Children will understand the story first. To help older children, alert them to the "down" direction of verses 6-8 and the "up" direction of verses 9-11. Point out the call for us to be as obedient in our lives as Jesus was in his (verse 6).

Old Testament: Isaiah 50:4-9a Children will hear in this suffering-servant song the words and phrases that Jesus could have said, or those that describe Jesus.

Watch Words

Hosanna! the big word for Palm Sunday, is a fun word to say over and over, knowing that it is a greeting meant only for Jesus. It need not be translated or defined.

Be sure to define *passion* as one title for the story of Jesus' death. Remember that its common use today is to describe sexual feelings.

The word *crucifixion* is used only in the Christian church today. Be sure to define and explain it.

Let the Children Sing

Palm Sunday Choices: "Lift up Your Heads, Ye Mighty Gates" is a song with which the crowds might have welcomed Jesus. Before singing it, point out that we will be singing about opening the gates of a city, and also of opening "the portals of our hearts," or getting ready to love and serve Jesus. "Tell Me the Stories of Jesus" is a Palm Sunday hymn many children know.

Passion Sunday Choices: "Were You There," with its repeated lines that tell the passion story, can be sung even by nonreaders. "O Sing a Song of Bethlehem" traces Jesus' whole life and ministry with simple words and tune. Avoid hymns that speak of "the cross" as a symbol for the passion events and those that are filled with abstract atonement language.

The Liturgical Child

1. Matthew's account claims that the whole city was stirred up. So, if there are other congregations nearby, plan palm processionals of choirs and congregations from several churches to an outdoor gathering place where a Palm Sunday litany is read and hymns sung. It is best that worship services in each sanctuary precede such a procession.

2. Act out Psalm 118:1-2, 19-29. The congregation, standing in place, takes the role of the welcoming crowd, reading verses 1-2. A worship leader in the pulpit, as the priest, reads verse 20. A second worship leader, taking the role of the king, enters from behind the congregation and stands about halfway up an aisle to read verses 19 and 21-23. The congregation replies with verses 24-29.

3. To confess fickle loyalty to King Jesus, pray:

Almighty God, on Sunday it is easy for us to say, "Jesus is Lord!" It is easy to sing about you as our King and make big promises about being your servants. It feels good to be among your people. But it is different at school and at work. Too often, we are ready to try anything to get good grades or to be successful. We ignore your rules to satisfy our own wishes. We listen when friends want us to try things we know are unloving and wrong. Forgive us. Help us remember that you are the King of all our lives, every day of the week, everywhere we go. Amen.

Assurance of Pardon: Jesus *is* Lord—the Lord of love and forgiveness. From the cross, he forgave the people who had praised him on Sunday and called for his death on Friday. And he forgives us too! Thanks be to God!

Sermon Resources

1. Instead of preaching a sermon, read all or parts of the passion narrative. Prepare a lively, dramatic reading. Consider illustrating the reading with slides or large pictures. Select a variety—some great paintings and some simple pictures from the church school picture files. If you plan ahead, you might even include some drawings done by children's classes, mounted on poster board or photographed on slide film.

2. Matthew's Gospel stresses the fickleness of

the crowd. On Palm Sunday, they shouted, "Hosanna! Save us!" Five days later, they shouted just as loudly, "Crucify him! Let his blood be on our heads!" In preaching about our fickle loyalty to King Jesus, tell stories about . . .

• a girl who recited a dozen memory verses about love in Sunday school, but played only with her chosen few friends at school.

• a boy who promised to give all the money he usually spent at the store to the Easter Hunger Offering, but kept putting it off to buy a candy bar "just for today."

• a grandchild who enthusiastically made Easter baskets for older church members, then complained about staying home for an hour that afternoon with Grandpa.

4. Collect and post on a bulletin board the children's Holy Week pictures from the Worship Worksheets.

Use the key below to decode these Palm Sunday shouts.

Code Key

A	B	C
D	E	F
G	H	I

J	K	L
M	N	O
P	Q	R

S	T	U
V	W	X
Y	Z	

Draw a picture of one story about Jesus that you hear today. Show how people felt about what happened.

Title: _____

EASTER

From a Child's Point of View

Gospel: John 20:1-18 or Matthew 28:1-10. The text from John is really two Easter stories: (1) the visit of Peter and John to the empty tomb; and (2) Mary's encounter with the Risen Lord. Both stories describe strong interplays of *fear* with joy, and confusion with understanding. Matthew's account, though it mentions the conflicting feelings and responses of Jesus' friends, is simpler and therefore may be the better choice for children.

For children, the heart of the story in both texts, and in all Easter stories, is that God surprised everyone. On Good Friday, it looked as if the bad guys had won, that hate was stronger than love. On Easter, God proved this was not so. Since few children comprehend the significance of death, they do not sincerely value the resurrection promises related to death. Easter is more a celebration of God's surprise in raising Jesus and proving that God's love is stronger than any other power in the world.

Children, especially girls, also appreciate the fact that God chose to announce the Easter surprise to a couple of unimportant women, rather than to the twelve disciples, to the state officials who had condemned Jesus to die, or to the religious leaders who planned his death. Since children often feel ignored when important things happen, they like the fact that God included the Marys. That inclusion alerts them to feel that God cares for them and might include them in any action in the future.

Note: During the Easter Season, the Old Testament reading is replaced with a sequential reading from Acts. On Easter, a choice is offered.

First Reading: Acts 10:34-43 or Jeremiah 31:1-6. Peter's sermon, in its context in Acts, focuses on God's salvation of the whole world, not just Jews. In the Easter liturgy context, it is more or less a summary of the good news about Jesus. Unfortunately, its reference in verse 38 to the kind of things Jesus did—"He went about doing good and healing"—is difficult for children to understand. To help them, cite specific familiar examples.

Because its many Old Testament references assume detailed knowledge of both Exodus and Exile stories, Jeremiah 31:1-6 is a definite second choice for children and those adult worshipers present on this day who do not know these stories.

Psalm: 118:1-2, 14-24. This selection of verses from Psalm 118 is a disjointed series of praises for God's saving activities. Children will more easily tune into its celebrative mood than to the meaning of its words. The last verse is the one most likely to be familiar and understandable as an appropriate Easter praise.

Epistle: Acts 10:34-43 or Colossians 3:1-4. The demand in Colossians makes little sense to literal-minded children when they hear it read. But its message can be restated to make the point more clearly. The point is that just as Jesus' resurrection changed him forever, so it also changes us forever. Jesus did not return to life as

84

he had lived it with his friends. Resurrected life was new and different. Jesus' friends could not go back to living as they had before. Matthew could not go back to being a greedy tax collector, and James and John could no longer let their tempers run wild. And we cannot live as if Easter never happened. They and we know about God's Easter surprise. They and we know for sure that God loves us (and all people) enough to keep loving us. Knowing that affects how we treat people and how we spend our time, money, and energy.

Watch Words

For children, *resurrection* is a church word about what happened on Easter. Use it frequently, but do not expect children to grasp its meaning as related to death, other than Jesus' death.

Alleluia! is an Easter praise word that means "Hurray for God!" "Good job, God!" and "Look what God has done!" Use it frequently today.

Let the Children Sing

"Christ the Lord (Jesus Christ) Is Risen Today!" follows every phrase with an Alleluia, so even nonreaders can join on the Alleluias. Older children will understand more and more of the phrases as they sing them.

"Christ Is Risen! Shout Hosanna!" celebrates God's surprising Easter turnaround of the Good Friday events. It is a good story hymn but does include some difficult poetic images (e.g., the tree blooming in the desert).

Children enjoy the change in mood from the sad verses to the upbeat chorus of the gospel hymn, "Up from the Grave He Arose."

If the choir sings the "Hallelujah Chorus," challenge the children to count the Hallelujahs.

The Liturgical Child

1. Children experience the feelings of Easter before they understand the story. So fill the sanctuary with flowers, hang sparkly white, shiny gold, or brightly colored Easter banners; wear stoles, and plan for grand music with brass accompaniment to announce God's big victory. Then, no matter how difficult the logistics of finding space for them, make sure all children are present for at least part of Easter worship. If nothing else, plan for them to come from their other activities to sit on the floor in the hall just outside the sanctuary to hear an Easter anthem.

2. Reading the Easter story is the main event of worship today. The Gospel accounts suggest dramatization, but the event and person of the resurrected Jesus are beyond everyday experience. Plays in which a human Jesus walks through the Easter events never satisfy either children or adults. So keep the events in the realm of personal imagination by presenting the Scripture story as a radio drama. Let the fear and joy of Jesus' friends show in your voice. Read the narration like a media commentator who is deeply awed and moved by what has happened.

3. Build a Prayer of Confession on our failure to believe in the power of God and in God's Easter surprise:

Almighty God, we sometimes live as if Good Friday happened, but Easter did not. We act as though we think the bad guys and hate and selfishness will always win. We are silent while others are hurt, as if we think no one can protect them. At times we even lie, cheat, and steal, as if that were the only way to get what we want and need. Forgive us. Help us remember that your power and love always win in the end. Give us the courage to live by that love. For we pray in the name of Jesus, who died and rose again. Amen.

Assurance of Pardon: Those who called for Jesus' death and those who killed him did not have the last word. Jesus forgave them all. Then God raised Jesus from death, proving once and for all that the loving, forgiving power of God is stronger than any force—stronger than greed or hate or fear. God loves us and will love us always. Thanks be to God! Amen.

4. After exploring it in the sermon, invite worshipers to join in the Easter witness by "preaching with Peter," using his words in Acts 10:34-43. If you do not have pew Bibles, print the text in the bulletin.

Sermon Resource

Retell the Easter story, exploring feelings as you go. Consider assuming the role of John or Mary Magdalene. Tell what happened and how you felt about it on Thursday, Friday, Saturday, and finally on Sunday morning.

Shade each space that has a dot in it to find an Easter greeting in this garden.

Write the correct letter in each numbered space to find another Easter greeting.

__ __ __ __ E
1 2 3 4 5 6 7 8 9

__ __ __ __ __ __ __ __ E
10 11 12   13 14 15

__ __ __ __ __ __ E;
16 17 18 19 20 21 22 23 24 25 26

__ E __ __ __ __ __ E __ E
27 28 29 30 31 32 33 34 35 36 37 38

__ __ __ E __ __ __ __ __
39 40 41 42 43 44 45 46 47

__ __ __ __ .
48 49 50 51

A= 11,21,24,39,46
B= 42
C= 37
D= 10,19,25,41,47
E= 9,15,26,28,33,38,43
G= 44
H= 2,8,14,20
I= 3,5,36,48,50
J= 34

L= 16,27,45
M= 23
N= 40,49
O= 17,35
R= 18,32
S= 4,6,22,31
T= 1,7,13,29,51
U= 30
Y= 12

SECOND SUNDAY OF EASTER

From a Child's Point of View

Gospel: John 20:19-31. This text includes two resurrection stories—Jesus' meeting the disciples on Easter evening and Jesus' encounter with Thomas. It also includes a statement of the purpose of John's Gospel. The stories are interesting to children for several reasons. First, they give clues about what the resurrected Jesus was like. He was different. He could now appear inside a locked room. But he was also the same Jesus. His friends recognized him by sight. He showed his crucifixion wounds, and he was kind to Thomas. From this, older children learn not only interesting information about the resurrected Jesus, but also what our own resurrections might be like.

The second point of interest is that Easter is not the final chapter of Jesus' life. It is the beginning of a new chapter. On Easter evening, Jesus is looking ahead. He gives his disciples two gifts—his peace and his Spirit—and then sends them to work. Their task is to forgive people. Jesus insists that anyone they do not forgive will not be forgiven. While it is possible to interpret this as authority to sit in judgment, it is more in keeping with the gospel to interpret it as a challenge to be sure all people are forgiven—because we are their only chance. That makes forgiving an important Easter activity for Christians, and for the church.

Finally, children who were not present when something exciting and important happened appreciate the story about Thomas. Jesus' treatment of Thomas, who had missed out on Easter evening and had lots of questions, reassures children that (1) Jesus understands their feelings when they are left out; and (2) no questions are too stupid or embarrassing to ask.

Epistle: I Peter 1:3-9. Both the message and the language of these verses make them somewhat remote for children. "Mercy," "living hope," "imperishable inheritance," and so forth are not in the daily vocabulary of most children and speak of concepts too abstract for their mental development. The writer's insistence that readers hold out through bad times in this life, for the sake of salvation in the next, has little impact on children, who live in the present and immediate future.

However, if they are told that this is a letter to Christians who were being tortured and killed for being Christians and that the writer of this letter wanted them to know that being a Christian *was* worth being tortured or killed, older children can explore the possibility that being a Christian is also worth whatever teasing or grief they take today. In other words, if being a Christian was worth being fed to a lion, then it also must be worth being called a sissy when you refuse to smoke a joint or join the gang in a cruel prank.

First Reading: Acts 2:14a, 22-32. This section of Peter's Pentecost sermon focuses on the interpretation of Psalm 16. Peter's intricate exegesis and point are beyond the interest and mental ability of children. Older children may follow the description of Jesus' life and death in verses 22-24 before they get lost in the argument about David. Read this mainly for the adults.

Psalm: 16. This is the psalm Peter interpreted as being prophetic of the resurrection, but his interpretation means little to children. Furthermore, the psalmist uses such poetic images as "my cup" and God's "counsel" to speak of trusting God's plan, and the obsolete terms Sheol and the Pit to speak of death. Consequently, the psalmist's simple trust in God is lost in the verbiage.

Watch Words

Today's texts are filled with abstract theological terms such as *salvation*, *mercy*, and *faith*. Remember that this is a foreign language to children. Whenever possible, describe in concrete terms what Jesus said, did, and promised.

If you focus on Thomas, be careful about your use of *believe*. Children *believe* in Santa Claus, they clap during Peter Pan to show their *belief* in Tinkerbell, they *believe* their team will win the championship this year, and they *believe* in God. As middle-elementary children begin to sort out the realities involved in life, they often conclude that *believe* is a "less sure" form of *think*, or even a well-intended distortion of reality, and thus relegate their belief in God to the same status as their belief in Santa Claus.

So, redefine *believe* to be even stronger than *think*. What you *believe* makes a difference in how you live. For example, before he met the resurrected Jesus, Thomas did not know what to think about what his friends claimed. But when he finally met Jesus, he not only thought that it was true that Jesus had been raised from death, but he knew that fact would make a difference in what he did every day, from that day on.

Let the Children Sing

"O Sons and Daughters, Let Us Sing" has one set of verses for Easter Sunday, and a second set related to Thomas's story, for the second Sunday of Easter. Its words are fairly simple and include a chorus of Alleluias for nonreaders. Sing it after reading the Gospel lesson.

"Breathe on Me, Breath of God" is a good choice if the service emphasizes Jesus' gift of the Spirit. Consider working through parts of it in the sermon.

"I've Got Peace Like a River" is a good response to Jesus' Easter-evening gifts of peace and the Spirit.

The Liturgical Child

1. The Gospel stories are the heart of today's worship for children. Like last week's stories, they need to be presented in a way that leaves listeners free to "see" the events in their imaginations. Again, present the stories as radio dramas. Practice the way Jesus and Thomas speak their words, and how you will read the narrator's part.

2. Respond to Jesus' challenge to forgive. In a bidding prayer, offer worshipers opportunities to forgive a variety of people and groups. Include members of our families; friends who have wronged us; people we do not like because we need to forgive them so often, and we do not expect them to ever treat us any better; groups of people (cliques, other nations, other races) who constantly abuse us; and so forth. After describing each group, identifying its possible members, and offering a public prayer of forgiveness, invite worshipers to pray silent personal prayers of forgiveness.

3. If your worship regularly includes an Affirmation of Faith, point it out this morning. Explain why your worship includes this opportunity to say, "I believe . . . ." Challenge worshipers to think about what they are saying and what it will mean for them if they really believe these things. Many creeds follow each "I believe" with several statements. Today, repeat "I believe" before *each* one. Or, turn the statements into questions to the congregation, to which they are invited to respond, "Yes, we (or I) believe that."

Sermon Resources

Celebrate questions. Review Thomas's questions about Jesus' body and recall the story of Jesus' questions in the Temple when he was twelve years old. Point out that questions are not the opposite of believing, but are tools with which we build our beliefs. No genuine question is too stupid or silly to ask. We are to remember this about our own questions, and about the questions of others—especially those of younger children who ask many questions that may sound dumb to us. This is a great opportunity to push church-school attendance.

Happy Easter!

Because Easter is so wonderful, we celebrate it for 50 days. That includes 7 Sundays! Today is the second Sunday of Easter.

Listen for 3 Easter words in worship today.
Draw a butterfly each time one is said.
Draw a flower each time one is sung.

Alleluia!

Forgiven

Believe

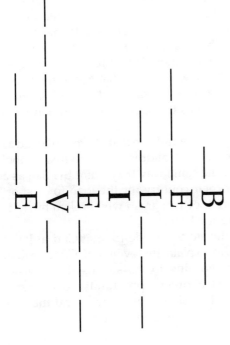

Believe is an important word.
Believe means. . .

I know it.
I feel it.
I will do it.

Thomas believed in Jesus. He knew about Jesus. He loved Jesus. And he did what Jesus asked him to do. These 6 words tell what we do when we believe in Jesus.

LOVE FORGIVE CARE
FOLLOW OBEY SERVE

Write each word in the correct spaces below.

— B — —
— — E — —
— L — — —
— — I — —
— E — V —
— — — E

THIRD SUNDAY OF EASTER

From a Child's Point of View

First Reading: Acts 2:14a, 36-41. Children need to be reminded of the context of this event. Peter told a crowd that they had witnessed the murder of Jesus, who was God's Messiah, and that God had raised Jesus from death. Their response was, "What shall we do about this?" Children who know the Easter stories might ask the same question and receive the same answer: You should change your ways to follow Jesus, and you should be baptized. Exploring the crowd's question presents an opportunity to identify their response to Easter. Exploring our answers presents an opportunity to outline your tradition's understanding of baptism and/or confirmation as a way of responding to God's Easter surprise.

Psalm: 116:1-2, 12-19. The Jewish psalmist's prayer of thanksgiving, with its references to Temple offerings of wine for recovery from a near fatal illness, is often used by Christians to thank God for resurrection. Children have little understanding of Temple rites and such a vague concept of death that it makes genuine appreciation of personal resurrection impossible. So read this psalm for the adults.

Epistle: I Peter 1:17-23. Children make no sense of this complicated text as it is read. But if its message is paraphrased, they appreciate the writer's insistence that we can count on God's love always. Jesus' resurrection, in this case, is proof that God loves and forgives us and that God's love is powerful enough to reach us wherever we are—even beyond death. That truth provides all children with courage for facing frightening situations and assures grieving children that God still loves and cares for those who have died.

Warning: Ransom and atonement interpretations of God's love confuse children. For literal thinkers, they pose difficult questions: "Who did God pay the ransom to?" "If God expects us to forgive each other for free, how come God made Jesus pay for our forgiveness?" "How can Jesus' death make me forgiven?" So avoid atonement theology. Speak instead of God's love, which is so powerful it reaches us even after we die.

Gospel: Luke 24:13-35. This simple story can be understood as it is read, from almost any translation. Children are interested in what kind of "body" the risen Jesus had. They need to be invited to speculate, but also to be told that no one knows exactly what Jesus' resurrected body was like. What we do know is that Jesus did not stay dead, that there were some changes in his body, but that from what he said and did, his friends recognized him as the same Jesus who had been crucified.

The story also identifies a loaf of broken bread as a symbol for Jesus. Children can claim this symbol for Jesus in the same way they claim the flag as a symbol for their country, or the logo for a sport team, before they can grasp why broken bread is appropriate for Jesus.

Finally, the story is evidence that God in Jesus was ready to explain the events of Good Friday and Easter morning to his surprised, confused friends. It is another opportunity to celebrate God's unimaginable Easter surprise and the care God takes to help us understand it.

90

Watch Words

Though *broken bread* is a good symbol for Jesus, do not confuse children by applying it more generally to the sacrificial love of God.

Remember, for younger children, *resurrection* is what happened to Jesus on Easter. Older children begin to understand that it has something to do with God loving us beyond death. So in exploring the message of First Peter, avoid terminology such as *living the resurrection* or *the resurrection life*. Instead, talk specifically about how we face "hopeless" situations, and how we treat one another because we know God's Easter surprise.

Let the Children Sing

Invite worshipers to sing "On the Day of Resurrection," imagining themselves as the Emmaus travelers, running back to Jerusalem and remembering what had happened. The abstract language of "O Thou Who This Mysterious Bread" makes it less child-accessible.

Keep the Easter Alleluias going with "Come, Christians, Join to Sing."

Celebrate God's love throughout our lives with "Now Thank We All Our God."

The Liturgical Child

1. To recall Jesus' recognition by the Emmaus travelers, display a large broken loaf of bread on the Communion table. Perhaps a floral display using wheat could feature the broken loaf.

2. If baptisms are part of today's worship, invite children to gather near the baptismal font to discuss what is to happen. People to be baptized, or parents of those to be baptized, might be asked to share why they want to be baptized or how they plan to keep their baptismal promises to their children. Following the discussion, allow the children to remain where they can see.

If no baptism is scheduled, either invite children to meet you at the font for a discussion of baptism, or simply move to the font during the part of your sermon that deals with the meaning of baptism. Scooping water up in your hand as you speak about its use will make what you say more vivid.

3. Affirm faith in God's Easter love with a litany such as the following. The congregation's response: *"God loves us forever."*

We know God because we know Jesus. In Jesus, God lived among us. He loved people and taught them how to love one another. He healed people and told them to take care of one another. He refused to give up loving and teaching and healing, even to save himself from being killed on a cross. But Jesus' love could not be killed. Jesus rose from death.
(RESPONSE)
So when we feel alone, when we feel we have no friends, when we feel that even the people in our family do not care about us, we remember Jesus, and we know . . .
(RESPONSE)
And when we miss people we love who have died, we remember that God still loves and cares for them, in mysterious ways we know little about.
(RESPONSE)
When we face problems that seem impossible to solve, we remember that God knows about those problems and that God works with us and through us to solve all problems.
(RESPONSE)
When we are bravely trying to love people who do not seem to want our loving care, when we are trying to stand up for God's ways among people who have other plans, when we are being teased or ignored because we are Jesus' disciples, we trust God, because . . .
(RESPONSE)

4. Feature the Doxology. Before singing it, identify, as one of God's blessings, the powerful Easter love that can reach us anywhere, anytime.

Sermon Resources

1. To prepare yourself to speak about baptism with words and ideas children can understand, check church school resources. Most denominations produce one or two excellent books which explain baptism to young children. Their language and stories are often appropriate for sermons.

2. If you focus on remembering God's resurrection love in "hopeless" situations, describe some situations that lead children to despair: fighting parents headed for divorce; a parent with a serious problem such as addiction or emotional distress; a feeling of being hopelessly behind at school. At this point in the year, some students who continue to have difficulty with reading, math, or other skills sense that their teachers have consigned them hopelessly to failure.

PICK A PENCIL

Peter told people to repent and be baptized. Draw or write about a change you need to make.

OR

If someone is baptized today, draw a picture of the baptism or write a prayer for that person.

Draw a path through the word trail. Then write the letters from the word trail in the spaces below to find out what Cleopas learned on his way to Emmaus.

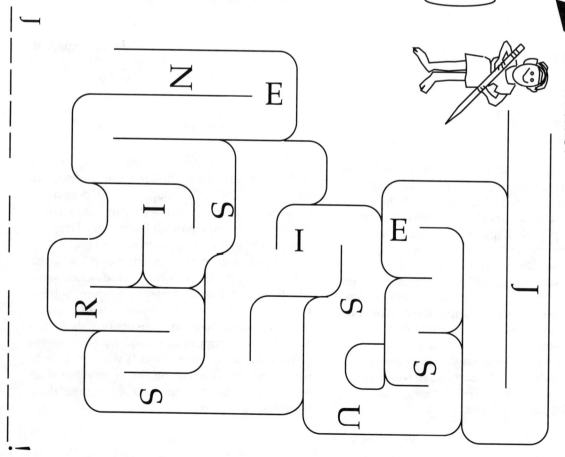

Answer: Jesus is risen !

Third Sunday of Easter/ © 1992 by Abingdon Press.

FOURTH SUNDAY OF EASTER

From a Child's Point of View

Gospel: John 10:1-10. This text offers two shepherd-based images of Jesus. Children respond more readily to comparing Jesus to a shepherd than to the door of a sheep gate. The former compares a person to a person rather than to a thing, and the care given by the shepherd is more significant to children than the security and freedom provided by the door.

The point that the shepherd knows each of the sheep by name is crucial to children. It is the promise that God knows them, loves them, and calls them as individuals, rather than as members of any group. This truth is especially significant to children who spend most of their lives in groups (in a class at school, in after-school care, at a day-care center). Such children often sense that adult leaders know them simply by the way they act in the group rather than by who they are as individuals, with their own experiences, dreams, and feelings.

To understand what it means to recognize the voice of the shepherd, children need to hear about the practice of penning all the village sheep together for the night. In the morning, each shepherd would enter the fold with a unique whistle or call. The sheep of each flock recognized their shepherd's voice and followed it. Younger children are satisfied with knowing this background and hearing the text. Fifth- and sixth-graders are ready to explore the way we recognize God's voice. That is, it is a loving voice (the voice that says we are no good is not the Good Shepherd's voice). It calls us to love and share (the voice that says, "If you want it, take it," is not the

Good Shepherd's voice). It directs firmly and gently, rather than threateningly (the voice that says, "Come with me, or . . ." is not the Good Shepherd's voice). And it invites and challenges us to be our best (the voice that says, "You don't need to worry about that—it's too hard," is not the Good Shepherd's voice).

Psalm: 23. Though many children and most adults know this as the Shepherd Psalm, it could be more accurately titled "God is Like." The psalmist compares God to two once familiar human figures—the shepherd (vss. 1-4) and the host (vss. 5-6). Unfortunately, those figures are no longer as familiar to today's children. Most children have little contact with sheep or shepherds, and no children have met a host who poured oil on their heads! Younger children are content to hear the jobs of a shepherd and a host described. Older children are interested, but they need help in identifying the details of those jobs in the phrases of the psalm. Once they understand the details of the shepherd's job, most children find great security in the psalmist's comparison. Pictures that depict Jesus as the Good Shepherd are often favorites with children. Perhaps they imagine themselves as the sheep loved and cared for by Jesus, the Shepherd, with the same love they lavish on their pets.

Epistle: I Peter 2:19-25. This text is difficult for children for two reasons. First, the shepherd image used to describe Jesus' suffering death is derived from atonement theology based on the Temple sacrifices. Adults who understand atonement theology can see the connection between the shepherd's suffering on behalf of the sheep and Jesus' suffering. Children do not have the ability to think in this way.

Second, the writer's main point, that we should suffer injustice meekly, as Jesus did throughout his trial and crucifixion, seems to contradict adult encouragement to stand up for their own rights and the rights of others. So either bypass this text, or focus on it by digging into its challenging instructions for our relationships with those in authority who treat us poorly.

First Reading: Acts 2:42-47. This is a description of the church on its best behavior. The activities described are familiar to children: studying God's Word, enjoying church friends, worshiping, taking care of one another, serving people beyond the church. The text comes to life for children when it is illustrated with current activities in which they participate in their own church.

Watch Words

Do not assume that children know all the shepherd words—*flock, fold, rod, staff.* The most familiar staff to many children is the "shepherd's" crook used at swimming pools to reach swimmers who are in trouble.

Let the Children Sing

Before singing a hymn based on Psalm 23, point out its biblical base. Choose a hymn version of the psalm with which your congregation is familiar and, if possible, one with contemporary, rather than Elizabethan, vocabulary.

The repeated phrases in the chorus of "He Leadeth Me: O Blessed Thought" almost make up for the complex vocabulary of its verses. Most other "shepherd" hymns involve abstract concepts that make little sense to children.

The Liturgical Child

1. Include Good Shepherd art in worship. Hang a banner featuring shepherd's tools. Carry a shepherd's crook in the processional and display it prominently during worship. Display and explain the shepherd's-crook cross Chrismon ornament. If your sanctuary includes a Good Shepherd stained-glass window or painting, be sure to refer to it.

2. Psalm 23 is one psalm many congregations can read in unison with more than the usual feeling. The New Revised Standard Version is most child accessible. But if the King James Version will be read by the worshipers in a way that radiates their love of it, children will hear the message of the psalmist in the feelings shown in the voices.

3. Create a responsive prayer about the care and leadership of the Good Shepherd. Praise God's loving care. Thank God for knowing us as individuals with unique talents, dreams, and needs. Ask for the willingness to develop those talents and work to make the dreams come true. Confess our tendency to ignore God's voice when it calls us to work we would rather not do. Pray for the attentiveness to recognize the difference between God's voice and other voices. The congregation's response to each prayer: "God, you call each of us by name."

Sermon Resources

1. Compare the work of a good shepherd to that of a good baby-sitter, a good tour guide or field-trip leader, or an older sibling who takes good care of younger brothers and sisters.

2. Describe (or demonstrate if you feel brave) the way people call or whistle for their pets. Then describe the way parents call their children and children call their parents. Point out that we can tell from a call not only who is being called, but what is expected, and even how the caller is feeling. This leads into exploring the Good Shepherd's call to the sheep.

3. *And Now Miguel* by Joseph Krumgold (Harper & Row, 1984) tells about twelve-year-old Miguel, who is working to become one of the men in his family of New Mexican shepherds. Chapters 4 and 5 describe the care of sheep. The painting of matching numbers on ewes and their lambs to keep them together catches the attention of worshipers of all ages and demonstrates the importance of the shepherd's work.

4. When discussing First Peter, identify some

of the "masters" most likely to trouble us today. Some that trouble children include teachers, coaches, or group leaders who do not like or understand them; baby-sitters who view them as burdens rather than as people worth knowing; and older brothers and sisters who do not appreciate the persons they are now. Describe ways of following Jesus' example in dealing with such people.

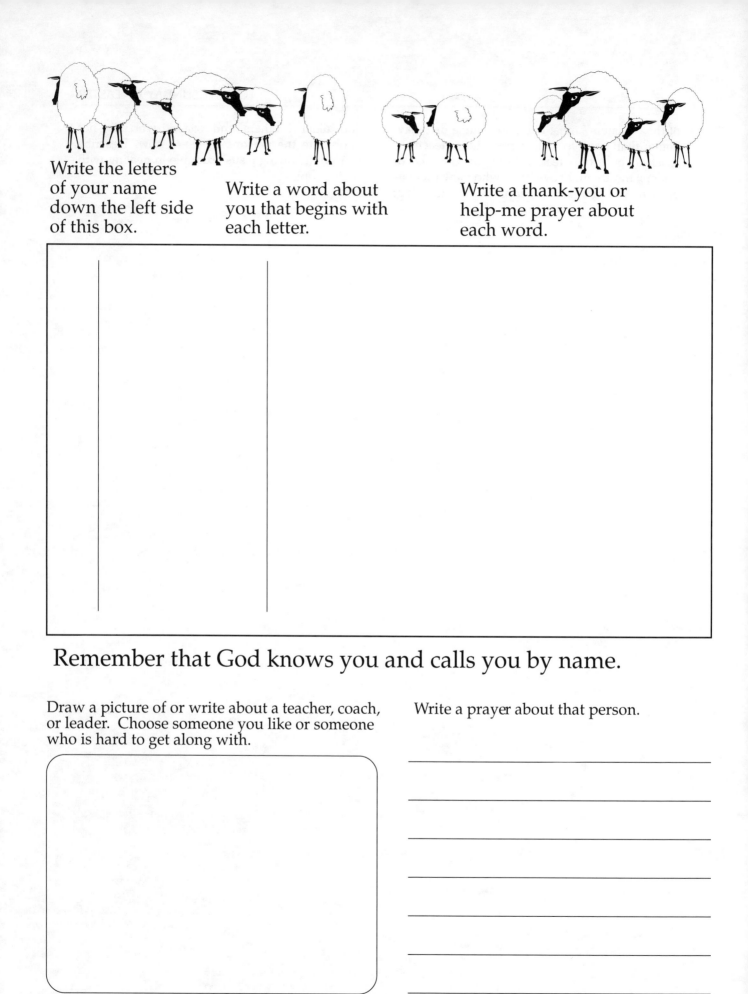

Write the letters
of your name
down the left side
of this box.

Write a word about
you that begins with
each letter.

Write a thank-you or
help-me prayer about
each word.

Remember that God knows you and calls you by name.

Draw a picture of or write about a teacher, coach,
or leader. Choose someone you like or someone
who is hard to get along with.

Write a prayer about that person.

Fourth Sunday of Easter/ © 1992 by Abingdon Press.

FIFTH SUNDAY
OF EASTER

From a Child's Point of View

First Reading: Acts 7:55-60. To appreciate this text, both adults and children need to hear the whole story of Stephen's trial and stoning but they do not need to hear the content of his statement to the Council.

Stephen is a potential hero. He stood up for Jesus and Jesus' ways even when it made others angry, and he remained loving and forgiving as people were killing him with stones. Because children often risk the anger of their peers when they stand up for Jesus' ways, they appreciate the way Stephen stood up to the Council. And because they have experience in tripping over stones or even being hit with a stone, they identify with Stephen's pain and the difficulty of forgiving people who are throwing stones at you. Stephen is a hero because he "has the guts to make a stand" and because he "can take it"—he can take abuse from others and keep on loving and forgiving. Christian children are called to be as heroic as Stephen.

Psalm: 31:1-8, 15-16. This lament which seeks God's rescue in a time of trouble is included among today's lections because it uses a "rock" as a poetic image of God's protection. Unfortunately, all translations are filled with generalized defense and refuge language unfamiliar to children. However, if before the psalm is read, you introduce the image of God, protecting us as a rock wall or a cave protects people from enemies or storms, older children will catch the meaning of a few lines. Younger children will hear its meaning more in the expression of the reader than in the psalmist's words.

Epistle: I Peter 2:2-10. This text compares Christians to newborn babies who must be fed carefully, to the stones in the wall of a temple, and to the king's priests. Even older children are bewildered by this profusion of abstract images. So it is best to focus on one, probably that of stones in the wall. Once the function of the cornerstone is explained, older children can grasp that Jesus is God's cornerstone, and can respond to the challenge to get in line to become part of the wall of Jesus' temple. "Getting in line," however, needs to be described in terms of doing what Jesus did and following Jesus' teachings. People who lie, cheat, and hate do not fit into the wall of the temple for which Jesus is the cornerstone. We must avoid such activities if we want to be part of Jesus' temple/church. Be careful about including more than one or two of the many stone images in this passage, since concrete thinkers are quickly confused.

Gospel: John 14:1-14. Jesus' complex, repetitive statement here holds two messages of interest to children. The first is that God is with them always. The second is that if they want to know what God is like, they should read about Jesus, because God was speaking and acting through Jesus. Neither message will be apparent as the text is read, but will need to be spelled out in the sermon.

Though many children have heard, and some may have memorized the words of John 14:6, they do not understand it. The concepts of "the way,

97

the truth, and the life" are entirely too abstract for their mental abilities.

Watch Words

Defense, fortress, and *refuge* are general terms that are unfamiliar to children. *My rock* is an old description of God's protection and is lost on literal thinkers.

Let the Children Sing

Sing Easter praises to God and Jesus with the Alleluias of "Come, Christians, Join to Sing."

"Christ Is Made the Sure Foundation," based directly on the First Peter lesson, is used frequently in most congregations. Its difficult language, however, makes it one children must learn over the years. Before singing the hymn, help that process by pointing out the "cornerstone" phrases in the first verse.

In response to Stephen's heroism and as commitment to be one of the stones in the wall of Christ's temple, sing "I Sing a Song of the Saints of God" or "Lord, I Want to Be a Christian."

Avoid hymns with complex "rock" imagery such as "Rock of Ages."

The Liturgical Child

1. Use rocks in the floral display at the center of the chancel. Challenge children at the beginning of worship to listen for clues in the hymns, prayers, and readings, to find out why there are rocks on the table today. Or simply refer to the rocks during worship.

2. Before reading Psalm 31, give each worshiper a small rock. (Children might gather them before the service and pass them out in baskets during worship.) While the rocks are being passed out, talk about the security of rock walls around cities, the safety of a concrete (or rock) basement during a storm, and the protection of a cave when sleeping or hiding. Introduce the psalm as a poem in which God's loving care is compared to such protection. After reading the psalm, encourage worshipers to carry their rocks in their pockets during the week, as a reminder of God's protecting love.

3. Introduce Stephen, read Acts 6:8-15 and

summarize his message—that the religious leaders had often resisted what God was doing, so it was not surprising that they had killed Jesus. Then conclude with Acts 7:54-60. Read dramatically. Plan and practice the way Stephen will say his lines and how the false witnesses will sneer their accusations. Let the intensity and anger of the mob be heard in your voice as you narrate their actions.

4. If your church has a cornerstone, tell its story and note its location during worship. Suggest that worshipers go to look at it after church.

5. Create a prayer based on Christ the Cornerstone. Thank God for calling us to become living stones in the temple Christ is building. Note ways we depend on Christ. Pray for guidance to live as Christ did (following the direction of the cornerstone). Pray for the church/temple. Conclude each prayer with, or have the congregation respond with, *"Christ, you are the Cornerstone"*:

> Lord, all of us have our own ideas about what the church should be doing. Remind us that your ideas are the ones that matter. Give us the patience to pray and search the Bible, so that we know what you want the church to be doing. (RESPONSE)

Sermon Resources

1. Build a sermon around the rocks in these passages. Illustrate it with several rocks which can be produced from behind the pulpit at the appropriate times. Use a large concrete block or building block to remind worshipers of the cornerstone, several smaller rocks to recall Christians who became living stones in Christ's temple (consider drawing crosses on them with a marker while you speak), and a jagged rock for all the rocks thrown at Stephen.

2. Talk about heroes and heroines. Tell about some of your own hero/ines at different times in your life. Challenge worshipers to identify some of theirs. Children's hero/ines often include sport figures, TV or movie superheroes, teenagers or adult friends they admire, and so forth. Older children tend to give greater status to real people than to the fictional characters younger children often cite. Talk about how our heroes and heroines can affect what we do and say. Then introduce Stephen as a candidate for hero status among Christians.

Shade each rock in this wall that has a dot in it to find an important message.

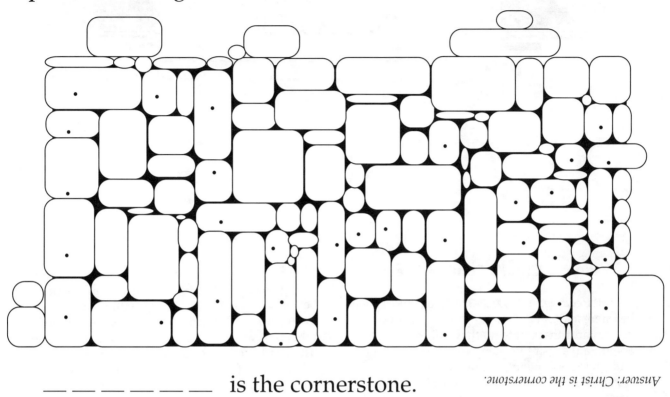

_ _ _ _ _ _ _ _ is the cornerstone.

Draw one of your heroes or heroines on top of this stand. Then write words about him or her on the stand.

Name

Talk to God about this heroic person.

Fifth Sunday of Easter/ © 1992 by Abingdon Press.

SIXTH SUNDAY OF EASTER

From a Child's Point of View

First Reading: Acts 17:22-31. Older children will be interested in Paul's strategy in this sermon. To understand that strategy, they will need to hear about Paul's visit to Athens and some of the gods and goddesses people there worshiped.

Paul's sophisticated sermon leads children to ponder what God is like. Paul says God is bigger and more powerful than anything we can imagine. God is too mysterious to be painted or carved into a statue. God created the whole universe and everything in it. God created all the people and spread them out around the world. This means that all of us are God's children, part of one human family. But even though God is so much more than we are, God is very close to us, loving us and caring for us. And God wants us to know God. God lived among us as Jesus so that we could know God. Paul's final point—that because we know about God through Jesus, God will judge us—raises questions about the responsibility that comes with knowledge. These questions complicate the day's theme for children. So, for clarity, focus on what God is like and save the matter of responsibility for another time.

Gospel: John 14:15-21. This complex theological statement is not a text one would choose to explore with children. But when it is linked with the Acts lesson, it offers another opportunity to explore the mysterious God. The phrase in verse 20, "I am in my Father, and you in me, and I in you" (NRSV), invites further exploration of the ways God is close to us. Children quickly agree that because God was in Jesus, Jesus loved people,

healed them, and even died rather than stop loving them. But they need encouragement to believe that God is also deep within each of us, loving us and giving us the power to love others—if we will listen. One of the best ways to listen is to follow Jesus' commandment to love others. Part of the mystery is that the more we love others, the more aware we become of God's loving presence; and the more we are aware of God's loving presence, the more we are able to really love others.

Epistle: I Peter 3:13-22. This text urges Christians who are suffering because they love others, as Jesus commanded, not to give in but to keep loving, and be ready to explain their actions to those who ask why they are doing what they are doing. The writer reminds them that Jesus also suffered for loving them. If the passage is illustrated with examples of children who suffer the consequences of trying to love the unlovable at school or in the neighborhood, the lection offers children the same encouragement it offers adults.

The allusions to Noah's ark and to baptism require more explanation than their meaning for children merits.

Psalm: 66:8-20. This psalm requires that readers know the broad sweep of Old Testament events and understand the significance of Temple sacrifices. Verses 10-12 are a series of poetic images, each requiring some explanation for children. These problems and the psalmist's understanding of God-sent suffering make this psalm inaccessible to children.

100

Watch Words

Introduce the word *mysterious* to describe God, who is more than we can even imagine. Surround the word with everyday examples of God's power and love, which provoke wonder and security rather than fear of the unknown and incomprehensible.

Avoid describing the mystery of God in big theological words such as *omnipotent, omnipresent,* or *omniscient.*

Let the Children Sing

Praise the mysterious God by singing "I Sing the Almighty Power of God," "How Great Thou Art," or "For the Beauty of the Earth."

Sing "Immortal, Invisible, God Only Wise" only after pointing out some of the mysterious words and phrases that describe God, who is more than we can ever imagine—*immortal, invisible, in light inaccessible hid from our eyes, unresting, unhasting, and silent as light.*

Ask a children's class or choir to lead the congregation in praying for God's presence by singing "Kum Ba Yah, My Lord." They may want to illustrate the song with hand motions as they sing.

The Liturgical Child

1. Praise God with a litany. The congregation's response: *Praise God, who is greater than we can imagine.*

> God, you are the Creator. You created the world and everything in it. You spun out galaxies and stars. You formed the mountains and the oceans. You imagined and made elephants and ants, whales and minnows, corn and roses and people. (RESPONSE)
> God, you are forever. We know that everything you made has a beginning and an end. Even mountains are born and die. But you always have been and always will be. (RESPONSE)
> God, you are more than a father or mother. You made us, and you know all there is to know about each of us. You are always with us, always ready to respond when we pray. (RESPONSE)
> God, you are greater love than we can imagine. You came among us as Jesus to show us that love. You care for us and forgive us, even when we do not deserve it. (RESPONSE)

2. To set the Acts reading in context, tell about Paul's visit to Athens, describe some of the city's shrines to gods and goddesses, tell how he came to the Council, then clear your voice and assume the role of Paul. Read the words as you think Paul would have said them to that erudite crowd. With your hand, sweep the crowd as you read verse 22. Then point behind you to imaginary shrines in the distance.

4. If you sing the Gloria Patri weekly, feature it today. After it is sung at its usual spot in the service, interrupt briefly to examine *what* we sing about the mysterious God, and *why* we sing that at this particular point in worship. Then invite the congregation to sing it again.

Sermon Resources

1. Begin the exploration of what God is like by citing some of the unanswerable questions children ask about God. Who was here before God? (No one. God always was. Before anything else, God was.) Who made God? (No one. God has always been. There was never a time before God.) How can God hear everyone's prayers at once? (We don't know how. We just know God can.) How can God care for everyone in the world at the same time? (We don't know how. We just know God does.) Where does God live? (God is everywhere.) What does God look like? (We cannot see God.) Point out that most of these answers do not really satisfy our curiosity, because God is more than we can measure or describe or understand. People have been thinking about God and living with God for thousands of years, but we still do not know everything about God—and never will.

2. Tell stories about God's presence as experienced by people doing mission work, people observing the beauty and power of God's creation (mountains, rainbows, intricate flowers), people worshiping with other Christians (Christmas candlelight services, Communion in different situations), and people struggling with difficult problems (illness, fears, family fights).

3. *The Great Gilly Hopkins* by Katherine Paterson (Harper & Row, 1987) is the story of the persevering love of fat and simple Trotter, the last in a long line of foster mothers and the sixth-grade teacher of Gilly Hopkins, a very difficult child to love. The book is filled with realistically humorous examples of suffering love that can be appreciated by worshipers of all ages.

Draw a picture of a time when you feel God close to you.

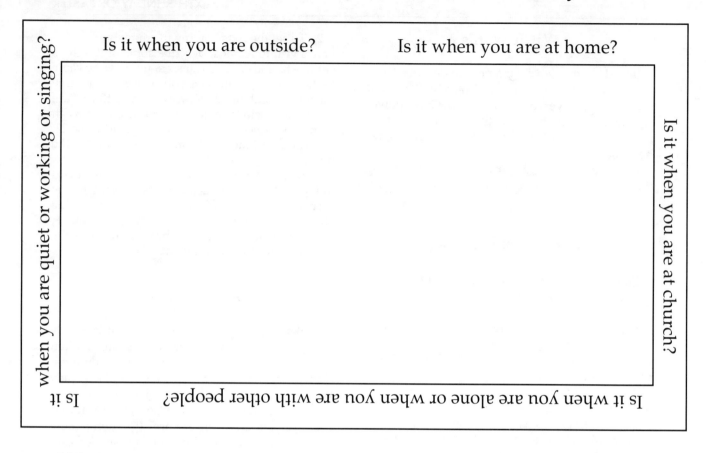

Is it when you are outside?   Is it when you are at home?

Is it when you are quiet or working or singing?

Is it when you are at church?

Is it when you are alone or when you are with other people?

Cross out the extra letter in each word to learn what Jesus said.

Jesus said . . .

IT TAM TIN YOUR SAND

YOUX SIN MET

" __ __ __ __ __ __ __ __ __ __

__ __ __ __ __ __ __ ."

SEVENTH SUNDAY OF EASTER

Note: On the Seventh Sunday of Easter, you may choose between the lections for this Sunday and those for Ascension Day. The resources for Ascension Day are found in Year C of this series.

From a Child's Point of View

Today's readings provide a sober conclusion to the joyous Easter season. As Jesus ascends (Acts 1), he instructs his disciples to take up his work and become witnesses. The other readings point out that this work will not always be easy. Strong evils are at work, and at times Christians must suffer. None of the readings is particularly attractive for children or easy for them to understand. Children will respond more readily to the general theme of preparing to take up hard and dangerous work for God.

First Reading: Acts 1:6-14. At the end of the Easter season the spotlight turns from Jesus to the gathering new church. In verses 6-11, Jesus returns to "the Father," having completed his mission, and tells the disciples that they are now to be witnesses throughout the world to what has happened. The two men in white (vss. 10-11) emphasize this by telling the disciples to stop looking up in the sky and to move on. Older children can see this as Luke's bridge from his Gospel account to what Jesus did to his Acts account of what the first Christians did.

The child's paraphrase of "in Jerusalem, in all Judea and Samaria, and to the ends of the earth" is "at home, in school and around the neighborhood, and all around the world."

Epistle: I Peter 4:12-14; 5:6-11. This writer was speaking to Christians who were being physically tortured and killed. While it is tempting to apply its teaching to lesser sufferings such as teasing peers, to do so robs it of its power. It makes more sense, even to children, to explore these promises as preparation for suffering such as the original readers faced, in solidarity with those who suffer today, as they did then.

The writer insists, and history agrees, that we should not be surprised by such suffering. Children need to be told that many Christians often suffer for being God's people, and they need to prepare to suffer heroically, should that be needed. The writer includes guidelines for suffering Christians: Remember that you are not the only one who has suffered (Jesus and many Christians suffered); keep alert so that you do not give in to temptations in the attempt to save yourself from suffering; and trust God to be with you.

Gospel: John 17:1-11. The language, repetitive phrases, and complex sentence structure of this prayer are impossible for children to follow. But they can appreciate that Jesus, knowing he would be betrayed and killed, worried about and prayed for his friends. His prayer was that God would take care of them as he had while he was on earth. He most wanted them to be protected from temptations, fears, and discouragement, so that they would stay close to God.

Psalm: 68:1-10, 32-35. The poetic images and references to Exodus events make this psalm difficult for children. However, it can be introduced as a reminder to those who suffer that God is powerful and will win in the end. If it is read with strong conviction, children will hear the confident mood of the psalm and will catch one or two of the lines.

Watch Words

Define the disciples' task of being *witnesses* for Jesus in terms of witnesses at a trial, or witnesses who tell news reporters what happened.

Persevere, endurance, and *steadfast* are words related to suffering which children neither use nor recognize.

Let the Children Sing

Sing at least one hymn of Easter Alleluias, such as "Come, Christians, Join to Sing."

Sing your commitment to be disciples with "I Sing a Song of the Saints of God" or "God of Grace and God of Glory."

Spirituals such as "Jesus Walked This Lonesome Valley" or "Nobody Knows the Trouble I See" grow out of and communicate the feeling of suffering in today's texts. Children respond to these feelings when sung by the congregation, choir, or soloist. "We Shall Overcome" is another spiritual that fits the day's theme and can be sung easily by children.

The Liturgical Child

1. Hang banners or display a painted wooden cross made by suffering Christians in Central America, or mount posters from Amnesty International to recall those who suffer for their faith today.

2. Pray your way around the world, focusing on places where Christians are suffering. Include those who fight apartheid and other forms of racism, those who live in countries where people "disappear," those who have been forced to flee and are trapped in refugee camps, those who are in prison because they stood up for what they believe, and so on. After describing and praying for people in each place, pause to allow worshipers time for their own prayers.

3. Paraphrase Jesus' charge to the disciples and the benediction of I Peter 5:10-11:

In the name of the Risen Jesus, our Lord, I charge you to be his witnesses at home, in *(your community)*, in *(your state)*, and even to the ends of the earth. And may the God of grace, who has called you, be with you, and support you, and make you strong. To God be the power forever. Amen.

4. As the end of the school year approaches, include in the church's prayers the concerns of children, such as exams, grades, class parties and trips, relief from homework, anxiety about summer camps, new child-care arrangements or baby-sitters, and so forth.

Sermon Resources

1. *Sounder,* by William H. Armstrong (Harper & Row, 1969), describes the suffering of David Lee, the son of poor black Louisiana sharecroppers. David Lee's father is sentenced to a year in a labor camp for stealing food for his family. The boy misses his father and must work harder in the fields to make up for his absence. Finally, his delight at his father's early return (he was lamed in an accident) is interrupted by an invitation to attend school in another town. Though David Lee wants to go, he feels he should stay with his father.

Others in the family and town suffer also. A white woman risks being arrested and shunned by other whites when she tries to find out where David Lee's father has been sent. The sufferers of all ages display the discipline described in I Peter. Borrow the book or video from the public library or rent the video.

2. Identify specific ways in which your church witnesses and helps its members be witnesses: global mission offerings, local projects in which members of your church participate, the examples set by members who live as disciples every day at school and on their jobs, and the classes and groups that help people live as good examples. Be sure to include offerings for which the children kept coin boxes, did sponsored work (hunger walks, etc.), or made special purchases, such as animals or equipment, for people in other countries. Interpret children's and adults' church school classes and activity clubs as ways to learn how to be better witnesses every day. Encourage children to witness to their friends by inviting them to these activities.

A witness has to know exactly what happened. Listen carefully when **Acts 1: 6-14** is read. Find Jesus' instructions to his disciples in these groups of letters.

" _ _ _   _ _ _ _   _ _   _ _

_ _ _ _ _ _ _ _ _ ."

Draw a picture of or write about one way you can be God's witness at school or after school with friends.

Me? A witness?

Yes! I am!

PENTECOST

Note: Consult the Pentecost materials in other years of this cycle for additional resources. Year C includes many more suggestions for the general celebration of Pentecost.

From a Child's Point of View

First Reading: Acts 2:1-21 or Numbers 11:24-30. The Pentecost story interests children, but it is hard for them to follow as presented in Acts 2. The opening events of verses 1-4 (especially in the NRSV) catch children's attention. But the long list of unfamiliar ethnic groups (vss. 8-11) distracts them from the crowd's response. And they can make little sense of Peter's explanation (vss. 14-20). With adult help, they can understand the inclusiveness and promises of verses 17 and 18, but their literal minds will be baffled by the "portents in the heavens" of verses 19-21. For these reasons, the story needs to be retold in the sermon.

For Jews, the name Pentecost came from its being the fiftieth day after the first sabbath after Passover. For Christians, it is the fiftieth day after Easter. Children can remember this connection by the reference to a pentagon, a five-sided figure—the best-known example is the Pentagon in Washington, D.C.

The gift the Spirit brings, in Numbers 11:24-30, is ecstatic prophecy. Moses' point was that a few should not hoard such gifts of the Spirit, but wish them for everyone. Because ecstatic prophecy is hard to explain to today's children, and because children do not have the experience to understand Moses' point, focus on the other stories about the Spirit today.

Gospel: John 20:19-23 or John 7:37-39. In John's account (chap. 20) of the giving of the Holy Spirit, the details differ from those in Acts. Some very alert older children will notice those differences and wonder which writer was telling the truth. But most children simply hear them as two stories about God's Spirit coming to be with us. The preaching point for all ages is that Jesus did not desert us to return to heaven. Instead, God, who was with us as Jesus, is now with us as Holy Spirit. So, on Pentecost we celebrate two ways to know God: We know God by reading and thinking about Jesus, and we experience God's powerful Spirit working deep within us. If the message of Christmas is "God is with us!" the message of Pentecost is "God is *still* with us—and always will be!"

To keep the Pentecost symbols of wind and fire at center stage and avoid overwhelming children with too many symbolic images on one day, go lightly over the text from chapter 7. Living water which flows out of believers' hearts is almost impossible to explain satisfactorily to literal thinkers. And the promise of the coming of the Spirit is not as important to children as the story of its coming.

Psalm: 104:1a, 24-34, 35b. If they are told before the reading that this psalmist was praising God for creating all the animals in the oceans, and they are urged to listen for a sea monster named Leviathon, children will understand what the psalmist says and join happily in the praise. The New Jerusalem Bible's translation is especially easy for children.

Epistle: I Corinthians 12:3b-13 or Acts 2:1-21 (if it was not the First Reading). The Corinthians text describes individual talents as one evidence of the presence of God's Spirit. Paul insists that God gives each of us talents, with which we are to love and serve others. Each talent is a valuable source of power for the church, and each talent-bearing person is valuable. Unfortunately, Paul lists talents that are now unfamiliar to most children. Hearing a paraphrase that includes more familiar talents such as singing, patience in caring for sick people, willingness to cook for the homeless, and so on, helps children understand Paul's message. The challenge to children is to identify their own talents as gifts from God, to appreciate those talents, and to use them in doing disciples' work. They are also to appreciate the talents of others as God's gifts.

The inclusion of the image of the body of Christ (vss. 12-13), on a Sunday filled with Pentecost images of fire and wind, complicates rather than clarifies Paul's message for children.

Watch Words

Use *Pentecost* repeatedly to build familiarity with the name of this less-well-known holy day.

Speak of *Holy Spirit*, rather than *Holy Ghost*, which has Halloween connotations.

The term *gifts of the spirit* means little to children until they hear their *talents, skills,* and *abilities* described as *gifts of the spirit.*

Let the Children Sing

Older children can read and sing the simple words of "On Pentecost They Gathered" to retell the Pentecost story. For younger children, singing "Happy Birthday" to the church best captures the reality of the day.

Celebrate God's gift of the Holy Spirit with "Every Time I Feel the Spirit" or "Breathe on Me, Breath of God."

Commit yourselves to using the Spirit's gifts with "Take My Life, and Let It Be Consecrated" or "Lord, You Give the Great Commission." Discuss the meaning of the repeated chorus of the latter before it is sung.

The Liturgical Child

1. Ask a children's class to tie small red bows onto safety pins, to be given to the worshipers as a sign that they and their talents are among God's gifts to the church. Children may pass out the bows during worship, or they could pin them to worship bulletins before the service.

2. Pray a responsive prayer to praise and thank God for being present with and working within your congregation. Be specific: Cite mission projects in which people sense God moving; describe the spirit that is giving life to the church school or the music of the congregation. The congregational response to each prayer: *God is with us!* For example:

> Lord of all the world, we recognize that you were moving among us as we welcomed the Hsus (*or other family from another culture*). We were all nervous at first. But as we worked on language and going to school and getting new jobs, we have come to love one another. We have learned again that you love all people, everywhere on the earth. And we have learned again that with you, we have the power to take care of one another. (RESPONSE)

Sermon Resources

1. The Holy Spirit is God with us. Identify the ways we sense God's powerful presence in some common experiences shared by children and adults: admiring something God made, such as a rainbow or a newborn puppy; singing together in worship; sharing the fun and fellowship of a church supper or retreat; doing God's work together; finding in God's strength the courage to face frightening situations.

2. Describe a sequence of birthday gifts, such as a tricycle, followed by a bicycle with training wheels, followed by a multispeed bike, followed by—if you're really lucky—a car. Point out that such gifts often require the giver to work with the recipient in learning how to use the gift well and responsibly. Then compare these human birthday gifts to the birthday gifts in the form of talents, which God gave the church. Explore how God works with us to teach us how to use our talents well and responsibly. Instead of flowers, place one or more beautifully wrapped gift boxes in the worship center, or set them on the pulpit.

Listen carefully when **Acts 2: 1-21** is read.

Number these pictures to show what happened first, second, and third.

A

B

C

Answers: A.2, B.3, C.1.

Write the letters of your name across the page. Turn each letter into a drawing of one of your talents.

My name is CAROLYN. This is me drawing this page for you.

TRINITY SUNDAY

Note: *Trinity* is not a particularly easy concept for most adults, and it is even more challenging for children. Consult Trinity Sunday in Year C of this series for information about children's understanding of the Trinity in general and suggestions about structuring the worship around God's Trinitarian nature.

From a Child's Point of View

Old Testament: Genesis 1:1–2:4a. This story of the seven-day creation of the world is familiar to most church children. They enjoy identifying what was created on each day. Fifth- and sixth-graders enjoy learning, from the creation of the domed sky in verses 6-8, that the writer(s) thought the world was like a flat plate covered by an inverted bowl, rather than like a ball suspended in space. Knowing that the scientific redefinition of the shape of the earth did not change our understanding of the God who created it provides budding scientists and historians with a crucial understanding to serve as a foundation for their learning and thinking about the world.

Psalm: 8. Children share the psalmist's awe when looking at the world, and his wonder at the role people play in that world. Most of the words and ideas are concrete enough to be understood by all children. The meaning of those that are not can be communicated in the tones and inflections of a dramatic reading.

Gospel: Matthew 28:16-20. In Matthew's Gospel, Jesus sends his disciples into the world in God's three-part name. They are to do the work of God,

who created and cares for the world; of Jesus, who loved and forgave us; and of the Holy Spirit, who is working to make the world the wonderful place God intended that it be. Children often learn about God by identifying what God does and what God calls us to do.

Epistle: II Corinthians 13:11-13. Paul concludes his letter with the hope that the Triune God will be with his readers and support them. Children can learn about God by the ways God acts on our behalf. God created the world and all of us, and God has a good plan for each of us. God in Jesus teaches us how to live and forgives us when we do not do as we should. And God's Spirit lives with us to enjoy life with us and works in us to give us the power to do hard work.

Watch Words

Children first understand *Trinity* and *Triune* simply as words we use at church to talk about God. The connection to a *triangle* helps them to recall and define the word.

Remember that God is neither male nor female. If you prefer not to speak of God in feminine images such as *Mother*, do avoid overusing masculine images and pronouns.

Let the Children Sing

"Now Thank We All Our God" is probably the best general praise hymn for the day. Second choice is either the familiar "Holy, Holy, Holy!" in which

109

difficult vocabulary is balanced by a repeated opening phrase, or the less familiar "Holy! Holy!" which has simpler vocabulary.

Consider three hymns, one for each person of the Trinity. To God the Creator, sing "For the Beauty of the Earth" or "This Is My Father's World." Sing "Jesus Loves Me!" or "Tell Me the Stories of Jesus" for Jesus the Son. And try "Breathe on Me, Breath of God" for the Holy Spirit, especially if you sang it last week to celebrate Pentecost.

The Liturgical Child

1. The creation story is familiar and loved. It is also long. To keep everyone's attention, ask seven readers to read one day each. In a small sanctuary, readers standing in a semicircle might be heard clearly. If microphones are needed, readers can stand near the microphone and take turns. If two mikes are available, alternate days can be read from each mike. Readers may include people of all ages, or they may be all from one class. One practice session is essential.

2. To help worshipers share the psalmist's awe, invite them to line out Psalm 8. (Lining out psalms and hymns was part of worship every Sunday in colonial America. A worship leader read or sang a line, which the congregation then repeated.) Instruct worshipers to repeat your tone and voice inflections, as well as your words. Then read the psalm dramatically, one or two lines at a time. Speak majestically the lines about God's glory and majesty. Emphasize the thoughtfulness of the questions in verses 3 and 4. Decide carefully which words to emphasize in verses 5 through 8. (The meaning can be shaded by emphasizing either the "Yous" or the names of the animals put into human care.)

3. Base both the Charge and Benediction on the Trinitarian formula:

Go now to join God the Creator in caring for the earth and all the plants and animals that live here. Tell people about Jesus. Take up Jesus' work of loving the people no one else loves. Pay attention to places where God's Spirit is at work building peace, and do what you can to help.

And as you go, remember that the God who created you watches over you; that Jesus loves you and forgives you; and that God's Spirit will be with you, to comfort you and give you more power than you ever imagined you could have. Amen.

4. At a World Mission conference several years ago, a missionary told of a young Chinese boy who heard the Great Commission from the King James Version ("and lo, I am with you alway"). Because his name was Lo, he felt God speaking directly to him. Tell this story to invite worshipers to hear Jesus speak to them as you repeat the Great Commission as the Benediction.

Sermon Resources

1. Children enjoy the old story about the blind people who learned about an elephant by touching it. The one who touched one of the legs thought an elephant is like a tree; the one who caught hold of the trunk decided an elephant is like a snake; and so on. Older children have the ability to understand that this can be compared to trying to describe God. God is so big that none of us will ever know all there is to know about God. But we can keep exploring God: We can read the Bible, we can pray; and we can talk and work with others at church.

2. To explore our commission from the Triune God in Matthew 28:19-20, describe God's presence and work in the world in terms of the Trinity. Children recognize God the Creator quickly in the beauty and power of the world. And though they enjoy sunrises and sunsets, most children are more responsive to rainbows and animals, and they are fascinated by baby anythings. Many have experience with puppies, kittens, and baby brothers or sisters. They respond enthusiastically to calls to join God in caring for the created world. Ecology is their science.

Children are also comfortably familiar with stories about Jesus. Jesus is perceived by children as One who loved and took care of people, especially people with needs. They also know from his stories that Jesus wants us to join him in that work (the good Samaritan story may be best known). The preaching task is to identify those around us every day who need this loving care.

Holy Spirit is harder for children to respond to because it operates in the abstract. The best introduction is for adults to say, "I feel God's Holy Spirit with us," in high moments of worship, mission, and church fellowship, so that children can collect experiences with the Holy Spirit. So cite times when you have sensed the presence in your congregation, then challenge worshipers to recognize and interpret such experiences to one another, and especially to their children.

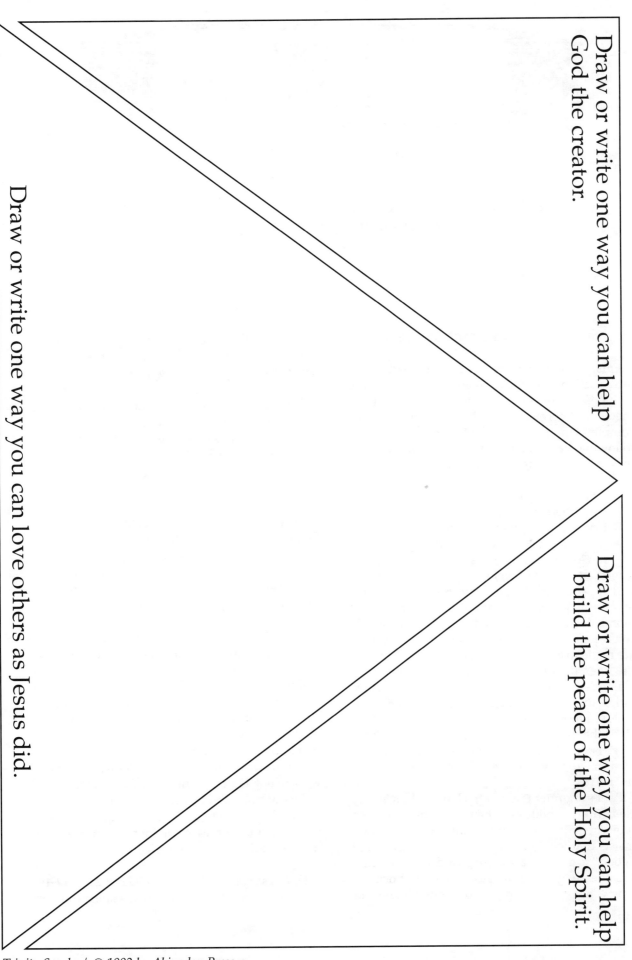

Listen carefully when **Matthew 28: 16-20** is read. Remember that Jesus is speaking to you, too.

Draw or write one way you can help God the creator.

Draw or write one way you can help build the peace of the Holy Spirit.

Draw or write one way you can love others as Jesus did.

Trinity Sunday/ © *1992 by Abingdon Press.*

PROPER FOUR

(Sunday between May 29 and June 4 inclusive, if after Trinity Sunday)

From a Child's Point of View

Epistle: Romans 1:16-17, 3:22b-28 (29-31). This introduction to a series of readings from Romans includes no fewer than seven major abstract theological terms, set in long compound and complex sentences. Children have no chance of following the text. Fortunately, most of the terms will be explored individually in the weeks ahead. Today, the crux of Paul's message is that we can do nothing good enough to earn God's love, and we don't need to, because God's love is a gift.

Before exploring Paul's arguments about the Law, it is important to be aware that just as there are stages of mental development, there are stages of moral development. Interviews in which people of all ages were asked to respond to ethical problems indicate that our earliest moral decisions are based upon the probable consequences for ourselves. Our first decisions are made to avoid punishment or pain. Between the ages of four and eight, children begin to make decisions to gain rewards and pleasure rather than to avoid pain. In middle childhood, children look beyond themselves, making decisions that will make them look like "good" boys or girls. That is, they make decisions that will gain the approval of the authoritative people in their lives.

Paul's arguments about the Law make sense to elementary children when presented in the thought patterns of the "good" girl/boy. Paul insists that we do not need to earn the status of "good" to gain a place among God's people. God has already given us a place. We do not need to worry about avoiding God's punishment or earning God's rewards. Following God's rules is not like completing all the requirements for a Scout badge or practicing a sport or musical instrument to get on the team or into the band. Following God's rules is more like practicing because we are *on* the team or *in* the band, and we want it to be the very best team or band possible.

Verses 27-28 speak clearly to "church kids" who have been following the rules and consider themselves "good" girls/boys. The paraphrase: "Do not think you are better than other people because you follow the rules better than they do. Remember that you did not *earn* your place among God's people. God let you in because God loves you. And God loves everyone else just as much." For older children who compare and rate each other mercilessly, this is an important lesson.

Gospel: Matthew 7:21-29. Because preadolescents do not have the mental ability to understand the comparison between building a spiritual life and building a house, they hear in this story the not very surprising truth that houses built on strong foundations are more durable than those built on weak foundations. However, when the two houses are presented as symbols (like flags) for those who follow Jesus' teachings and those who do not, children understand that it is smarter to follow Jesus and be represented by the strong house. That preference is in keeping with Jesus' message and serves as a foundation for later understanding.

Old Testament: Genesis 6:11-22, 7:24, 8:14-19. Most of the children know Noah's story and will enjoy hearing it. Without adult help, however, children often interpret it as a warning against disobeying God's rules. They easily fall back to first-level moral reasoning to conclude that God can and will destroy those who disobey. God becomes a frightening, punishing judge. Tell the rest of the story, especially the rainbow promise in Genesis 9:8-15, to emphasize God's loving care of Noah and the animals, rather than the punishment of the guilty.

Psalm: 46. The Good News Bible offers the only translation of this psalm that children can understand, and even there the image of the river running through the city of God puzzles literal thinkers. The theme of the psalm and several key verses, however, speak clearly to children of God's powerful trustworthiness. When the "refuge" (vs. 1) is paraphrased as "safe place," it offers real security to children for whom life is a series of battles. Likewise, the "be still" (or "stop fighting" of the Good News Bible) calls for children to stay calm and remember that God is in charge. Both verses are short enough to be easily learned by heart during worship. Stories that contain verses which help us to be calm and secure in a tough spot encourage children to learn such verses.

Watch Words

An *ark* is a *boat*. The Romans text speaks of the *Law, righteousness, faith, grace, redemption, atonement,* and being *justified*. These words are overwhelming!

Grace is the key word for today. (Focus on the others as they reappear in the Romans readings of coming weeks.) Although for most children, *grace* is a girl's name or a mealtime blessing, in today's readings, it is God's love, which cannot be earned but is given as a gift.

Let the Children Sing

Martin Luther's hymn "A Mighty Fortress Is Our God" is familiar but filled with difficult vocabulary and ideas.

Explore *grace* and use the term frequently before expecting children to sing "Amazing Grace!" with understanding.

Sing "I Sing the Almighty Power of God" or "We Plow the Fields and Scatter" to praise the powerful God of Noah.

The Liturgical Child

1. If you focus on Noah's story, ask a children's class to prepare a display of animals leaving the ark. This could be placed in the worship center, perhaps instead of flowers. Children could make clay animals one week and paint them the following week; an adult or teenager could create a freestanding ark and a rainbow for a backdrop. Or the children could make fabric animals and mount them on a banner to carry in the processional and display during worship.

2. To recover the original format of Psalm 46, present it as a responsive reading. A reader reads verses 1-3, 4-6, and 8-10, pausing after each section for the congregation to respond: *The Lord Almighty is with us; the God of Jacob is our refuge.*

The Good News Bible is helpful for children.

Sermon Resources

1. To explore Paul's message, describe two teams with very different approaches to choosing their members. The first team looks at each prospect thoroughly. Candidates must try out in front of the others. People with friends already on the team are more likely to make the team. Candidates with good equipment to bring to games also have a better chance of being chosen.

The second team welcomes anyone who wants to play. The coach works with all those who sign up to play the best possible games and enjoy being a team. According to Romans, God's team is like the second team—and we're already signed up. We don't need to worry about being good enough at the tryouts or earning anyone's favor.

2. The story of Noah is included in the readings for this day, in the readings for the first Sunday of Lent in Year B, and among the many readings of the Easter vigil. So consider devoting the whole service to celebrating and exploring this rich story. Devote the sermon to telling the story in your own words and expounding on it. Good resources include Bill Cosby's recorded monologue "Noah," on the record or cassette *The Best of Bill Cosby*, and Peter

Spier's delightfully detailed picturebook *Noah's Ark* (Doubleday, 1977).

Note: Remember, as we enter "ordinary time," that the texts within a Proper often explore unrelated themes. Therefore you probably will want to enlarge the appropriate half of a Worship Worksheet and omit the activities unrelated to your theme. In fact, it will be necessary to enlarge some worksheets to provide sufficient space for children to complete the activities.

Draw or write what you think it was like inside Noah's ark.

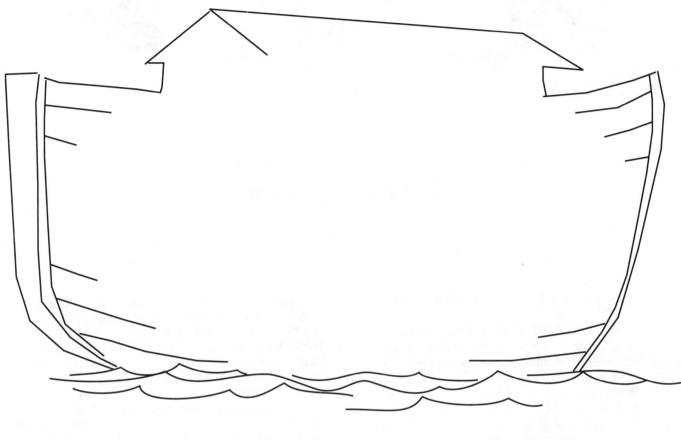

Grace is another word for God's love. God accepts us as friends. We do not have to earn God's friendship. It is a gift. That is grace!

Write the words love, care, friend, accept, and gift in the correct spaces below.

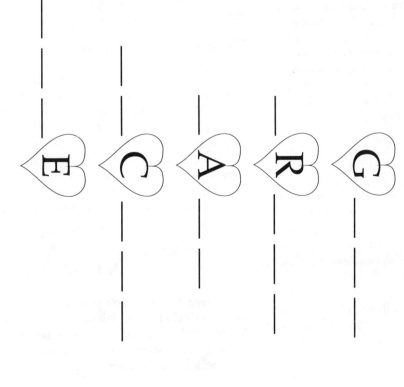

G _ _ _

R _ _ _ _ _

A _ _ _ _ _

C _ _ _

E _ _ _ _ _

Listen for the word **grace** in worship. Draw a ♡ every time you hear it.

PROPER FIVE

*(Sunday between June 5 and 11 inclusive,
if after Trinity Sunday)*

From a Child's Point of View

Old Testament: Genesis 12:1-9. This simple, familiar story poses no vocabulary or concept obstacles for children. Abram's response to God's offer speaks clearly to children about their response to the promises offered to them. Coaches promise that children will play well if they practice with *their* team. Teachers promise that children will be able to do interesting, exciting things as they grow up, if they *study* hard. Peers promise that children will have fun if they join *their* group and do things *their* way. Commercials promise fun and happiness if certain products are purchased. Because children must decide which of all these promises to accept and whether they are willing to do what is asked, they appreciate Abram's decision to leave his home to claim God's promise that God would make the family he did not yet have great.

Epistle: Romans 4:13-25. This is Paul's commentary on living by God's promises. Children need to explore the detailed description in verses 18-25, about why it was hard for Abram to believe God's promise, before they can make sense of the generalizations in verses 13-17. Even then, those generalizations must be put into simpler words and phrases than those Paul uses. As a summary, God gave Abram a gift, a promise, and all Abram had to do was accept the gift and live as if the promise would come true. God has offered us the same gift/promise, a place among the people of God. All we need do is accept that gift and live as God's people.

Gospel: Matthew 9:9-13, 18-26. This text offers children three more stories about living faithfully. Matthew the tax collector leaves his job to follow Jesus. A woman who has been sick for twelve years (longer than young children have been alive) works her way through a big crowd, believing that if she can just touch Jesus, she will be healed. A Jewish leader risks trouble from other Jewish leaders by publicly asking Jesus to bring his dead daughter back to life. Without adult help, children cannot recognize the risks these people took "to faith," but they deeply appreciate those risks, once they are described and explained.

Psalm: 33:1-12. This might be introduced as the song of God's faithful people. Children easily follow the calls to praise God with music and enjoy paraphrasing the calls to include modern instruments. When it is lifted up for individual attention, they enjoy the mental picture of God collecting all the oceans of the world into a bottle (vs. 7, NRSV) and understand its point about God's power. And they are ready to agree with verse 12. In fact, reading verse 12 as part of the introduction to the psalm may help children understand and claim the whole psalm.

Watch Words

Faith is living as if God's promises are true. *Faith* is living as God's people, following God's rules about loving. Fifth- and sixth-graders who are learning about parts of speech enjoy, and get the point of, turning *faith* into a verb, to speak of *faithing.*

Let the Children Sing

Most well-known hymns about faith are filled with Elizabethan English and abstract theological jargon. Children often learn the words of one or two of their congregation's favorites before they understand their meaning.

"O for a World," recorded by the Medical Mission Sisters (included in the *Presbyterian Hymnal*), sets new, simple words, which fit today's texts quite well, to a familiar tune.

The Liturgical Child

1. To help children hear what God said and how Abram responded, enlist two readers for the Genesis text—one to read the narrator's part, the other to read God's words.

2. The Matthew text blends three stories. To help children keep up, instruct them to listen for three people: Matthew (the tax collector); a woman who had been sick for twelve years; and a father whose daughter had died. This will be especially effective if you refer to these people as you explore the stories during the sermon.

3. After exploring today's stories, invite the congregation to read in unison an affirmation prayer about faithful living:

> God, we dream of being faith-filled people.
> Like Abram and Sarai, we know you have invited us to be your people. Give us the courage to live as your people every day.
> Like Matthew, we want to follow you. Help us follow your teachings.
> Like the sick woman, we trust your power. Heal the hate and greed and selfishness that make our lives so unhealthy.
> Like the father whose daughter died, we know that your love and power go even beyond death. So we trust those who have died to your care, and we live bravely, knowing that even when we die, you will be with us.
> God, we dream of being your faith-filled people, and we trust your power to make your promises come true. Amen.

Sermon Resources

1. The stories of Abram and Sarai, Matthew, the woman in the crowd, and the father whose daughter died assume much background that must be spelled out for children, and for many adults. So retell the stories in your own words, expanding on key details, pointing out the risks each faithful person took, and describing the significance of what they did. Compare their situations to those of people your children know or are aware of today.

2. Describe faith by comparing three faithful people. The first likes sports and has athletic ability. This person joins several teams, eats foods that build a strong body, exercises regularly, watches sports events on TV, and reads about sports heroes.

The second person likes to draw and draws well. This person belongs to the art club at school, takes painting lessons, spends birthday money on paints, pays more attention to the pictures than to the words in books, and reads about great artists.

Children can recognize in these descriptions two people who have God-given gifts, have accepted their gifts, and are enjoying and developing them. They are faithful to their gifts.

The third story speaks mainly to older children and adults. This person believes that God made him or her part of a family that includes everyone in the world. So this person treats everyone with kindness, stands up for kids who are teased or abused by other kids, refuses to laugh at jokes about people's color or nationality, and contributes Christmas money to build a house for a family living in a shack. This person is faithful to God's gift/promise that we are all one family.

3. Other examples of faith that children understand include jumping off a diving board for the first time, with someone watching who promised to help you if you need it (faith in what you have been told and shown, and in your potential rescuer); riding a bicycle down a steep hill (faith in your own abilities); and telling a friend a secret (trusting friend not to tell). In each case, what you think and hope must be blended with what you do.

Abraham, Matthew, and a sick woman each had a promise from God. Each one did something brave to claim that promise. Find the correct path from each person to his or her promise. Write the letters from that path in the spaces at the end of the path to learn what each person did.

1. ABRAHAM

2. A SICK WOMAN

3. MATTHEW

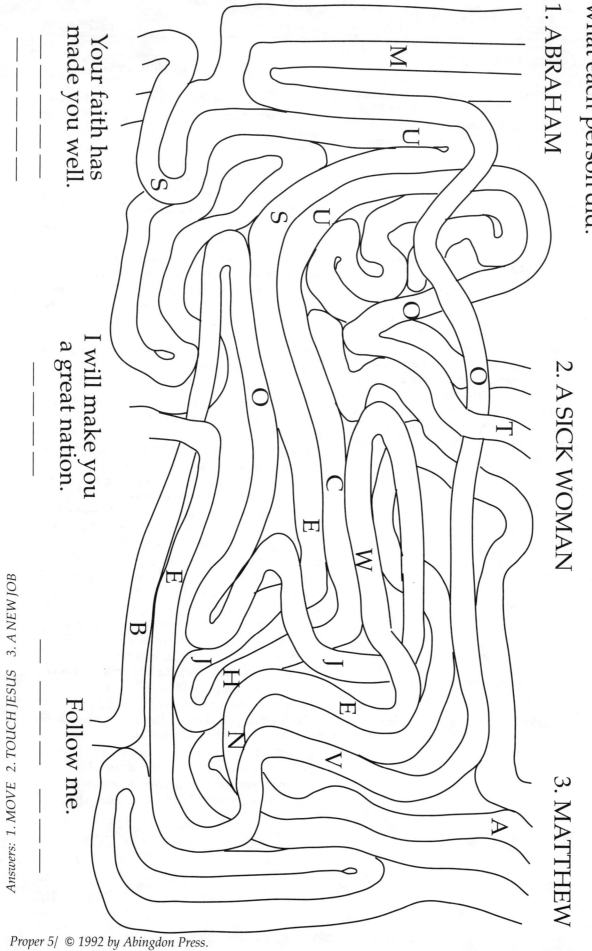

Your faith has made you well.

__ __ __ __

I will make you a great nation.

__ __ __ __

Follow me.

__ __ __

Proper 5/ © 1992 by Abingdon Press.

PROPER SIX

(Sunday between June 12 and 18 inclusive, if after Trinity Sunday)

From a Child's Point of View

Old Testament: Genesis 18:1-15 (21:1-7). Children can keep up with the events in this interesting two-part story when it is well read. They are fascinated by God appearing as not one person, but three people. From this they learn that God can come to us in any form God chooses. Children follow the events of the story with the curiosity shared by listeners of all ages. Even the youngest child knows that people almost one hundred years old do not have babies. Older children know why that is the case. All share in Sarah's disbelieving laughter as she eavesdrops from inside the tent, and in her happy laughter as she plays with her "surprise" son. With adult guidance, children can learn from the story that nothing is impossible for God and that God often surprises us when we think we are hopelessly trapped.

Epistle: Romans 5:1-8. Paul engages here in very adult, abstract logic, totally beyond the thinking abilities of even the oldest children. He speaks about justification attained through Christ, who died in order that we might be reconciled with God.

The underlying idea that does make sense to children is that God wants to be friends with us so much that God does not wait for us to decide we want to be friends. Instead, God comes to us while we are still enemies, to make friends with us. Celebrate that amazing, undeserved love, rather than trying to explain it. There are no theologically sound explanations of the way God used Jesus' death to make friends with us that will satisfy literal thinkers.

Gospel: Matthew 9:35–10:8 (9-23). The description of Jesus' work (9:35-36) is easier for children to adopt as an example for themselves than are the instructions for the mission of the Twelve (10:5-23). The latter describes unfamiliar activities (casting out unclean spirits, cleansing lepers, etc.), while the former speaks in familiar generalities (teaching, proclaiming the good news, healing, having compassion). Older children respond especially readily to Jesus' call for workers to show and tell others about God's great love.

Because children need lots of help to decipher the significance of the instructions in 10:9-23, and they can be frightened by the warnings about family betrayals, it may be wise to stop the reading with verse 8. If you do read on, you will find that the instructions about taking pay mean little to children. You will need to explain that verses 11-15 are directions for what to do when our good efforts are not accepted. And you will need to explain the animal images. Though few children choose to be sheep among wolves, many are attracted to the possibility of being clever as a snake but gentle as a dove. The snake's cleverness lies in going a little this way and a little that way to get to the goal.

Psalm: 116:1-2, 12-19. The references to Temple thank offerings and sacrifices make this a difficult psalm for children. Therefore the best use of it may be to raise the question asked in verse 12 and ponder modern answers—that is, I will keep the promises made at my baptism; I will worship with God's people; and so forth.

Verse 15 can disturb children. So choose The

119

Good News Bible's "How painful it is to the Lord when one of his people dies!" rather than other translations, such as the NRSV's "precious . . . is the death of the faithful."

Watch Words

In Romans, *reconciliation* describes "making friends," and *justified* is defined as "being good enough."

If you speak of going on *missions,* define them as *assignments* or *tasks.* Contrast these kinds of missions to the assignments of spies.

Let the Children Sing

Sing "Now Thank We All Our God," to name God's many blessings.

Try "Child of Blessing, Child of Promise" or "Wonder of Wonders, Here Revealed," two new baptism hymns with simple vocabulary. Sing them to celebrate Isaac's surprising birth or God's powerful love (Romans).

"Lord, Make Us Servants of Your Peace" invites us to dedicate ourselves to mission by singing Saint Francis' famous prayer.

The Liturgical Child

1. The Genesis text is easily followed when it is read with dramatic inflection worthy of the good story. It also can be presented as a readers' theater by four readers (Abraham, the visitors, Sarah, and God). Or it can be pantomimed by a youth or adult group, as a narrator reads.

2. Celebrate God's power with a litany about laughter. The congregation's response to each account: *Is anything impossible with the Lord?* Before the reading, help the congregation practice saying the response with a feeling of happy amazement at what God does.

Abraham and Sarah were old and childless. They thought they would be the last of their family. Then when they were nearly one hundred years old, God promised that their family would be great. They laughed about having a baby at their age. (RESPONSE)

Moses and the Hebrew slaves saw the army of Pharaoh behind them and the Reed Sea in front of them, and they thought they were dead. But God cleared the way across the sea, and on the other side, they laughed and sang to God. (RESPONSE)

Jesus was arrested, tried, and killed on Friday by people who thought they had gotten rid of a troublemaker. But on Sunday, Jesus rose from death. Christians have been laughing and singing about God's power ever since. (RESPONSE)

God interrupted Paul on his way to arrest Christians in Damascus and called him to become a church leader instead. The frightened Christians were suspicious at first, but then, how they laughed about what God had done. (RESPONSE)

(Briefly tell one or two stories about God's action in your congregation, community, and world. For example, I would speak of the laughter as the Berlin wall came down, and the laughter at a church work party to help someone in need.)

3. If you are focusing on the sending of the Twelve, invite each worshiper to write on a slip of paper the group or person to whom he or she will pass God's love this summer, and place that paper in the offering plate as it is passed. Promise confidentiality and instruct the ushers to respect this promise. (See the Worship Worksheet.)

Sermon Resources

1. Speak about some of the things it is hard for children to believe God can do: Change a bully into a friend; do something about serious family problems; and make a difference in problems that, to them, seem hopeless.

2. Ask people to imagine what might happen if members of your congregation, of all ages, took Jesus' instructions to the Twelve seriously for the summer. Point out that Jesus did not send his disciples far away, but told them to go to work right where they were. He told them to volunteer and not expect to receive much reward. Then help worshipers identify where God's love is needed in your community. Be as specific as possible. Challenge each worshiper to select one person or group to whom he or she will pass God's love this summer. Warn them that it will not be easy (Matt. 10:16, 17, 22) and promise that God will be with them, helping them to say and do what is needed (10:18-20).

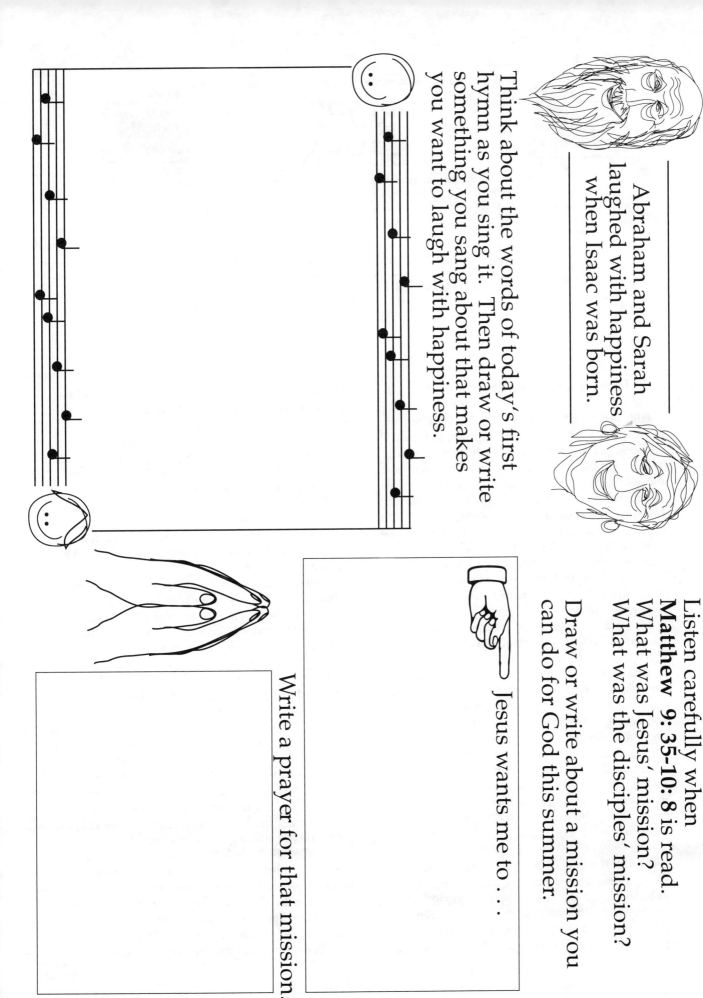

Abraham and Sarah laughed with happiness when Isaac was born.

Think about the words of today's first hymn as you sing it. Then draw or write something you sang about that makes you want to laugh with happiness.

Listen carefully when **Matthew 9: 35-10: 8** is read.
What was Jesus' mission?
What was the disciples' mission?

Draw or write about a mission you can do for God this summer.

Jesus wants me to . . .

Write a prayer for that mission.

PROPER SEVEN

(Sunday between June 19 and 25 inclusive, if after Trinity Sunday)

From a Child's Point of View

Old Testament: Genesis 21:8-21. Children are bothered by the casting out of Ishmael, as they will be bothered by next week's story of the near sacrifice of Isaac, because they hear the stories from the point of view of the children in the stories. They are offended by the fact that Abraham would turn his own son out into the desert, with God's blessing. (One skinful of water does not seem like much help in that situation.) For children who feel that their parents love another sibling better—and most children feel this occasionally—the story raises unthinkable possibilities about what might happen to them.

To avoid this frightening interpretation, present the text as the story of two mothers, who fought so much that even God could not figure out how they could live peacefully in the same tent. The problem was not that either God or Abraham loved Isaac more than Ishmael. The problem was that Sarah and Hagar bickered and fought so much that the only solution was to separate them. So God suggested that Hagar and her son Ishmael go away. Abraham did what he could for them (gave them water), and God took over from there, promising that Ishmael also would become the father of a great family. Keep the focus on God's loving care, even when we are at our worst.

Epistle: Romans 6:1b-11. Because the details of Paul's message are a result of baptism as practiced in Judaism and the Greek mystery religions, they are beyond the understanding of children. But Paul's point makes good sense to children if it is presented in terms of living as a "good" boy or girl

among God's people. (Review the information about moral development in Proper 4.) According to this kind of thinking, when you join a club or team, you follow the rules and work for the group's goals. So when you become one of God's people, you do what God's people do and follow the rules of God's people. If you do not want to live like God's people do, then you should not join. God's forgiveness is for people who make sincere mistakes as they try to be God's people. It is not an easy out for those who do not want to be God's people.

A related and equally important point is that belonging to God's people affects every part of life. Joining God's people is like being a new person. You cannot be one of God's loving people at church and be a selfish, me-first person at home or a cheating fighter on the soccer team. You must be God's loving person everywhere you go.

So read this passage for the adults, but explore its message with the children as well.

Gospel: Matthew 10:24-39. Jesus' point is that being a Christian means some people are not going to like the way you live. He makes his point with a series of sayings about facing opposition.

Verses 24-25 warn that just as Jesus was called mean names, his followers can expect to be called mean names. Though few children today have been called Beelzebub, Christian children sometimes are taunted with, "Isn't he/she swe-e-e-t!" when they live by Jesus' example.

Faced with daily harassment on the bus and playground, promises about what will happen in the next life (vss. 28, 32-33) mean little to children who live so much in the present. But verses 29-30 promise that God will care for them, even though others may make life miserable.

Verses 34-39 point out that Christians may even encounter opposition at home. Children, however, often miss that point and hear only Jesus' insistence that family loyalty is of secondary importance. Because they are so dependent on their parents' care, that is frightening to them. Ease their fears by listing other loyalties that also should be secondary—winning a game, keeping a popular friend, doing what the group is doing, being a member of a club or gang, and so forth. (Do not let the family turmoil referred to here be confused with that caused by the jealousy between Sarah and Hagar.)

Psalm: 86. If this is introduced as the prayer of a person trying to live as one of God's people (Romans 6) or of a Christian facing the kind of opposition Jesus described (Matthew 10), children will appreciate occasional lines in it.

Watch Words

If you focus on the Genesis story, introduce and use *mercy* to describe God's treatment of sinners like Sarah and Hagar—and us. If *mercy* appears in your regular order of confession, point it out and explain its use there.

Do not expect children to make any sense of talk about *dying and rising with Christ.*

Let the Children Sing

In response to the feuding of Sarah and Hagar, sing "Let There Be Peace on Earth." Or sing "Blest Be the Tie That Binds," as a reminder that we have good reasons not to fight.

Commit yourselves to being one of God's people, even in the face of opposition, with "Lord, I Want to Be a Christian."

The Liturgical Child

1. Base a Prayer of Confession on the bickering of Sarah and Hagar:

Lord, we confess that we often bicker, fight, and feud, just as Sarah and Hagar did. We treat others as if we are better than they are. We boast about

what we have that they do not have, and what we can do that they cannot do. We fight to make sure we get everything that is our right and that they get nothing more than is their right. We act as if there is not enough of anything to go around. Forgive us. Teach us how to get along so that we do not doom ourselves to lives of fighting. We pray in the name of Jesus, the Prince of Peace. Amen.

Assurance of Pardon: God loved both Sarah and Hagar. Even when they fought, God did not give up on them. God separated them and took care of them and their sons. God does the same with us when we fight. God keeps on loving us, caring for us, separating us when necessary, and working toward that day when we will all live together in peace. That day will come. We have God's word for it. Thanks be to God!

2. To help children pay attention to each of Jesus' sayings about facing opposition, either have each saying read by a different reader, or have a single reader pause between each saying (vss. 24-25, 26-27, 28, 29-31, 32-33, 34-39).

3. As you pray about standing up to opposition, be sure to pray for courage to stand firm in the locker room, at the pool, in close ball games, in the cabin at camp, and in other situations in which children must make their witness during the summer.

Sermon Resources

1. Children delight in a sermon that features the bickering of adults rather than that of children. But they also need examples of bickering that include children: (1) being shut up in a mountain cabin with no TV, in the rain for the third day, having played all their games and worked all their puzzles twice; (2) being in the back seat of a car on a long trip; or (3) having arguments over sharing a room, with lines drawn down the middle.

2. To explore the Romans text, tell a story about a boy who played on the Eagles team, but only when it suited him. He wore the team cap everywhere, and boasted about the team, and went to team parties. When he showed up, he was a fairly good player. But he did not always show up for practice, or even for games. If a friend invited him to the movies or to go swimming, he went there instead.

Finally, the coach confronted him and demanded, "Either be a real Eagle, or don't be an Eagle. Stop pretending to be an Eagle only when you feel like it."

Draw or write the names of people with whom you are most likely to fight.

Write a prayer about getting along with them.

Get the message through! Put each of the scattered letters into the right words below.

A A A A U E E E I O Y

Jesus said,

"D _ N _ T B _ _ FR _ _ D."

(Matthew 10: 31)

The psalm writer prayed,

"T _ _ CH M _ Y _ _ R W _ _ , _ L _ RD."

(Psalm 86: 11)

PROPER EIGHT

(Sunday between June 26 and July 2 inclusive)

From a Child's Point of View

The story of Abraham's near-sacrifice of Isaac is frightening for worshipers of any age, but particularly for children, who are totally dependent upon their parents. Therefore, preaching on this text demands great sensitivity to the fears and needs of the children in the congregation.

Old Testament: Genesis 22:1-14. Because children hear this story from Isaac's point of view, they may wonder whether God would ask their parents to prove their faith by killing them, and whether their parents would do it. About the only way to head off the terrifying possibilities this suggests is to introduce the story of Isaac as one of the scariest stories in the Bible. Point out that it frightens both parents and children. It scares children because they wonder if God would test their parents that way, and how their parents would respond. It scares parents because most parents, though they trust and want to obey God, would rather kill themselves than hurt their children.

That puts the focus on testing. Children need to know that all of us will face difficult decisions about how we treat people and how we live, and in these situations, we must be brave and do what is right. They also need to be reassured that God, who does the testing, loves us. Isaac was never in any danger. God was not about to allow Abraham to kill him. Likewise, God will not test us with tasks that will destroy us or those we love.

Psalm: 13. Children, for whom time seems so much longer than it does for adults, empathize with the psalmist's repeated question, "How long?" They know what it is to wait and endure, and they are generally pleased to find a psalm that reflects their impatience. It helps to paraphrase verse 5: "I wait patiently because God's love lasts forever."

Epistle: Romans 6:12-23. Children know what is expected of a slave. They also are encouraged to avoid "being a slave" to anything. So they need help to understand Paul's assumptions that we all are slaves to something, and the only question is, To what will we enslave ourselves? Exploring the slavery of professional athletes and musicians to their crafts, the slavery of an addict to a drug, or the slavery of a person to a project such as a soup kitchen, helps older children to grasp Paul's point. The challenge then is to explore the way we live out our slavery to God each day.

If you prefer to avoid the image of slavery, develop the image of being an instrument or tool ready for God's use (vs. 13). Speak of the jobs God is doing and the things we can do to help get that work done.

Gospel: Matthew 10:40-42. These verses are based on the rewards of hospitality. Older children begin to understand that there are different kinds of rewards for being friends with different kinds of people. Though they will not grasp Jesus' three examples, they can explore the difference in befriending popular people who will include them in fun parties, befriending tough people who will get them in trouble, and befriending those who have nothing to offer but who need a good friend.

Watch Words

Testing is a difficult concept. If you use it, relate it less to school tests and more to a team that tests itself against the ability of another team.

Speak of *slavery* to persons (God or Jesus) or activities (football, drugs), rather than to abstract concepts such as *righteousness*, *law*, or *sin*.

Describe what *instruments* and tools do, then ask children to do similar work, rather than ask them to *become* the instruments or tools.

Let the Children Sing

Sing of testing with "Fight the Good Fight," which is filled with contest images familiar to children, or "God of Grace and God of Glory," with it's repeated chorus.

Commit each part of your body to be used by God, with "Take My Life, and Let It Be Consecrated."

The Liturgical Child

1. Read Psalm 13:5-6 as a call to worship, or ask a children's class to repeat it together at the front of the sanctuary. They can join their parents during the opening hymn. Rephrase the first verse from the New Revised Standard Version: "I trust in God's everlasting love; my heart shall rejoice in God's salvation."

2. If you focus on testing, explain the meaning of this line in the Lord's Prayer: "Lead us not into temptation, but deliver us from evil." Then use the phrase as the congregation's response in a litany prayer:

> Lord of our lives, You made us, and we are yours. But all around there are temptations for us to pretend that we can do whatever we want and that we are the only ones who matter. We need your help and protection, so we pray . . . (RESPONSE)
>
> Lord, your world is filled with beautiful, interesting things. Commercials promise that if we buy these things, we will be happy. It is easy to believe those promises and to spend our lives getting and enjoying things. So we pray . . . (RESPONSE)
>
> Creator God, you made us and gave us talents. People urge us to use those talents to be the best and to come out at the top. It is easy to forget that winning isn't everything. It is tempting to ignore the rules and the needs of others as we work hard to win. So we pray . . . (RESPONSE)
>
> God, our Father and Mother, we are part of your big family. But we think so much about what we are doing, what we want, and what we need that we tend to overlook the needs and wants of others. We easily forget those we do not see. We even forget those we are with every day. So we pray . . . (RESPONSE)
>
> Lord of the world, we live in a rich and powerful nation. Remind us that we are responsible for the use of that power. Be with our leaders when they are thinking of using power unfairly to get our way. So we pray . . . (RESPONSE)
>
> Lord, when we pray "lead us not into temptation but deliver us from evil," we remember thankfully that "thine is the kingdom and the power and the glory, for ever and ever." And we say, let it be so! Amen.

3. *Benediction:* Go forth from this place to be God's slaves. Do what God has commanded. Take care of others, as Jesus did. Tell the good news of your Master's love. And as you go, remember that God goes with you. The power of your Master is working through you and supports you in everything you do.

Sermon Resources

1. In chapter 15 of *On the Banks of Plum Creek* (Harper & Row, 1953), one of the Little House on the Prairie series by Laura Ingalls Wilder, Laura nearly drowns in a stream swollen by spring rains. She had been strongly warned against playing in the stream, but on the first warm day after a long miserable winter, she put just her toes in, then her feet . . . then she was caught in the current!

2. Describe the functions of several kinds of tools or instruments. For example, a military tank is a tool for destruction, while a tractor is a tool for farmers to grow things. Similarly, a piano, when banged at, makes irritating noise, but when played by a trained pianist, makes beautiful music. Describe children (of all ages) who cause trouble wherever they go and those who spread happiness and fun. St. Francis' prayer, "Make me an instrument of peace," makes sense to children after such an exploration of tools and instruments.

Pay attention to the words as you sing, "**Take My Life and Let It Be Consecrated.**" Then draw ways you can serve God with your hands, feet, voice, and heart.

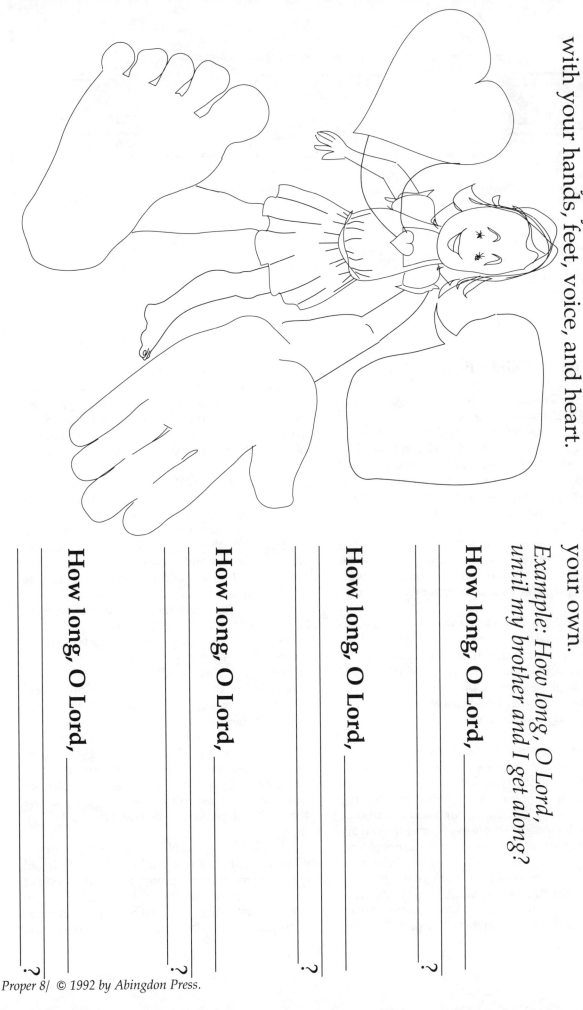

Read the 4 "how long" questions at the beginning of Psalm 13. Then write 4 "how long" questions of your own.

Example: How long, O Lord, until my brother and I get along?

How long, O Lord, _____ _____ ?

How long, O Lord, _____ _____ ?

How long, O Lord, _____ _____ ?

How long, O Lord, _____ _____ ?

PROPER NINE

(Sunday between July 3 and 9 inclusive)

From a Child's Point of View

Old Testament: Genesis 24:34-38, 42-49, and 58-67. Children, who are generally interested in wedding stories, are fascinated by this story of how Isaac and Rebekah met and were married. They enjoy hearing the details of the arranged marriage and with help can appreciate the underlying assumption of the story that God is concerned about and involved in all parts of our lives—in this case in whom we marry. God had a good plan for Isaac and Rebekah. Abraham's servant recognized it. Rebekah and Isaac accepted it and followed it. We are called to watch for signs of God's plans for us and to respond as they did.

Psalm: 45:10-17. Children will be interested to find this wedding song among the psalms. Though the sexual stereotypes in the psalm have a Middle Eastern or fairytale bias that will need to be dealt with in the sermon, the very presence of the psalm indicates that God cares about all parts of our daily lives—including our marriages.

Epistle: Romans 7:15-25a. Children, like many adults, become hopelessly tangled in Paul's complex sentences and logic. But they understand, with painful clarity, Paul's basic message that we never live up to our good intentions. During elementary-school years, children struggle to recognize the intentions of others and themselves. Adults repeatedly urge children to forgive others because "he or she didn't mean to do it." But the same adults apply different standards when asking, "Why did you do it? Good girls (boys) do not do that. Don't you want to be a good girl (boy)?" The answer to the question is, of course, "I don't know why I did it. I didn't mean to, but . . . ." Children appreciate hearing that everyone has the same problem. Living up to our good intentions is something all of us work on, but never achieve.

Gospel: Matthew 11:16-19, 25-30. Although this passage speaks of children, much of its message is too sophisticated for children. Both Jesus' point that some people will never be satisfied with God's activity (they had criticized the asceticism of John the Baptist and accused Jesus of gluttony) and the Wisdom references in verses 25-27 require intellectual skills children do not possess.

Verses 28-30, while they are familiar, present two problems. The first is that children have little knowledge of yokes, a problem that is fairly easily solved. Beyond that is the fact that Jesus was addressing Jewish adults overburdened with Pharisaic demands about following God's rules. For them, the rules (the Law) had become a burden rather than an asset. Six- to twelve-year-olds, on the other hand, are at the stage of moral development when rules are seen as good, useful ways of relating happily with one another. Children really do not want relief from rules—at least not from good rules. Therefore, the promise Jesus offered his Jewish listeners means little to them.

It is, however, possible to explore that promise as the offer of a plan for our lives that is designed especially for us or our group. Jesus promised not to force us into a plan, or yoke, that fits someone else, or that others wish would fit us. Instead, Jesus promised a plan/yoke that is uniquely ours.

Consider linking these verses with the Genesis story to encourage worshipers to be as responsive to God's plan (a marriage) as the Old Testament families were, rather than as unresponsive to God's plan (the work of Jesus and John) as Jesus' critics were.

Watch Words

A *yoke* is a harness (usually wooden) with which horses or oxen pull wagons or plows. A *yoke* is also the work God has for us to do. Just as an ox yoke is carved to fit a particular animal, so God's plan for us is designed to fit us.

Should these texts lead you to speak of *predestination*, simply tell children that God has a plan for us, just as God had a plan for Rebekah and Isaac.

Let the Children Sing

Praise God, the Creator and Planner, with "For the Beauty of the Earth" or "All Creatures of Our God and King," with its repeated Alleluias.

Commit yourselves to God's plans with "I Sing a Song of the Saints of God," or with "Be Thou My Vision," if children frequently sing it elsewhere.

The Liturgical Child

1. If you can find a horse or ox yoke, display it in the chancel. Use it to explain the fit and function of yokes.

2. Prayer of Confession:

God, sometimes we do not understand ourselves. We know right from wrong, but that could not be proved by what we do. We are full of good intentions. We want to treat our family and friends kindly. We want to help people who need our help and make friends with people who are lonely. We dream of standing up bravely for your justice. But when the time comes to do those things, we forget or get busy or simply chicken out. Forgive us for all the good we do not do.

Lord, we also know what is wrong. We are against cheating, lying, and language that is used in anger. But we sometimes cheat in order to win. We lie when it keeps us out of trouble. We say angry words, which embarrass us even as we say them. All too often we go along with the crowd, rather than pointing out that what the crowd is doing is wrong. Forgive us for the wrong we do knowingly.

At times, God, we are ready to give up on ourselves. All we can do is ask you to forgive us and pray that you will not give up on us. Amen.

Assurance of Pardon: We are not alone. Paul insisted that all people have sinned and been less than God intended for us to be. But God loves us and forgives us. God accepts our apologies and urges us to keep trying. God promises to work with us and in us and through us, to do what is right. Thanks be to God.

Sermon Resources

1. Use the story of Rebekah and Isaac as an opportunity to talk about marriage as part of God's plan for some people. Tell other marriage stories (your own if appropriate), in which partners consider their marriage part of God's plan. Admit that we sometimes misread God's plans and make unhappy marriages. Encourage parents to tell children how marriage has been part of God's plan for their lives. Suggest signs to look for in deciding whether a potential marriage is part of God's plan.

2. Shoes (for working people) may be the closest modern equivalent to yokes (for working animals). So talk about wearing shoes that are too big (walking out of them), or too small (ouch!), the wrong style (you wore dress-up shoes to a party where everyone was playing soccer), or shoes that would be OK for someone else but not for you (Mom wants you to get plain tennis shoes, but you want high-tops with irridescent laces). Describe the difficulties of wearing shoes that are not quite right and the pleasure of wearing shoes that are just right. This leads to talking about jobs that are just right for us.

3. If you wear a clerical stole in worship, describe its function as a reminder of the yoke to which you are fitted as a preacher. Talk about how you feel about that yoke and how it affects your life. Name the invisible yokes you see others wearing.

4. Among your examples of failed intentions, include some from childhood, such as intending to get along with your brother or sister while your parents are gone, or meaning to stay in the yard so you'll be there when dinner is ready, or meaning to sit with the new kid at lunch, and so forth.

Listen to the story in **Genesis 24**.

Draw a picture of something that happened in that story.

OR

Write a prayer for Rebekah as she leaves home.

Show your picture or prayer to your pastor as you leave worship.

To find a promise from Jesus, reverse the order of these letters and write them in the spaces below.

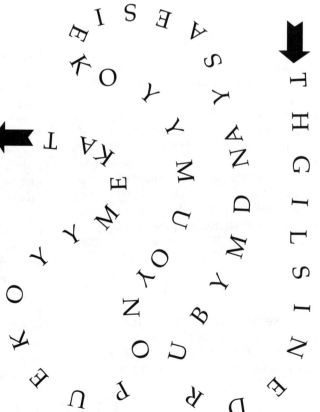

"TAKE _ _ _ _   _ _ _   _ _ _ _ _ _ ."

PROPER TEN

(Sunday between July 10 and 16 inclusive)

From a Child's Point of View

Old Testament: Genesis 25:19-34. Children enjoy this very believable story about a feuding family of less than heroic people. They revel in the differences between the red-haired outdoor boy and his soft, stay-at-home twin brother, who were fighting even before they were born. They appreciate the narrator's honesty in admitting that the parents played favorites. From this story, we can conclude that if God would use these people, there may be hope for us and our families.

A central theme of the story is the overthrow of primogeniture. Though children enjoy speculating about how primogeniture would change their position, they realize that it is history. What is real for them is that they have an equally strong interest in enforcing an ordered world today. Older brothers and sisters should be allowed to stay up later and do things younger ones cannot. If I had to wait until fourth grade to get a bicycle, then my little brother should have to wait until fourth grade for his. If the sixth-graders have gone on an overnight trip at the end of camp each year, there will be outrage if that trip is cancelled or changed. Children like an ordered world—especially if the order works to their advantage—as much as adults do. This story challenges that preference by insisting that God breaks out of such orders.

Epistle: Romans 8:1-11. The abstract language and concepts of this text make it impossible for children to hear or read with understanding. But they can explore its message through what Paul said about two different kinds of people. One kind of people view life from their own self-centered position. Their first concern is always "What's in it for me?" The second kind view the world from God's point of view. They see themselves as members of God's family, living in God's world. Their concern is to be happy, productive parts of that family and world.

This second worldview, however, is hard for children to grasp because they are sharply focused on understanding and learning how to function in the world around them. Even those who are growing up with God's worldview operate from a self-centered perspective. Only accumulated experience and the mental development of adolescence will enable children to grasp Paul's distinction between these two ways of living.

Gospel: Matthew 13:1-9, 18-23. From a child's point of view, the seed on the path stands for people who totally ignore God. Some of them do not go to Sunday school or worship. Others go, but pay no attention. In either case, they ignore God. The seeds on the rocky ground stand for people who love to go to church on Sunday, know all the stories about Jesus and sing about God's love, but give up quickly when hard disciples' work is needed at home, on the team, or among friends. The seeds that are choked out stand for the people who have decided that always winning and having great clothes, wonderful toys, and popular friends is more important than love and sharing. The seed in the good soil stands for those who hear about God and are disciples every day.

Psalm: 119:105-112. This is part of the big acrostic psalm praising God's torah, or law. Verse

131

105 is most familiar, but its imagery is strange to literal thinkers. They need to hear the psalmist's praise stated more prosaically: When I read the Bible, I know what I should do and how I should act. Older children stretch to compare using a flashlight to find our way at night with thinking about what we learn from the Bible in order to figure out what we should do in difficult situations.

Watch Words

Remember that *pottage* and *blessing* need to be defined. *Sower* is often heard by nonagricultural children as *sewer*, one who sews. So introduce this as the story of a *farmer* who *sows* seed.

Avoid Paul's comparison of the *flesh* and *spirit*. Children often confuse this pairing to mean that any body-centered activity (sports, health) is bad, while any activity that deals with religion (praying, reading the Bible) is good. This seriously skews Paul's intent.

Let the Children Sing

Praise God with "For the Beauty of the Earth" which includes thanks for families.

The Medical Mission Sisters have written a lively rendition of today's parable, "The Sower," which makes a fine children's choir anthem (in *Knock Knock;* order book from Vanguard Music Corp. or record from Avant Guard Records, 250 W. 57th St., New York, N.Y. 10019).

Most hymns about the Bible are filled with abstract images and difficult words. "Wonderful Words of Life" is the best choice for children. Even nonreaders can join in on the chorus if encouraged.

The Liturgical Child

1. Take advantage of midsummer relaxed attitudes to present the whole Jacob story dramatically. To complete the story, add Genesis 27:1–28:5, Jacob's theft of the blessing, which is not included in the lectionary. Have a narrator read Genesis 25:19-25. Then present the scenes in Genesis 25:29-34 and 27:1–28:5 as plays. After each section, offer a preaching/commentary on that section. Perhaps a group of older children and youths could meet during the week to prepare the narration and two scenes.

2. Pray for relationships within families. Offer opportunities for parents to pray for children, for children to pray for parents, and for siblings to pray for one another. Pray about fights over space in the house, who watches what on TV, who gets to do what. Remember that all households do not include a mother, a father, and a couple of children, and plan your prayers accordingly.

3. Ask four youths and/or adults to dance or pantomime the growth of the four kinds of seed as the parable is read. Dress the four earthily in jeans and plain T-shirts, unless you have brown or green tunics (perhaps shepherd costumes from Christmas) and people willing to wear them.

Sermon Resources

1. Introduce the "triangle theory" of personal relationships. According to this theory, people within families relate in threes, forming triangles. Within each triangle are three pairings, which may be strong, weak, or destructive. These triangles tend toward balance. The best balance is three strong pairings. The most dangerous is one strong relationship and two destructive ones. The most common and fixable is one strong relationship and two weak ones (e.g., Rebekah, Jacob, and Esau). Family counselors help their clients analyze the triangles in their families and work on the unbalanced ones. A therapist might urge Jacob to find ways to strengthen his weak friendship with Esau. As their relationship improved, the relationship between Rebekah and Esau would tend to improve also, since we tend to accept the friends of our friends as friends and their enemies as our enemies. Thus this triangle would move toward a healthier balance, and the potential for family problems would decrease.

Use the triangle theory to analyze the problems of the Genesis family. Then urge worshipers to apply the theory to their own families—perhaps drawing the triangles in a blank space on their bulletins—and to work for changes that might make a difference. Older children understand this theory and are capable of using it to make significant changes in the health of their families.

2. Compare the family in Genesis with some of the families on television, perhaps the Simpsons and the Cosbys.

Listen as **Matthew 13** is read. Finish the pictures to show what happened to the seeds . . .

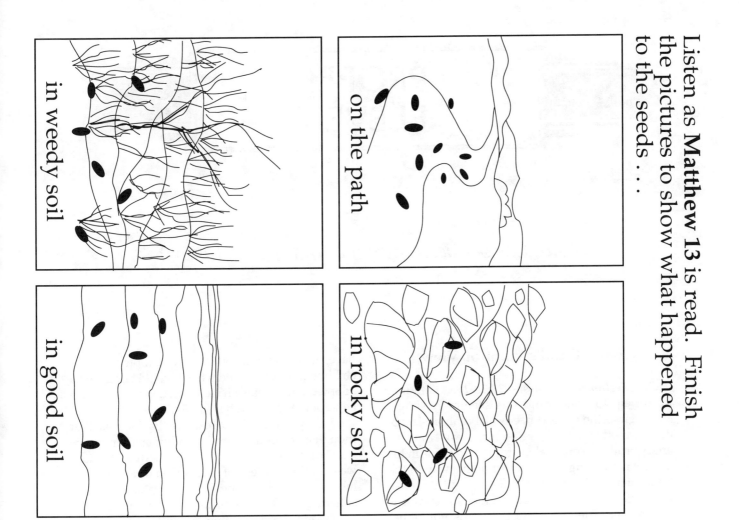

on the path

in weedy soil

in rocky soil

in good soil

Listen to the story about the family in **Genesis 25: 19 - 34.** Then draw a picture of your family. Talk with God about each person you draw. Tell God what you like to do with each one. Tell God about problems you have in your family.

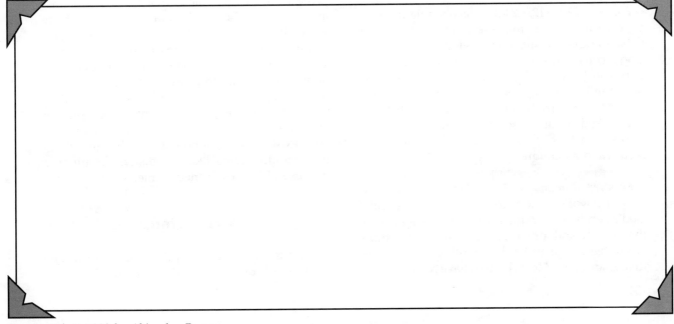

PROPER ELEVEN

(Sunday between July 17 and 23 inclusive)

From a Child's Point of View

Old Testament: Genesis 28:10-19a. Children need help to understand this seemingly simple story. First, the context needs elaboration. Jacob, on his mother's advice, has run away from his angry brother. Totally alone for the first time in his life, he is sleeping in the desert on his way to the home of his unknown uncle. Scared and alone, he meets God in a dream. The ladder to heaven is God's way of telling Jacob that he is not alone. There is always communication between heaven and earth—between God and people. The vision is reinforced by God's words, promising to be with Jacob, to protect him, and even to get him back home. The story invites children to claim for themselves God's promise that no situation is so bad that God will not be with them.

Psalm: 139:1-12, 23-24. Jacob might have prayed this psalm in the desert. It invites children to bask in God's complete knowledge of them and God's constant, caring presence. Some children can expect such care from no one, even in their own family. But children from secure homes also sometimes feel (rightly or wrongly) that they are overlooked, underloved, and unappreciated. So God's constant presence provides important security to all children.

Epistle: Romans 8:12-25. Paul describes the powerful work of the Spirit, which adopts us into God's family, is working toward the re-creation of the world, and prays for us. The most child-accessible image in Paul's complex argument is that of adoption. Most children have read about or

have met children who were adopted. Many children have wondered what it would be like to be adopted and at times have wished that they could be adopted into another family.

So they are ready to explore Paul's idea that though all of us are born into a human family, we may be adopted into God's family. In this adoption, we gain the privilege of calling God our father and mother and of sharing in the hopes, joys, and sufferings of God's family. We look forward to the new world God is creating, we suffer with the rest of the family while we work and wait for the creation of that world (just as Jesus, our older brother, did), and we enjoy the protection and loving care of God's Spirit. Do not expect children to gather any of this from the reading of the text.

Gospel: Matthew 13:24-30, 36-43. The unstated problem in this parable is that the roots, stems, and leaves of the good plants and those of the weeds become so tangled that the weeds cannot be pulled out without damaging the good plants. This problem needs to be explained in detail for nongardening children. Even with this explanation, children will not comprehend the subtle entanglements of good and evil. They simply need to accept Jesus' claim that the good and evil must exist together for now. To children for whom next month seems like the distant future, the promise of harvest remedies means little.

Watch Words

Spirit is God at work in the world and in our lives. Speak of *weeds* rather than *tares*.

Let the Children Sing

Conclude each verse of "We Are Climbing Jacob's Ladder" with the words "children of the Lord," rather than "soldiers of the cross."

"Come, Ye Thankful People, Come" is based on Jesus' parable. Explore it verse by verse in the sermon before the congregation sings it.

For Jacob and the writer of Psalm 139, sing the version of Psalm 23 most familiar to your congregation.

If Communion is celebrated, sing "I Come with Joy to Meet My Lord," to emphasize that this is the table of God's family.

The Liturgical Child

1. Ask that the floral display illustrate Jesus' parable by including both weeds (perhaps thistles or thorny branches) and garden flowers. Refer to the display.

2. Lead a responsive prayer based on God's promise to Jacob. The congregation's response is that promise: *Know that I am with you and will keep you wherever you go.*

> When we are frightened by new places, new jobs, new responsibilities, new people, or new ideas, remind us of your words to Jacob. (RESPONSE)
> When we feel trapped by problems we cannot solve and stuck with people with whom we cannot get along, let us hear what you said to Jacob as he ran from his angry brother. (RESPONSE)
> When we feel as totally alone as Jacob felt when he was alone in the desert, when we feel abandoned by our friends, when we feel lost, help us remember your words. (RESPONSE)
> When we lose hope that anything will ever be any better than it is now, when our own problems seem too big to ever be solved, when hunger and injustice and war seem unavoidable, when it looks as though the evil always wins and the good loses, speak quietly to us. (RESPONSE)
> Speak quietly to us, Lord, and give us the courage to rise up as your children. Make us constantly aware of your loving, powerful presence with us. Teach us to depend upon that power to do surprising things in your name. We pray, remembering Jacob, and in the name of Jesus. Amen.

3. If Communion is part of your worship today, present it as the dinner table of God's family. Mention the dream which promised a banquet at which God's children of all places and times will gather. Invite people to think of that feast as they eat and drink at the Lord's Table today.

4. Invite children (either all the children in the congregation, or a class that has received a prior invitation) to sit with you in the chancel. Explain that Jesus once told a story to a big crowd. Read Matthew 13:24-30. If children are comfortable with such conversation, talk briefly about what they think Jesus' story meant. Then point out that Jesus' friends were puzzled by the story too, and later when they were alone, they asked Jesus to explain it. Read Matthew 13:36-43 and make one of Jesus' points briefly before the children return to their seats.

5. To give worshipers an opportunity to pray Psalm 139 in the first person, as it is written, line it out (read one line at a time, the congregation repeating each line as it is read). The words and phrases of the Good News Bible are easiest for this.

Sermon Resources

1. At the bottom of the ladder from heaven, Jacob, running away from his angry brother, slept in the desert, frightened and lonely. Invite children to draw their own pictures of the ladder from heaven to earth and, at the bottom of that ladder, draw a situation in which they feel as frightened and lonely as Jacob did. Discuss their pictures with them briefly as they leave the sanctuary, and remind them that God will be with them in the situation they drew.

2. Tell the story of a person who was adopted into God's family. Tell how the person was adopted in baptism, what s/he did as part of God's family, how s/he suffered as part of God's family, and who knew and loved that person as a Christian brother or sister. The story of Nelle Morton, who lived as a member of God's family in the South, participating in civil-rights movements and caring for people with mental disabilities, is available on video or film from many church libraries. Her story speaks to people of all ages.

The GOOD WORDS and EVIL WORDS below are as tangled together as the roots of the good plants and weeds in Jesus' story. Can you find all six words? (There are some extra letters you won't use.)

Good:
SHARE
KIND
LOVE

Evil:
GREED
CRUEL
HATE

Draw a picture

OR

Write a prayer for

a time when you need God's "I'm with you" promise.

God said to Jacob, "I am with you and will keep you wherever you go."

Proper 11/ © 1992 by Abingdon Press.

PROPER TWELVE

(Sunday between July 24 and 30 inclusive)

From a Child's Point of View

Old Testament: Genesis 29:15-28. In the story of Jacob's weddings to Leah and Rachel, Jacob meets his match in Laban, who tricks him just as Jacob had tricked his own brother and father. On one level it is a morality story, teaching that trickery leads only to more trickery and unhappiness. To put it another way, when we will do anything to get what we want, we end by being unhappy. It is a negative proof-text for the Golden Rule.

But in the context of the Patriarch's saga, the story also insists that God was working, even through the likes of Jacob. God loved Jacob, rascal that he was. In a sense, Jacob could be the patron saint of kids who are continually in trouble at home and among their friends. If linked with Paul's affirmation, this story claims that not even our own scheming and meanness toward one another can separate us from the love of God.

Psalm: 105:1-11, 45b or 128. Children easily hear the short praises with which Psalm 105 begins. If challenged, they listen for the names of Abraham, Isaac, and Jacob, about whom they have been hearing the last few Sundays. But few will grasp or share the psalmist's praise of God's faithfulness to the covenant.

Psalm 128 is a wedding song for the groom. It matches the song for the bride in Psalm 45 (see Proper 9). Like its counterpart, it is filled with sex-role stereotypes and images that are no longer appropriate.

However, if these problems are pointed out, the text can be read for Jacob's wedding, to celebrate God's care for families.

Epistle: Romans 8:26-39. Beneath Paul's abstract theological jargon (*predestination, justification, election,* etc.) are two basic truths that are very important to children. The first is that God is all powerful and is in complete control. There is no power that can overcome God's power. Occasionally it may look as if certain evil powers are winning, but they will not last. God will win in the end. The second truth is that this powerful God loves us and takes care of us. Even if we suffer (vss. 35-36), God will be with us.

The key verses for children can be paraphrased: "If God is for us, what does it matter who is against us?" (8:31b); and "I am convinced that absolutely nothing in the universe can separate us from God's loving care" (8:38-39). To help children understand Paul's final point, paraphrase verses 39-40, replacing Paul's list of evil powers with a list of powers that frighten us today (nuclear bombs, neighborhood bullies, not having enough money for food and clothes, etc.). These two verses give children a deep sense of self-esteem and security, based on God's love for them.

Gospel: Matthew 13:31-33, 44-52. The term *kingdom of heaven* leads concrete thinkers to assume that Matthew is speaking of life after death. So begin by explaining that Matthew was speaking about being one of God's people now.

The two parables about pearls point out the value of being one of God's people; they challenge listeners to set aside their other pursuits in order to do something better—to be one of God's people. For children learning to make choices, this is a call to make choices that will make God proud. Those choices include deciding whether to join

137

the soccer team that plays on Sunday or to attend church school; deciding whether to tell that mean but very funny joke; and deciding how to treat people who are not good to you.

The parables about the mustard seed and the yeast claim that small things can have big results. For adults this is fairly obvious. But children, who long to do really big important tasks, need to hear repeatedly that saying kind words and doing loving deeds each day make big contributions to building God's kingdom. Similarly, the everyday habits of God's people (worship, going to church school, helping other people, etc.) make a big difference in our lives.

The parable of the net may frighten children who fear being left out or found not good enough. It says that many people are swept along with the work and activity of God's people, but not all of them really belong. Deemphasize the threat by focusing on the happiness of being chosen from the net by God.

Watch Words

Paul leads us to speak of *predestination, election, justification,* and to describe the powers of the world in cosmic terms. Such vocabulary is beyond children's comprehension.

For children, a *parable* is simply a story Jesus told.

Let the Children Sing

"Be Thou My Vision" uses the treasure images of the parables. "All Things Bright and Beautiful" praises the God who values small things.

Praise the God of Paul's faith with "Praise to the Lord, the Almighty," which has phrases and vocabulary simple enough for older children, or "God Will Take Care of You," which has a much repeated phrase and an easy chorus.

The Liturgical Child

1. Ask that the floral display in the chancel include large flowers. See if you can obtain enough seeds of the chosen flower for the worshipers. Enlist the services of one or more first- or second-grade class(es) to tape one seed on each worship bulletin for the day. Refer to the seed and the flowers during the sermon.

2. Have five different readers read the five short parables. Third- and fourth-graders can prepare these readings successfully with adult help. Introduce the readings in this way: Jesus told five parables about the kingdom of heaven. Each one began, "The kingdom of heaven is like . . . ." Listen for God's Word in each of these parables.

3. Pray about the powers we fear might separate us from God's love and care. Children fear many of the same powers that adults fear, such as war and money problems. In addition, children fear the outcome of family fights (What will happen to me if my parents get a divorce?) and failure (What if I get straight Fs or make the mistake that loses the game?). Children are intimidated by the power of specific people or groups who seem to be "out to get them." Many children fear new experiences such as going to camp or to a new school.

Sermon Resources

1. Tell a series of vignettes in a rhetorical pattern. In each vignette, describe someone who refuses to do small things and concludes that "it doesn't really matter." Retell the event, this time including a small loving deed and its consequence, with the person concluding, "It really did matter after all." Include people of different ages in different situations. For example:

Kurt ran out the door. As he swung his camp bag over his shoulder, it hit Kim who was toddling around on the porch. Kim screamed. Kurt frowned. Kim always seemed to be in his way. Then Kurt said to himself, "It really doesn't matter," and he kept running.

On another day, Kurt ran out the door, but he watched for Kim this time. He stopped to give Kim the special handshake he had taught her, and then ran down the sidewalk. Kim yelled after him, "Bye, Kurt." It really did make a difference.

2. See the Worship Worksheet suggestion about drawing ads for the treasure that is God's kingdom. At the beginning of the sermon, urge children to draw an ad to share with you as they leave and/or to post on a bulletin board.

3. Explore tricks and their results. Describe fun tricks, such as April Fools Day jokes. Describe

mean tricks that are planned to make fun of people. Then focus on tricks that are planned to get what we want. Recall the trick that Ursula the Seawitch played on Vanessa in the movie "The Little Mermaid," so she could become queen of the ocean; the trick Jacob played on his father to receive the blessing of the first-born son; the trick Laban played on Jacob, to "marry off" both his daughters.

You have seen ads or posters that tell people why they should join a group. Draw an ad or poster that tells people why they should join God's people.

Hey— look at this!

Looks good to me.

Decode this message. In the space below each letter, write the letter that comes before it in the alphabet.

OPUIJOH DBO TFQBSBUF VT

_ _ _ _ _ _ _   _ _ _   _ _ _ _ _ _ _ _   _ _

GSPN UIF MPWF PG HPE.

_ _ _ _   _ _ _   _ _ _ _   _ _   _ _ _ .

Answer: Nothing can separate us from the love of God.

PROPER THIRTEEN

(Sunday between July 31 and August 6 inclusive)

From a Child's Point of View

Old Testament: Genesis 32:22-31. Although the ambiguities of this text are beyond the understanding of children, most children, especially boys, enjoy the story of God coming to Jacob as a wrestler, to wrestle all night. Wrestling is an activity they know and generally enjoy. A God who will wrestle is a God who will meet them on their own turf and is therefore attractive. A God who will wrestle is also strong, active, and willing to get dirty—another plus. And since this particular match sounds as if it were between friendly rivals, rather than between enemies fighting to the death, God must be willing to wrestle with friends like Jacob, and like us.

For younger children, thinking about God as one who wrestles (like a father or older brother) is attractive and reassuring.

For older children, wrestling with God can begin to be defined as struggling with God about doing right and wrong things. Again, it is reassuring to know that this divine, basically friendly wrestler will "pin" them until they do what is right.

The story also describes conflict as acceptable, even inevitable. Jacob was always struggling with someone, but God still accepted him. Our lives may be as rough and tumble as Jacob's was, and still be acceptable to God.

Psalm: 17:1-7, 15. This psalm, with its legal context and language, is one for adult Bible scholars. Children will find more meaning in the other texts for the day.

Epistle: Romans 9:1-5. With a little adult interpretation, children can understand Paul's grief over the Jews and can admire his willingness to trade his salvation for theirs, but the passage has little significance for children or their lives.

Gospel: Matthew 14:13-21. The story of the feeding of the five thousand is familiar to most church children. From it they learn that Jesus cared about people's needs. He used his powers to heal and to feed the crowd. We can expect God to be as aware of, and as responsive to our needs as Jesus was to the needs of those people. We are also called to follow Jesus' example, using our powers to meet the needs of the people we meet.

With adult direction, children can connect the bread and feeding in this story with that of Holy Communion. For younger children, Communion is primarily a way to show that we remember and love Jesus and want to be one of his followers. They understand that when Jesus wanted to leave us a reminder of himself, a good choice was bread, such as that he broke and shared in his many meals. Remembering this story as an example of Jesus' loving care is good Communion preparation.

Watch Words

The Genesis and Matthew texts, which are the most child accessible, offer no vocabulary traps. The legal language of the psalm is foreign to children, and Paul's message is so filled with unfamiliar words that it is difficult to follow.

Let the Children Sing

"I Sing the Almighty Power of God" is a good praise hymn for either the wrestling God or the feeding Jesus.

For Communion, choose a hymn in which bread references are concrete rather than symbolic. "Let Us Break Bread Together" is a good choice.

The first and second verses of "Fight the Good Fight" speak of fights (wrestling matches) and races reminiscent of Jacob's life.

The Liturgical Child

1. Even if you are not celebrating Holy Communion today, place five loaves of bread on the table to point to the connection between the five loaves with which Jesus fed the crowd and the bread of Communion.

2. Pray for hungry people in different places around the world, and for the hunger-relief efforts of your church. The congregation's response to each prayer: *Give us this day our daily bread.* For example:

> Lord, in Russia, potatoes are rotting in the fields and people will go hungry in the cities. Help our Russian brothers and sisters find ways to get the potatoes harvested so that they can eat this winter. (RESPONSE)

> (OR)

> Father, some of us in our own town do not have food to eat today. Watch over the food we give to the food bank. Help get it to those who need it. And work through us for the day when no one in our town will go hungry. (RESPONSE)

3. If you focus on wrestling with God, refer to another "wrestling" match (Job 38–39) in the Call to Worship:

> When Job challenged God to a debate, God replied from a whirlwind, "Who is this that darkens counsel by words without knowledge? . . . I will ask *you* questions and *you* can answer *me*. . . . Where were you when I laid the foundation of the earth? . . . Have you commanded the morning? . . . Can you send forth lightning? . . . Do you give the horse it's power?" And Job was silent. Let us worship God.

Sermon Resources

1. Gilly is a sixth-grade foster child who has always struggled with her string of teachers and foster parents. She is bright but very difficult to love, though she desperately wants to be loved. Katherine Paterson's award-winning novel *The Great Gilly Hopkins* (Harper & Row, 1978) describes the way Gilly wrestled with the love offered her by an angel in the form of Trotter, an unlikely foster mother. In the critical scene, Gilly is literally pinned under the overweight woman. Excerpts from this book or a recounting of its story provides a modern-day parallel to the Jacob story that both parents and children can understand.

2. Encourage the practice of mealtime blessings. Offer sample blessings for families, and others for individuals on their own in public places. Here are some suggestions for children and their families:

● "Blessed art thou, O Lord, King of the Universe, who brings forth bread from the earth." (This traditional Jewish blessing is great for sandwich lunches.)

● Sing the Doxology together.

● Tell God one thing you really like about the meal you are about to eat, and say, "Thank you."

● At home, take turns around the table, each member thanking God in your own words for one good thing you especially appreciate that day. The last person adds, "And thank you for this food. Amen."

Provide a chart for the week, on which individuals or households can track their success at establishing the habit of mealtime blessings. Print the chart on the back of the bulletin or as a bulletin insert.

3. When preaching about Jesus feeding the crowd, explore the meaning of the phrase "Give us this day our daily bread" in the Lord's Prayer. Children (and many adults) need to be reminded that we pray not just for ourselves, but for everyone and that we should think about what is required of those who pray that the hungry be fed.

Listen carefully to the Scripture reading. Then draw a picture of what happened in that story. If there are 2 readings, choose one to draw.

One way we can thank God is to pray before we eat. Write a prayer to pray before each meal this week.

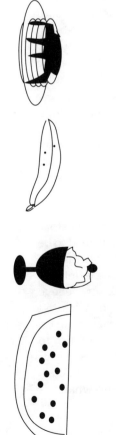

PROPER FOURTEEN

(Sunday between August 7 and 13 inclusive)

From a Child's Point of View

Old Testament: Genesis 37:1-4, 12-28. Children, particularly those whose parents are continually after them to get along better with their brothers and sisters, love this Bible story. It tells of a set of siblings who treated one another worse than most children ever do. Though many children daydream about the possibility of life without a particularly pesky brother or sister, most would not go to the extremes that Joseph's brothers did to realize their dream.

Though the suggested lection omits Joseph's dreams (vss. 5-11), including them explains why Joseph's brothers hated him so much. It was not simply that he had the misfortune to be the favorite of a father who should have known that playing favorites so blatantly leads to trouble. Joseph was a braggy pain in the neck. His brothers had good reason to detest him.

Children also can hear in this story a warning that family bickering can get out of hand. Boasting, as Joseph did; playing favorites, as Jacob did; letting hate build up, as the brothers did, can lead to explosions such as kidnapping and attempted murder.

The only hope is that families can identify their problems and work to solve them before they get out of hand.

Psalm: 105:1-6, 16-22, 45b. This storytelling psalm describes Joseph's life after his brothers sold him. Unfortunately, the psalmist uses pithy phrases to recall whole events and assumes that readers can fill in the details. Few children can, so either tell the whole story or choose another psalm for the day.

Epistle: Romans 10:5-15. This passage is an appeal to Jews to abandon legalism and accept grace. It is addressed to adults who have had enough experience in trying to live by the letter of the Law that they can see the problems. They knew exactly what Paul was talking about. Children, however, are at a stage of moral development when rules are seen as a good way to order our relationships with one another. Many children believe they can and do keep the rules perfectly. It will be several years before they learn from experience what legalism is all about. Furthermore, children live unconsciously by grace, trusting adults to provide their basic necessities. So Paul's appeal is not a meaningful text for childhood.

The ideas in verses 12-15 are more child accessible. Paul insists that we are brothers and sisters of all Christians, no matter how different they look or act. He further points out that we are called to make sure that every person in the world hears about God's grace.

Gospel: Matthew 14:22-33. This is another story that fascinates children. However, they need to be told clearly that the point of the story is *not* that we can walk on water or do other nature-defying deeds, if we only believe in God, or believe strongly enough that we can. Jesus had invited Peter to walk on water. The point is that we can do whatever Jesus commands or invites us to do—even deeds that look dangerous and hard. The key is trust. Jesus insists that we, like Peter, can trust God to give us the power to do whatever God asks.

Watch Words

Trust is more familiar than *faith,* and speaks more precisely of the issue in the Gospel text. Using the two interchangeably builds children's understanding and comfort with *faith.*

Paul's use of *the Law* in referring to the Jewish approach to living for God makes little sense to children.

Let the Children Sing

"God of Grace and God of Glory" is usually sung in reference to the church at work in the world, but it also can be sung by the church at work in our families. Even the youngest children can join in praying the repeated "Grant us wisdom, grant us courage" as they face family problems.

Before singing "Give to the Winds Thy Fears," point out the "storm" words that connect verses 1 and 2 with Peter's story. Then paraphrase the last two verses: (3) If you let God be the leader, you'll fin that God leads you well; (4) Praise God, who is worthy of our trust.

The Liturgical Child

1. Ask a group of elementary boys to pantomime the Genesis story as it is read. You will need ten brothers (one being Reuben), Joseph, Jacob, the man Joseph met at Shechem, and one or more slave traders. If space or available actors is limited, you might reduce the number of brothers to three or four. If possible, provide costumes. During rehearsal, work on ways to show feelings with facial expression and body posture. (This is a good opportunity for informal discussion about how we express anger.)

2. See the suggestion about praying for feuding families in Proper 10.

3. Read the story of Jesus walking on the water with all the drama you would use in telling a good story around a campfire. Read faster and louder as you describe the disciples' fear of the storm and the figure as it walked toward them. Read the disciples' line, "It is a ghost," the way you think they would have said it. Let the tone of your voice communicate Peter's feelings and Jesus' calm.

Sermon Resources

1. Speak to parents and children about solving family problems before they grow too big. Point out the similarities of the problems in Joseph's family and those in many families today. Describe some ways the members of Joseph's family might have worked on their problems. Encourage families to identify and work on their problems before they get out of hand.

2. Devote the sermon to the whole story of Joseph and his brothers, or tell it up to the point when the brothers went to Egypt for food, which is among next Sunday's lections. Take time to relate the details and explore their meanings. Interpret the events as you tell them. Few children or adults recall all the subplots, and therefore enjoy hearing and thinking about the whole amazing saga.

3. Childhood parallels to Peter's mid-walk loss of trust include the panic felt when you suddenly realize that you are riding your bike without training wheels for the first time, or when you realize that you have swum halfway across the pool for the first time. A parallel that is even closer to Jesus' point is realizing in the middle of what you are saying that you are standing-up to the gang and becoming frightened of your power and its consequences.

4. After the movie *Superman* was released, several children were injured when they attempted to fly. They mistakenly thought they would be able to fly if they "believed" strongly that they could. Describe the difference in what these children did and what we do when we trust or have faith in Jesus.

5. Enlarge only the appropriate half of the Worship Worksheet. If both sections are printed on the same page, children will not have enough space to work.

Listen carefully as **Matthew 14: 22-33** is read.

Draw a picture of what happened.

Below are words from the story about Peter trusting God.

stePped
bravE
ChrisT
watEr
daRe

Write your name in a column below (top to bottom). Add a word to each letter to tell how you trust God.

Draw or write about one problem in your family.

Write a prayer about that problem.

Proper 14/ © 1992 by Abingdon Press.

PROPER FIFTEEN

(Sunday between August 14 and 20 inclusive)

From a Child's Point of View

Old Testament: Genesis 45:1-15. Before children can understand this story, they need to hear about the brothers' sale of Joseph and be told that Joseph rose from slavery to leadership in Egypt.

Their focus then is on Joseph's refusal to take revenge on his brothers. If anyone was ever in a perfect position for satisfying, justified revenge, it was Joseph. Younger children are amazed that Joseph could forgive his brothers after what they did to him. And they often conclude that if Joseph could forgive his brothers then they ought to be able to forgive people for lesser crimes. But Joseph did not forgive because he had become a loving, forgiving person. Older children can begin to understand, if it is pointed out to them, that Joseph forgave because he had a vision that was more important to him than getting even with his brothers. He knew that God was using him to keep his family (and everyone in Egypt) alive through a famine. So, like Joseph, children learn that there are more important things than getting even with those who hurt you.

Psalm: 133. The opening verse and theme of this psalm is one children appreciate: "How good it is when we all get along happily together" (paraphrase). The two examples, however, are strange. Although it was a treat for the psalmist, being anointed with oil sounds slimy and yucky to us today. So explain anointing briefly, laugh at it, and note that in a few thousand years, people probably will think some of our treats just as awful. Though few children have seen the beauty of the dew on Mount Hermon (or even pictures of it), they can identify beautiful places they do treasure. Children get most effectively into the spirit of the psalm when they create their own verses to describe people living together happily (e.g., like a family trip to the beach when the weather is perfect and everyone gets along well together).

Epistle: Romans 11:1-2a, 29-32. The question about the Jews is a grown-up's question. Unless they have been raised with blatant anti-Semitism, few children have pondered the question or find Paul's answer particularly meaningful. The underlying message that is important to children is that God cares about everyone and does not write off any person or group.

Gospel: Matthew 15:(10-20) 21-28. The story in verses 21-28 confuses children. Jesus' turning away the pleading mother seems totally out of character. Even when the cultural situation and Jesus' point are explained, children remain distressed by Jesus' words and actions.

The teachings in optional verses 10-20 about what comes out of our mouths are, however, very important to children. Though older children are curious about Jewish eating customs, the main point of the passage for all children is that we need to discipline our tongues. We can do a lot of damage with words. Children recognize name calling, cruel teasing, angry words aimed at hurting others, lies, and bad stories told on others (both tattling and gossiping) as some of the defilers that come out of our mouths.

Watch Words

Forgiveness in Joseph's story means *refusing to get even with those who hurt us.*

Defiles means *gets us into trouble with God* (e.g., what comes out of our mouths can *get us into trouble with God*).

Let the Children Sing

"Forgive Our Sins as We Forgive" is one of the few hymns that focus on our forgiving one another rather than on God forgiving us. After some help with the words, older children can sing along. Consider omitting verse 3, which breaks the focus by speaking of God forgiving.

"Let There Be Peace on Earth" recalls Psalm 113 and Joseph's willingness to forgive. It also may be used to commit our mouths to peacemaking.

"Go Forth for God," with its identical opening and closing lines, is a hymn with which the congregation can send its children to live as God's people at school. Though younger children cannot keep up with all the vocabulary within the verses, they can sing the opening and closing lines and do appreciate that the congregation is singing for them.

The Liturgical Child

1. To create a litany prayer of confession, the leader offers a series of confessions related to our individual and corporate failures to forgive one another. The congregation's response: *Forgive us our debts (trespasses) as we forgive our debtors (those who trespass against us).*

2. Emphasize that we should take care about what comes out of our mouths; both in our homes and with other people.

Prayer of Confession:
God, you created us with mouths to speak. You made us able to say kind words, to talk about important ideas, to laugh together at shared jokes, and to tell stories of your love. We confess that we often misuse your gift. We are more quick to use angry, hurting words than kind ones. We are easily drawn to mean gossip, rumors, and even lies, and we easily forget to tell about the good that others do. We too often hear ourselves laugh *at* people instead of *with* them. We are truly surprised, embarrassed, and ashamed of some of the things that come out of our mouths. Forgive us. Work within us until our words are the words you would speak, for we pray in Jesus' name. Amen.

Assurance of Pardon: When Jonah ran away rather than speak God's good words in Nineveh, God caught him with a fish and brought him back to speak the words. When Jesus called James and John to be his disciples, they were known as "sons of thunder" because of their mouthy tempers. When Saul set out, muttering threats against the Christians at Damascus, Jesus stopped him in his tracks and sent him to preach God's good news. The God who created their mouths was able to reform them. And God can do the same with our rebellious mouths. Thanks be to God! Amen.

3. The beginning of a new school year is an intense and important time for children and youths. There is excitement about new clothes and school supplies, new experiences such as having a locker or riding a bus, and new teachers and friends. At the same time, there is fear of each of these new things and a fear of higher standards. Children for whom last year was difficult dread even harder work and the probability of more failures this year. Pray about both the excitement and the fears on the Sunday before school starts. Then the Sunday after classes began, invite children, parents, and adult friends to pray about the new year. Thank God for teachers, but remember that all students are not thankful for all their teachers. Pray about getting along with other students. And ask for help where it will be needed.

Sermon Resources

1. Devote the sermon to retelling the story of Joseph's confrontation with his brothers (Gen. 42–45). Take time to interpret and enjoy the detailed plot.

2. Being able to forgive requires being able to

see what has happened from a position other than our own. This is not easy for children whose early thinking is egocentric. To help them develop this ability, offer a series of examples: Forgiving a little brother who cut up your favorite book (he did not know any better); forgiving an older sister who yelled at you (she had a bad day at school); not throwing a tantrum when everyone else at the picnic got seconds (the fun of the picnic is more important than having seconds); Joseph feeding his brothers rather than getting even with them (God keeping the promises about Joseph's family was more important than what the brothers had done).

3. Conclude a sermon about forgiveness by having worshipers find "Forgive Our Sins as We Forgive" in their hymnbooks. Put the verses into your own words. Then invite the congregation to sing it.

Psalm 133 begins . . .

How good it is when people live happily together!

Draw a picture of or write about a time when your family or friends were happy together.

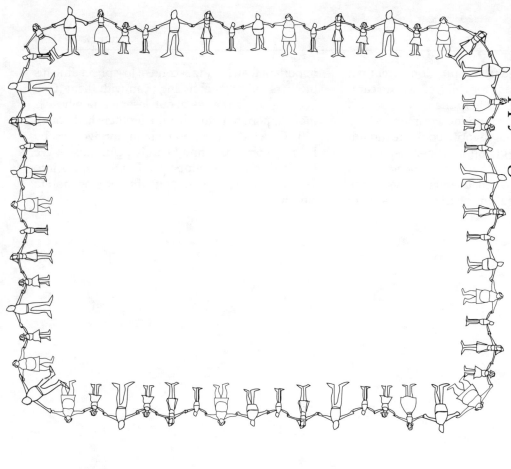

Listen carefully as **Genesis 45: 1-15** is read. Fill in the missing words in this story.

When his brothers came back to ___ ___ ___ to get more _{1.} ___ ___ ___, they brought _{4.} ___ ___ ___ ___ ___ ___ ___ with them. Then _{7.} ___ ___ ___ ___ ___ told them who he was. He told _{2.} ___ them how he became leader next to ___ ___ ___ ___ ___. He said _{3.} that what they had done was ___ ___ ___ ___, but that God had used _{6.} it for good. He asked them to bring his Father I ___ ___ ___ ___ ___ to live in Egypt. _{5.}

Write the letters from the numbered spaces above in the correct spaces below to spell the most important word in this story.

1. ___   2. ___   3. ___   4. ___   5. ___   6. ___   7. ___

Proper 15/ © 1992 by Abingdon Press.

PROPER SIXTEEN

(Sunday between August 21 and 27 inclusive)

From a Child's Point of View

Old Testament: Exodus 1:8–2:10. If you have been preaching on the Joseph saga, point out to the children that these Hebrews are the great, great . . . great grandchildren of Joseph and his brothers. Then simply read the text. Children need little help with it, especially if it is read from The Good News Bible.

Most church children are familiar with the story of the baby in the basket and enjoy hearing it read in the sanctuary. They particularly relish the heroic role of Miriam, the child who was left standing by the river all day to watch the basket. She stuck with her boring task, was on duty and alert at the critical moment, did some quick thinking, and made a courageous move in speaking to the princess. God used her good work to save Moses. So little kids do count. God chooses children, as well as adults, to do important work.

Psalm: 124. This psalm of deliverance assumes that the reader knows the outcome of the Exodus story. Even children who know it do not recognize it here. Therefore, as you invite them to hear or read the psalm, tell them that it was written after God had rescued the Hebrews from the pharaoh.

Though the psalmist probably was thinking metaphorically about the floods of life, children make more sense of the psalm if the floods are presented as the waters that flooded the slave babies killed by the pharaoh. The psalm then praises God, who saves people in such situations.

Epistle: Romans 12:1-8. For children, the sacrifices of the Old Testament were gifts people brought to God. Paul urges us not to buy gifts for God, but to make our whole lives gifts to God (12:1), and he tells us how to do so. First, we are to follow Jesus' teachings, rather than what others want us to do (12:2). We are not to follow the gang, or pay too much attention to TV commercials, or even listen to adults who tell us to do things we know are wrong.

Second, we are to remember who we are. We are important people, created with specific gifts. We are not to be stuck-up about our gifts, but learn to use them well to do our part of Christ's work. This text and the Romans text for next week make good back-to-school sermons. The Good News Bible offers the most child-accessible version.

Gospel: Matthew 16:13-20. Teenagers and adults are impressed by Peter's willingness to take an individual stand, independent of "what others say." Children, however, are at a stage of mental growth and faith development which requires them to choose between groups, rather than stand as individuals against groups. So for them, this is a story about how Peter chose Jesus as his leader, rather than choosing some other group or person. When Peter called Jesus the Messiah, he was making him the master of his life. Children are called to make the same decision Peter made. The church is made up of people who have made that same decision.

Watch Words

A *midwife* is a woman who helps a mother give birth to her baby at home. Before there were hospitals, most babies were born at home with the help of a *midwife*.

In recent lections, *faith* has been a matter of *trust*. That is the most significant definition for children. In today's Gospel text, Peter's *faith* is expressed in terms of what he thought or understood about who Jesus was. This is a very different definition, so be careful about how you use both *faith* and *belief* today.

Let the Children Sing

"I Sing a Song of the Saints of God" is a fitting tribute to the Exodus women and the heroes and heroines.

Every verse of "Ask Ye What Great Thing I Know" is a series of questions, to which the last line (the same in all verses) is the answer. Watching for this format can help children pay attention and keep singing.

Give your lives to God with "Take My Life, and Let It Be Consecrated."

The Liturgical Child

1. The Good News Bible formats Psalm 124 as a conversation between a leader and the congregation. Preserve that pattern with a worship leader and the whole congregation reading. Or ask a children's or youth class to present it as a choral reading. The pattern is:

Leader: verse 1
Congregation: verses 2-5
Leader: verses 6-8

2. Feature the part of one of the historic creeds that speaks about Jesus. In the sermon, discuss the meaning of the statements in that section. Suggest that during this discussion the worshipers, especially children, turn to that creed in the hymnal or prayer book. Following the sermon, invite the congregation to say that creed as an affirmation of their faith.

3. Before the offering (perhaps during the sermon), invite worshipers to draw or write on one side of a slip of paper a gift that God has created in them; on the other side, of the paper, draw or write one way they promise to give that gift back to God during the coming week. Suggest that they place the papers in the offering plate as a symbol of their intent. Promise confidentiality and instruct ushers to respect it.

4. See Proper 15 for prayer suggestions for the weeks before and after the beginning of school.

Sermon Resources

1. Miriam was a courageous, fast-thinking baby-sitter. Many older children are beginning to baby-sit for their own siblings and for neighborhood children. One of the most popular current book series for this age group is The Baby-Sitters Club, which recounts the adventures of four seventh-grade girls who band together to provide baby-sitting services. In Ann M. Martin's *The Truth About Stacy* (Scholastic, 1986), they compete with a club of older baby-sitters who do not take their jobs seriously. Things come to a head when the younger girls find three-year-old Jamie, without cap, boots, or mittens, playing unattended by the curb on a slushy day. The girls take Jamie back inside, tell his parents what happened, and confront the older girls with a baby-sitter test which proves their superiority as baby-sitters next morning at school (pp. 126-34).

2. The Exodus text tells of three courageous females. Be creative in unpacking their stories. Imagine several conversations Between Shiphrah and Puah as they respond to the pharaoh's orders. Consider having two costumed women act out the responses, "freezing" between conversations for your comments.

Or create a diary entry for Miriam, for the evening after she saved Moses.

Listen carefully when **Exodus 1: 8 – 2: 10** is read. Then write a page in Miriam's diary. Tell how she felt about what she did at the river.

MY DIARY

Date _____

IN EACH BLOCK

Write an "I believe" statement about Jesus.

OR

Draw a picture of something important that Jesus did.

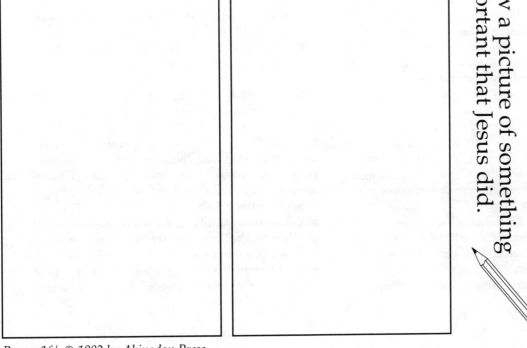

PROPER SEVENTEEN

(Sunday between August 28 and September 3 inclusive)

From a Child's Point of View

Old Testament: Exodus 3:1-15. Like Moses, most children are fascinated by the bush that burns but does not burn up. Unfortunately, their curiosity about how it happened and what it looked like often keeps them from hearing what God said to Moses.

When they do listen to the conversation, children learn two truths. The first is that when God sees something that needs to be done, God sends specific people to do it. In this case, God was aware of the suffering of the Hebrew slaves and sent Moses to rescue them. Similarly, when God sees people hurting today, God calls on people—people like us—to save them.

The second truth is that even great people like Moses are frightened by trying to do God's work. Moses' question "Why me?" is very like our response to setting aside our snack money to feed hungry people, or trying to befriend the kid everyone else ignores or teases. To explore this second point more fully, expand the reading to include the rest of Moses' attempts to avoid the job (Exod. 4:1-17).

Children, who tend to be interested in meaningful names such as those of Indians, are interested in God's name, "I am who I am" or "I am who I will be." In other words, God is bigger and "more" than we can ever describe.

Psalm: 105:1-6, 23-26, 45c. Verses 1-6 of the psalm call on worshipers to praise God, who is at work in the world. Verses 23-26 offer as an example the Hebrew experience in Egypt. The Good News Bible offers the clearest translation for children.

Epistle: Romans 12:9-21. At the beginning of a school and club year, children are keenly aware of and interested in rules. For them, this passage might be titled "Paul's Rules for Getting Along with People." Though the passage is somewhat of a hodgepodge, it can be restated:
- Treat every person as a friend.
- Always do what is right.
- Help people when they need your help.
- Pay attention to people's feelings. Laugh with those who are happy and comfort those who are sad.
- Do not act stuck-up or think you are smarter than you are.
- Ask God to be good to people who give you trouble.
- Do not try to get even with people who are mean to you. Instead, treat then kindly. (Your kindness will make them ashamed of what they did.)
- Do not give in to evil ideas or plans. Instead, find even better good ideas and plans.

Gospel: Matthew 16:21-28. This is a difficult passage for children to understand as it is read. Peter being called Satan by Jesus, talk of stumbling blocks and saving or losing lives, and references to the Son of Man—all these overwhelm children. However, when it is pointed out, children recognize the human inclination (shared by Peter) to avoid suffering and protect ourselves. They are as disturbed as adults are by Jesus' insistence that our lives will be best when we fight this inclination and sacrifice what we want and need in order to help someone else. Children need to hear examples from family and school life, in which children give up their TV show so that another family member can watch a favorite; do the most hated job in the household (maybe clean the cat's litter) for another family member; protect a little kid cornered by bigger kids, and so forth.

Text Connections: Though the word *cross* is not used in Exodus, the story about Moses can be an example of what it means to "take up your cross." The directives in Romans, however, cannot be used for this purpose. "Taking up your cross" involves much more than getting along with others. It requires putting yourself on the line, or suffering on behalf of others.

Watch Words

Cross is a Christian code word. It stands for a rich variety of related things. In today's texts it stands for suffering in order to take care of or to save others. Introduce *cross* as a code word, and be careful that all your references to it clearly fit this definition.

Let the Children Sing

The repetitive phrases and simple format of "Here I Am, Lord" catch the attention of children and invite them to answer God's call. "Take My Life, and Let It Be Consecrated" and "Lord, I Want to Be a Christian" are also discipleship hymns children can sing.

"I Sing the Almighty Power of God" is a good praise hymn for a holiday weekend when most people are outdoors.

The Liturgical Child

1. In preparing your reading of the Exodus passage, practice saying each of Moses' lines aloud so that they communicate his fear and make his attempts to wiggle out of God's call obvious.

2. Invite a children's class to lead the following version of the psalm, with each child reading one line. In a smaller congregation, ask younger children to read the short phrases, with older children reading the paragraphs at the end. The congregation's response to each: *Alleluia!*

Give thanks to God and call on God's name! *Alleluia!*
Tell everyone what God has done! *Alleluia!*
Sing to God! Praise God with music! *Alleluia!*
Tell of God's wonderful works! *Alleluia!*
Be glad that we belong to God! *Alleluia!*
Let all who worship God rejoice! *Alleluia!*
Go to the Lord for help! *Alleluia!*
Worship God continually! *Alleluia!*

Listen, you descendants of Abraham and Jacob. Remember the marvelous things God has done and the decisions God has made! *Alleluia!*

When the Hebrews moved to Egypt and settled there, God made them to increase in numbers. God made them stronger than the Egyptians, and the Egyptians hated them and treated them badly. Then God sent Moses and Aaron to rescue them with God's power. *Alleluia!*

3. Create a responsive affirmation with short descriptions of suffering and oppression, including global, local, and family problems. The congregation's response to each need: "God sees their suffering and says to us, 'Come, I will send you.' "

4. See Proper 15 for prayer suggestions for the Sundays before and after the opening of school.

Sermon Resources

1. Note that sometimes God sends a whole family to do a job. Describe the relationship among Miriam, Moses, and Aaron, and tell about their work. Cite examples of families in your congregation who do God's work together (e.g., walking on the CROP walk or packing clothes for a mission).

2. *The Integration of Mary-Larkin Thornhill* by Ann Waldron (E. P. Dutton, 1975), tells about a junior-high girl, the only white student at a black school in the 1970s. She and her family work through crisis after crisis as they make a stand for racial justice. This fictitious story, or similar stories of your own creation, help children to imagine themselves answering God's call as Moses did.

3. Develop a back-to-school sermon around Paul's advice in Romans. Open by explaining that though this sermon will speak mostly about living as a Christian at school, what is true for children at school is true also for architects, carpenters, businesswomen, and homemakers.

Make a series of posters based on Paul's advice:

Make your life a gift to God; Use your gifts well; Avoid evil and stick with good; Love one another; Respect all people; Work hard and do not be lazy; Serve God; Be joyful and hopeful; Be patient when you suffer; Pray!; Share with those in need. Give one poster to each of eleven children, to hold up in front of the congregation. Read them one at the time, noting that each gives good advice. Then select three or four for the sermon, take them with you into the pulpit, and prop each one up as you speak about it.

Draw the code symbol every time you hear the word, or say it, or sing it in worship.

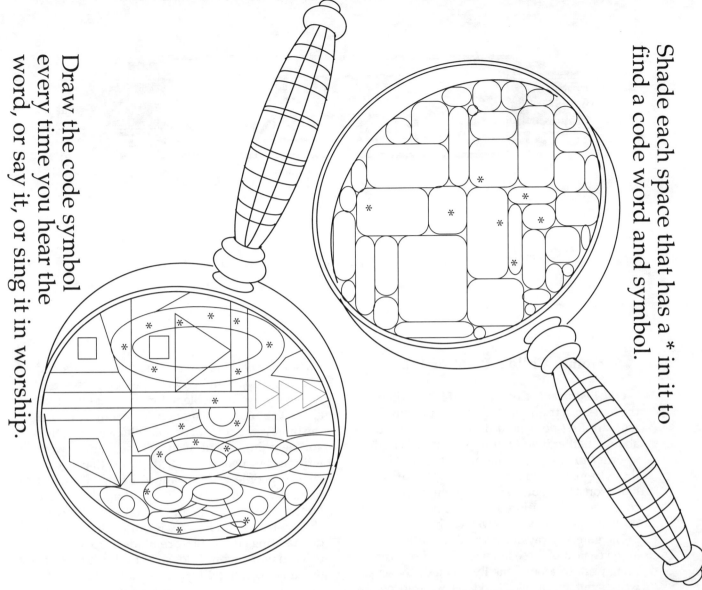

Find 2 orders for us as disciples by crossing out the extra letter in each word below.

1. STAKE   CUP   YEOUR   CHROSS   SAND

1. _ _ _ _ _   _ _   _ _ _ _   _ _ _ _ _   _ _ _

FOLOLOW   MEN

_ _ _ _ _ _ _   _ _.

2. IT   SWILL   SENDS   YOUR.

2. _ _   _ _ _ _   _ _ _ _   _ _ _.

Answers: 1. *Take up your cross and follow me.* 2. *I will send you.*

PROPER EIGHTEEN

(Sunday between September 4 and 10 inclusive)

From a Child's Point of View

Old Testament: Exodus 12:1-14. The killing of the first-born frightens children, especially those who are first-born, and it also raises questions about whether it was fair for God to kill children in order to straighten out an evil king. Though they appreciate the protection offered by the blood on the doorpost, many children remain concerned for the Egyptian first-born. There is no truly satisfactory answer to their concerns.

There are two ways to present this story to children in the context of these lections. First, if services are being planned around the Exodus texts for several weeks, put the focus of today's worship on the contest between the pharaoh and God. Read or tell of some of the plagues and how they made conditions worse for the slaves. The point is that no one, not even a powerful king, can outwit or find a way around God. The Passover is God's final word to the pharaoh and others like him.

But there is a second way to present the story. The central theme of the Passover, "God saves us," is repeated in the crossing of the sea, the text for next week. Since that story is easier for children, use it rather than the Passover to explore the "God saves us" theme.

A word about the lamb: Children whose meat comes from the grocery can be repelled by the directions for killing and cooking lambs. Remind them that every day, all people killed animals to eat. Moses' killing and cooking instructions did not seem weird to the slaves. What was different were the instructions about smearing blood on the doorposts, eating only unleavened bread, and eating while standing up and dressed for travel.

Psalm: 149. Verses 1-5 are easy to understand and share. The military images of verses 6-9, however, are a problem for worshipers of all ages. The only explanation for children is that the Bible is the story of people who were meeting and learning about God. These verses were written by people who thought that God's chosen people were meant to be the strongest military power in the world, but they were wrong. Jesus explained that God's people were chosen to love and serve. Reading such misunderstandings in the Bible reminds us to be ready to learn more about God, so as to clear up any of our misunderstandings.

Epistle: Romans 13:8-14. This passage falls into two separate sections. The first speaks more clearly to children. Verses 8-10 point out that Jesus' teachings about love fit well with the old rules—rules like the Ten Commandments. This point challenges older children, who are basing their moral decisions on what keeps or breaks the rules, to rise to the next level of moral reasoning. That higher level requires the evaluation of all rules by the principle, or spirit, behind them. Paul says that the Old Testament rules are good rules—not because they are in the Bible, but because they are based on love. He points out that if we always do the loving thing, we will find that we are following God's rules. A move from following rules to living by love is a big step.

The second section (vss. 11-14) expresses a sense of urgency, based upon a belief that time is short. Since time seems limitless to children, Paul's sense of urgency about the undated return of Christ is hard for them to accept.

158

Gospel: Matthew 18:15-20. Alert children will be the first to point out that this is one Bible teaching the church does not follow. The fact that procedures do exist for such disciplines evades the reality that they are followed only in extremely serious cases. To understand this passage, one must be able to explore textual problems that are beyond children. What children *can* understand is the truth that underlies this teaching: We are to work hard at resolving conflicts among ourselves. We are not to hide them, but admit them and work to solve them.

Watch Words

Do not assume that children are familiar with *Passover* terms. Define *Passover, first-born,* and *unleavened bread.*

Love is a key word in exploring both the Matthew and the Romans text. Remember that to many children, *love* is a mushy word or a term for sexual passion. Be sure to use strong terms in defining *love* as being about taking care of others. Use masculine as well as feminine examples.

Reconciliation is the adult word for settling a fight between friends. If you use it, take time to introduce it and make it the word of the day.

Let the Children Sing

"Let My People Go" ("Go Down, Moses"), probably the best known spiritual related to the Exodus, might be sung on several Sundays during an Exodus series. *The United Methodist Hymnal* offers eleven verses!

The triumphant music of "God of the Ages, Whose Almighty Hand" carries its message, even though its words are difficult for children.

If you link Communion with the Passover, sing "God of Our Life," which links past, present, and future.

Though "Let There Be Peace on Earth" is usually sung in reference to global peace, it can be sung as commitment to peace among individuals within the church and around the world.

The Liturgical Child

1. Divide the congregation into two groups, or have the congregation and choir read respon-sively the short praises of Psalm 149:1-5. Each verse includes two phrases. Verse 1 includes three, the first of which can be said by the whole congregation (or by choir and congregation). Encourage groups to read each phrase as if it were a crowd cheer for God.

2. To emphasize the connection between Passover and the Lord's Supper, use unleavened bread, matzoh, available in most large supermarkets. Point out that this is the bread Jesus used as he and his disciples celebrated Passover, at the time he instituted Communion.

3. *Prayer of Confession:* Lord, you have chosen us to be your family. We confess that we are a family that too often fusses and fights. No matter how hard we try, we seem to get into trouble with one another. Then we make matters worse by holding our angry feelings inside until we explode, by holding grudges, by trying to get people to side with us against those who have hurt us. Forgive us. Teach us how to solve our problems, instead of getting even. Be with us when we try to talk it out. Help us speak honestly but kindly. Remind us to listen, as well as to tell our side. Work with us to keep your family together. For we pray in the name of Jesus. Amen.

4. See Proper 15 for prayer suggestions for the Sundays before and after the beginning of school.

Sermon Resources

1. In a sermon about God's contest with the pharaoh, take time to describe each of the plagues. Enjoy some of the early ones: Name the places frogs were found (in your drawers, under your pillow); describe the discomfort of gnat bites on your elbows, behind your knees, in your ears. Comment on the growing seriousness of the plagues and the mounting worry about the consequences of the pharaoh's game with God. Help the children and the whole congregation relish the old family story of the way God beat the evil king and freed God's people.

2. To explore the relationship between rules and love, work through several situations in

which the rules of a game are changed. Describe a softball game in which the teams decide to allow the younger players four strikes, so they will have a better chance of getting a hit. Compare that rule change to the one demanded by a player who insists, in the last inning of a tied game, that s/he should be allowed four strikes instead of three.

Find 8 Passover words hidden in the lamb.

A B R E S C U E F
U N L E A V E N E D
R M O K J V E L D
D O O R P M P E J A T S
S S O R F P X L A S L R
K S D J Q S T A E O N
Q E S I R M B D M
R T F K Z

Draw a picture of people who need to make peace with one another.

Write a prayer for the people you drew.

H _____

E _____

L _____

P _____

PROPER NINETEEN

(Sunday between September 11 and 17 inclusive)

From a Child's Point of View

Old Testament: Exodus 14:19-31. The point of this story, like that of the Passover, is that the slaves were hopelessly trapped—in this case, between the Egyptian army and the sea. Only God could save them. And God did. God is the only hero and the only power worth trusting. (In planning an Exodus series, read the material on Joshua 3:7-17 in Proper 26 and plot the coordination of these texts in advance.)

Psalm: 114 or Exodus 15:1b-11, 20-21. The Exodus text includes Moses' and Miriam's songs of praise, in response to what God did by the sea. Both Moses' song and the psalmist's praises are long and filled with complex poetic images. Miriam's song is concise, and children quickly visualize the dancing and singing by the sea. So for their sake, read Miriam's song.

Epistle: Romans 14:1-12. This is a good passage for the first month of school. As the newness wears off, children begin to label others and be labeled—as brains, leaders, beauties, dumbies, troublemakers, nerds, and so forth. Comparisons of academic ability (who gets what grades and who is placed in the advanced and slow groups), athletic prowess, and popularity become the focus of attention. There is often friction on the playground, in the lunchroom, and on the bus during this period of settling into peer-assigned roles and groups.

Though Paul is speaking to adults who are judging one another's values and ideas, his message applies to the judging that children do at school. First, he sternly warns everyone neither to look down on, nor be intimidated by, any other children, because of what they wear, where they live, what they bring for lunch, or what kind of school work they do. They and all their classmates are God's children. Each of them will be judged by God. So children are to accept one another and treat one another well.

Second, Paul tells the children who must endure being labeled that the only judge to worry about is God. Though other kids (and even adults) may hurt us when they pin on us labels we do not want, their opinions do not count. God's is the only opinion that counts. Therefore we are to do our best to meet God's standards and not be upset by what others say about us.

Gospel: Matthew 18:21-35. Forgiving is not easy, no matter what our age. Verses 21-22 set the high standard. Jesus' point is that no one can keep count of that many forgiven offenses, so we must always forgive.

The parable that follows offers the reason for repeated forgiving: We must forgive because God forgives us. Children endorse this more as a fair system than as a natural personal response to God's forgiveness. They would prefer to accept God's forgiveness with no strings attached. But it seems fair that God asks us to forgive others as we have been forgiven.

Watch Words

Judged is not a word children use every day. So provide lots of common examples of ways we *judge* others. Also differentiate between having *good judgment* and the *judging* that Paul is condemning.

Help children understand *forgiveness* by exploring its financial meaning. In the parable, when the king *forgave* the servant's debt, it did not mean that the king gave the servant more time to pay the debt; rather, the servant did not need to pay the debt at all. Both he and the king could forget about it. This financial meaning clarifies the theological meaning.

Let the Children Sing

The first verse of "Come, Ye Faithful, Raise the Strain" retells the story of crossing the sea. Ask some children's classes or choir to sing it, accompanying themselves with homemade tambourines (and possibly other rhythm instruments). The congregation or adult choir can respond by singing the second verse, which compares this event to the resurrection. Children will miss the connection in the second verse, but all will share in happy praise, similar to that of Miriam and the tambourine-playing women beside the sea. (If your hymnal includes more verses, omit them to keep the comparison simple.)

Before singing "Forgive Our Sins as We Forgive," point out that verse 3 is based on today's parable. Though they will miss some of the difficult imagery in the hymn, children will enjoy the parable connection.

If the Romans text leads you to sing "Help Us Accept Each Other," remember that *acceptance* is an abstract word. Children will have difficulty understanding the meaning of the verses unless you have used *acceptance* frequently today and have offered numerous examples.

The Liturgical Child

1. The Gospel reading lends itself to being pantomimed by children as it is read. Actors needed include Jesus, Peter, the king, several servants, the unforgiving servant, the friend s/he refused to forgive, and possibly a jailer. The Scripture may be read by an older child or by an adult. In either case, it is essential that the reader and actors practice together in the sanctuary.

2. Before reading the Gospel text, place on the lectern a large sack, tied at the top, and one cardboard coin. Explain that in today's story, two people owe money. One owes about as much money as the sack might hold. The other owes about one big coin. As you read, point to the sack and the coin at the appropriate times.

3. Create a responsive prayer of confession in which a worship leader describes a series of sins. To each confession, the congregation responds: *"Forgive our debts (trespasses), as we forgive our debtors (those who trespass against us)."*

4. Prayer of Confession

God, you are our Father and Mother. All people are our brothers and sisters. But we forget that. We are quick to look down on people who dress differently than we do. We laugh at those who speak with different accents. We treat people with subtle differences according to the color of their skin. And, we often decide that those who disagree with us are stupid. Forgive us when we judge others. Remind us that you, and not we, are to judge. Teach us to look more closely until we can see in each person we meet a brother or sister, who is loved by God. Amen.

Assurance of Pardon: God does not judge as we do. God knows our thoughts, even the ones we do not speak. And, still God loves us, forgives us, and calls us "my children." Thanks be to God.

Sermon Resources

1. In *The Hundred Dresses* (Harcourt Brace, 1944), Eleanor Estes tells about some girls, led by Peggy and Maddie, who tease Wanda Petronski about her clothes, her accent, and her claim to have one hundred dresses at home—although she wears the same one to school every day. After Wanda moves, the girls discover how they had misjudged her. (This 80-page book, available in libraries, can be quickly read in sermon preparation.)

2. Many children read and enjoy Judy Blume's books, several of which describe the life of Peter Hatcher and his younger brother, nicknamed Fudge, who needed more forgiving than almost

163

anyone could come up with. In *Tales of a Fourth-grade Nothing* (Dutton, 1972), Fudge ruined a school project done by a fourth-grade committee and left in Peter's bedroom, then swallowed the only pet Peter was allowed, his turtle Dribble. To make matters even worse, everyone was worried about Fudge and not at all concerned about Peter's turtle. This book is filled with humorous, realistic examples of what it means for children to keep forgiving.

Write a psalm like the one Miriam sang by the sea. Finish each verse with one reason to praise God.

Sing to the Lord because _____

Sing to the Lord because _____

Sing to the Lord because _____

Pay attention to the hymns we sing today. Write the title of each hymn.

_____

_____

_____

_____

Draw a * by your favorite hymn.

Draw a picture to illustrate one verse of one hymn.

PROPER TWENTY

(Sunday between September 18 and 24 inclusive)

All today's texts are based on God's generous and loving care of us. Exodus tells of God feeding the wilderness travelers with manna and quail. Psalm 105 praises God for that and other care shown during the Exodus. Jesus' parable of the workers in the vineyard claims that God is loving, rather than fair. And Paul's letter to the Philippians insists that a loving God is working out a good plan through us. Our response to such generous love is trust and joy.

From a Child's Point of View

Gospel: Matthew 20:1-16. Younger children need help to grasp the details and significance of the workers' wages. Once they understand what happened, all children empathize immediately with the cry of the all-day workers, "It's not fair!" Children, perhaps more than adults, want life to be scrupulously fair. They want everyone to get exactly what they deserve—no more, no less. And they want everyone to be treated the same. If an older brother went to bed at eight when he was in second grade, he will insist that his younger brother do the same. Desserts must be served in equal portions, and cookies—especially the home-made ones—must be inspected carefully when shared by two or more. To fairness fanatics, Jesus says that God is not always fair. God, first of all, is loving and generous, to us and to others.

Old Testament: Exodus 16:2-15. The story of the manna and quail speaks powerfully to adults about trusting God, because adults generally consider themselves responsible for providing their own food. Children, however, depend on others for their food, so for them, the story is less challenging. It is simply another reminder that God takes care of us and that we are to trust God. In many ways, it is an example of the generous love that Jesus pointed out in his parable. Children's interest is caught mainly by the details about the sudden appearance of the manna and the quail.

Psalm: 105:1-6, 37-45. This psalm is a good review of the Exodus events. If you have been worshiping around these events, children will recognize most of the references in these verses.

Epistle: Philippians 1:21-30. This passage is based on adult experiences and concerns. Children can understand Paul's thoughts about the relative merits of living and dying, when they are explained to them, but the debate is not one most children experience or find meaningful. Similarly, Paul's reasoning in verses 27-30—that the firm stand of Philippians during persecution is a sign that Christ will prevail in the cosmic struggle—does not have much power for children. So read this text for the adults.

Watch Words

Manna may be a new term to your children. They will be interested in its qualities and in the way it suddenly appeared.

Before reading the Gospel, explain what a *denarius* is.

For children who have never seen one, a

166

vineyard is a garden where grapes are grown.

Do not let today's "trusting" texts lead you to speak of the *providence of God,* unless you make it the word of the day, define it, and use it repeatedly. To define it, point out the word *provide* in it and list examples of what God provides. Because many children who do recognize *providence* are likely to identify it as the capital of Rhode Island, point out that the city's name reflects the belief of its founders that it was a sign of God's *providence.*

Let the Children Sing

This is a good Sunday for praise hymns. Sing "For the Beauty of the Earth" or "Now Thank We All Our God" to praise God who provides generously. The repeated phrase and easy chorus make "God Will Take Care of You" a good choice for children.

"Guide Me, O Thou Great Jehovah" is filled with Exodus references. Point out some of them before the congregation sings the hymn and urge singers to watch for others. Invite the congregation to sing as if they were Hebrews in the wilderness.

Avoid "Glorious Things of Thee Are Spoken," which uses Exodus images in an abstract way that children cannot understand.

"Come, Christians, Join to Sing" reflects Paul's joy. Even nonreaders can join in on the Alleluias.

The Liturgical Child

1. Ask a children's group to fill a basket or platter with different kinds of bread to display on the Communion table during worship, as a reminder of all the bread God provides for us. Suggest that they include such things as hot-dog buns, a loaf of French bread, some pita bread, tortillas, corn bread, even bagels. In your prayers of thanksgiving include thanks for bread, in all its tasty shapes and forms.

2. If Holy Communion is celebrated, be sure to point to the similarity between manna and Communion bread. God gave the travelers in the wilderness manna to eat when they were afraid they would die of hunger. Communion bread reminds us that God sent Jesus to give us life.

Though this connection is too abstract for children to grasp fully, even the youngest can recognize that both kinds of breads are associated with God's life-giving care for us.

3. This parable of workers in the vineyard is another that lends itself to pantomime by children. Provide simple costumes and one large (2" wide) cardboard coin for each worker. In preparing the actors, focus on showing their feelings with both facial and bodily expressions. The actors and the reader, who may be an older child or adult, need to rehearse together in the sanctuary, to know where to stand and to get their timing smooth.

4. Invite a children's class to write a litany that describes God's loving care for us. The simplest format is a series of descriptions, each followed by a congregational response, such as "God loves us!" Have the group work several weeks ahead so that their work can be printed in the bulletin for congregational use. The children may lead the litany or participate in it as members of the congregation.

Sermon Resources

1. *Jacob Have I Loved,* by Katherine Paterson (Harper & Row, 1980), tells about twin sisters growing up on an island off the Carolina coast. It is written from the point of view of Louise, who feels that it is unfair that Caroline should be beautiful, have a fine singing voice, and be loved by everyone, while Louise feels plain, unloved, and not very special. Not until she is an adult does Louise realize that she also has gifts and that God has a plan for her that is just as fine as God's plan for Caroline.

2. Name some of the things we think would make us happy (e.g., receiving a Nintendo or some other gift, winning a big prize, having a room of our own). Compare those with other things that would make us truly happy (e.g., a picnic with our family on which everyone has fun together, or sharing secrets with an understanding friend we know we can trust). Use such examples to help young worshipers identify some of God's gifts that make them happy, then use them to differentiate between what we *think* will make us happy and what *really* makes us happy.

Today we are singing, praying, and thinking about God's providence.

PROVIDENCE means . . .

* God provides.

* God gives us what we need.

* God takes care of us.

* God created the world, and it is good.

THANKS, GOD

Turn your words into a prayer. Say "I praise the God of providence for . . ." before you say each example.

Write one example of God's providence for each letter of the word **providence**.

P _____

B R E A D

O _____

V _____

I _____

D _____

E _____

N _____

C _____

E _____

PROPER TWENTY-ONE

(Sunday between September 25 and October 1 inclusive)

From a Child's Point of View

Old Testament: Exodus 17:1-7. The story of the water from the rock parallels last week's story of manna and quail. In each case the people worry and complain, and God provides what is needed. Again, the key issue is to trust God, particularly for the necessities of life. For children, who must depend on others for these basics, the point is not very meaningful. Instead, they focus on the details and repetitive point in these stories. They may feel a little superior to the travelers who were such slow learners and will enjoy adding the story of water from the rock to their growing repertory of Exodus stories. (Review suggestions in Proper 20 about the providence of God and develop them if you did not do so last week.)

Psalm: 78:1-4, 12-16. This psalmist praises God for bringing water from a rock. If you have been worshiping around the Exodus texts, children will recognize the references to other events on the journey and appreciate the psalmist's point of view.

Epistle: Philippians 2:1-13. Paul urges the Philippians to live as Jesus did, and then quotes a hymn/poem about Jesus to illustrate what he means. Children will follow neither as they are read, but with help, they can appreciate Paul's point. The Philippians (and we) are to be as obedient to God's will as Jesus was. Though Jesus ruled the universe and rightfully should have been treated like a king, he was willing to come to earth as our servant in order to share God's love.

Therefore, we are to be willing to give up what is rightfully ours in order to be servants to one another and to share God's love. Because most children are deeply concerned about getting their fair share and missing out on nothing that is rightfully theirs, they are impressed by Jesus' willingness to give up what was rightfully his in order to serve us. (Check Palm/Passion Sunday of Years B and C for additional commentary and suggestions.)

Gospel: Matthew 21:23-32. The parable of the two sons is set in the context of a conversation between Jesus and some Temple leaders about the authority of Jesus and John the Baptist. The intricacies of the conversation are beyond children, but the parable is clear and speaks of a familiar childhood situation—obedience to parents. Children quickly realize that neither of these sons is a "good" son, but that the first is better than the second. With adult help, they can grasp Jesus' point about what it means to do God's will. For children, the point is that the Christian who goes to church and claims to know about God's love and to be a disciple of Jesus, but who does not follow God's rules or share God's love at school and in the neighborhood, is not doing God's will. In fact, the person who never goes to church, but who lives by God's rules and shares God's love, comes closer to doing God's will.

Watch Words

Follow up on last week's attention to *providence* by making *trust* the word of this week.

Few children know the meaning of the *mercy* or *compassion* of God mentioned in the psalm. Speak instead of God's *patient understanding* with the complaining, untrusting travelers.

A clearer word for *God's will* is *God's plan*. God's will is what God *intends* or *plans*. For example, a diner says to a waitress, "I will have fried chicken for dinner," or a teacher says to the class, "I will have quiet before we go on." Both are stating their *intent*. To do God's will is to follow God's rules and work on God's plan.

Let the Children Sing

Last week's Exodus hymns remain good choices. Singing "Guide Me, O Thou Great Jehovah" two Sundays in a row helps children to learn it.

If the focus is on obedience, sing "I Sing a Song of the Saints of God" or "Take My Life, and Let It Be Consecrated." Add verses to the spiritual "I'm Goin'a Sing When the Spirit Says Sing," such as "I'm going'a obey" or "I'm goin'a serve."

Praise the Christ of the Philippian hymn with "Come, Christians, Join to Sing"; nonreaders can sing at least the Alleluias. Even though it is not Christmas, sing "Infant Holy, Infant Lowly," which reflects Paul's hymn.

The Liturgical Child

1. Prayer of Confession:

Almighty God, you love us and take care of us just as you loved and took care of the travelers in the wilderness. But, like them, we complain and worry. We complain about the food we eat, the clothes we wear, the house we live in, the jobs we do. We worry that we are missing out on things that we deserve. We are jealous of anything others have that we do not. And, we worry that we will lose even what we have. Help us recognize all the ways you take care of us. Help us appreciate and enjoy your gifts. And teach us to trust you to give us what we need. Amen.

Assurance of Pardon: Even after God led them away from Pharaoh and through the Reed Sea, even after God fed them with manna and quail and made water flow from a rock, the people complained. God had every right to give up on them. But, God was patient. God took care of them and taught them and forgave them. God promises to do the same for you and for me. We have Jesus' word on it. Thanks be to God!

2. Invite the congregation to read in unison the Psalm section for the day from the Good News Bible.

3. Invite the children to sit with you at the front for the reading of the Gospel lesson. In your own words, tell the parable of the two sons, concluding with Jesus' question. Hear and briefly discuss the children's answers. Then inform them that Jesus told the same story to a group of church leaders and asked the same question. Urge them to listen for the story as you read the text from the Bible, perhaps holding in your lap the big Bible from the lectern. (Begin and end the reading with whatever admonitions customarily accompany the reading of the Gospel.) Then send the children back to their seats.

4. Offer a series of petitions about God's will being done, to which the congregation responds, *Thy will be done on earth as it is in heaven.* For example:

Creating God, who made and loves each of us, we know it is not your will that people should be homeless. When we see people sleeping on sidewalks, we hurt inside. But their problems seem too big for us. Give us the courage not to look away, but to look for a way to help. (RESPONSE)

Sermon Resources

1. If you begin the sermon with examples of our complaining and whining, include some children's complaints: School is too hard; My parents love my sister more than me; Coach doesn't like me, so I never get to play; I *never* get to . . . ; He *always* gets to . . . ; Everyone else has a . . . ; No one else has a little brother as pesky as mine; and so forth!

2. To recall the Exodus stories of God's care, present a series of teaching pictures or symbols. Find teaching pictures in the church-school files, or draw symbols on sheets of posterboard. These may be mounted on dowels set in buckets of sand, propped against a railing in the chancel, or displayed one at the time on an easel. As each is presented, recall God's care for the people in that situation.

Listen when **Exodus 17: 1-7** is read.
What were God's people complaining about?

Draw or write what you complain about most.

What do you think God would say to you about your complaining?

The letter I causes trouble when we use it too much. There are too many I's in the words below. Cross out the extra I's to find Paul's message.

LIET   THIE   SAMIE   MINID   BIE

___ ___   ___ ___   ___ ____   ____ ___   ___ ___

INI   YIOUI   TIHAT   WIAS   IIN

__ __   ___ ___   ____ ___   ___ ___   __ __

CIHRISTI   JIESIUS.

___ _____ ____   _____ .

PROPER TWENTY-TWO

(Sunday between October 2 and 8 inclusive)

From a Child's Point of View

Old Testament: Exodus 20:1-20. Elementary-school children are vitally interested in rules. They belong to many different groups which operate on different rules. They are aware that different families follow different rules. They evaluate rules by comparing them to other rules, and by considering how comfortable they make life in a group. Children are on the lookout for good rules. So the Ten Commandments, the rules of God's people, get their attention. They want to know what each one means and how one lives by it.

1. For literal thinkers, the first rule means that we are to sing and pray only to God. Talk of a "god" as something that is most important in our lives must wait until abstract thinking skills develop.

2. Even young children understand that we are not to make images of God, because God is bigger and different than anything we can imagine. No matter what we draw or sculpt, it will not be accurate.

Older children are often confused by the description of God as "jealous" because jealousy is an attitude they are taught to avoid. The phrase makes more sense to children when put, "I (God) care so very much about you."

3. For children, using God's name disrespectfully means saying "God" without real meaning in conversation, or saying God's name to express our own anger or frustration.

4. The human problem behind the command about the sabbath is that if we do not set aside specific times for rest and for worship, then we forget who we are and what is important. As children's sport teams begin to practice and play on Sunday mornings, children face the choice between church activities and sports. There is nothing sacred about Sunday school, but for most children today, it is their only chance to learn about God and clarify what is important. So if they join a team that meets on Sunday morning, it means they make no time at all for God. This must be challenged openly with both the children and their parents.

5. Even young children need to be told that the rule means we should treat parents with respect, rather than feel love for them. Children whose parents mistreat them need not feel guilty about their lack of loving feelings.

6. The basis for not murdering is respect for life. Children develop this respect in the way they treat animals, especially pets or small animals they may find.

7. Because of television, at a very early age, children know what adultery is. But the crux of this rule for children is still family loyalty. Family members are to support and look out for one another.

8. Stealing means the same thing at all ages.

9. For children, "bearing false witness" is telling lies about other people and sharing gossip they do not know to be true.

10. Do not *covet* means not to be greedy. Do not be jealous of the clothes, toys, special lessons, or homes of others. Again, children and adults can talk about the same problem with the same words—just different objects.

The Good News Bible offers the clearest translation of the Ten Commandments for children.

Psalm: 19:7-14. Because children appreciate good rules, they appreciate a psalm that praises God's good rules. Fifth- and sixth-graders, who learn about synonyms at school, enjoy looking for synonyms for God's rules in this psalm. If you name the synonyms and remind worshipers that Hebrew poets rhymed ideas, rather than sounds, children can follow this collection of rhyming ideas about God's rules.

Epistle: Philippians 3:4b-14. As usual, Paul is developing several themes at once. Children quickly become lost in them. Two themes, if lifted up separately, do speak to children. First, Paul claims that being a follower of Jesus is the most important thing in his life. He once made being a Jew the most important thing in his life, but now he has set that aside. He calls on children to make being a follower of Jesus central to their lives. All their other interests and the groups to which they belong are to take second place. Second, Paul compares being a follower of Jesus to being an athlete. We are to work as hard at following Jesus as an athlete works at winning a game.

Paul's references to a righteousness that is not based on keeping the rules, however, do not make sense to children, who are at a stage of moral development in which they use rules as the basis for ethical decisions (see Proper 4).

Gospel: Matthew 21:33-43. This parable is addressed to adults about an adult situation. Young children need information about contracts between tenants and landlords in order to make sense of the story on a literal level. All children need information about the function of cornerstones. Still, even with that information, children have difficulty grasping Jesus' warning to the Jews and do not find it particularly significant when they do grasp it.

Watch Words

Law, decrees, precepts, fear, commandments, and *ordinances* are synonyms for God's rules, which are expressed most concisely in the Ten Commandments.

Young children are unfamiliar with *tenants* and *cornerstones.*

Let the Children Sing

Dedicate yourselves to living by God's rules with "Lord, I Want to Be a Christian" or "Be Thou My Vision," if children sing it elsewhere. Though the middle lines are difficult for children, the repeated first and last lines of each verse make "Go Forth for God" a good choice also.

If the Philippians passage leads you to "When I Survey the Wondrous Cross," review the words and their connection to Paul's ideas with the congregation before singing it.

The sports images in the first two verses of "Fight the Good Fight" grab the attention of children.

The Liturgical Child

1. Use the Ten Commandments in a responsive prayer of confession or affirmation of commitment.

For a prayer of confession, a leader reads the Commandments one at a time, preceding each with the phrase, "God, you have told us . . . ," and following it with, "But we have . . . ." The congregation's response to each one: *Forgive us Lord. We have not kept your Commandments.*

For an affirmation of commitment, the leader reads each Commandment as above, with the congregation responding: *Lord, we will do our best.*

2. See Third Sunday After the Epiphany (Year C) for a structured reading of Psalm 19:7-14.

Sermon Resources

1. Since it is Worldwide Communion Sunday, note that one of the things that binds together the worldwide family of God is the Ten Commandments. We may look different, wear different clothes, live in different kinds of houses, and so on, but we all follow the same rules. Point out how those rules are lived out in several very different cultures (e.g., Japanese children bow to show respect to their parents; American children say "Yes, ma'am" or "Yes, sir").

2. To open a sermon on the Ten Commandments, ask several children to recite the rules of a group to which they belong. Boy and Girl Scouts can recite Scout laws. A member of a sport team might read the rules of conduct for players. A

younger child might bring the rules for his or her class at school. Hearing and comparing these rules sets the stage for discussing the rules for God's people.

3. If your church has a cornerstone, remind worshipers of its location and the meaning of any words on it. Tell where it came from and when and how it was placed. Refer to it in describing the function of a cornerstone. Urge children to find it after worship.

4. Use sports images to speak of knowing and following our rules (the Ten Commandments) with the same discipline and determination athletes apply to their sports. As you do, remember that children can identify ways that being a Christian is like being an athlete, but they cannot yet see life as a game or understand talk about the "game of life."

Unscramble these words to find the Ten Commandments.

I. ME NO HAVE BUT GODS

_____

II. IDOLS NOT WORSHIP DO

_____

III. NAME RESPECT SAY WITH GOD'S

_____

IV. HOLY SABBATH THE KEEP

_____

V. PARENTS YOUR HONOR

_____

VI. DO MURDER NOT

_____

VII. LOYAL BE FAMILY YOUR TO

_____

VIII. STEAL NOT DO

_____

IX. LIES DO TELL NOT

_____

X. NOT COVET DO

_____

Answers: Read Exodus 20:1-17.

Paul said he felt like a racer. Help him find his way through this race maze to the goal. Find Paul's advice to us in the path and write it in the blanks below.

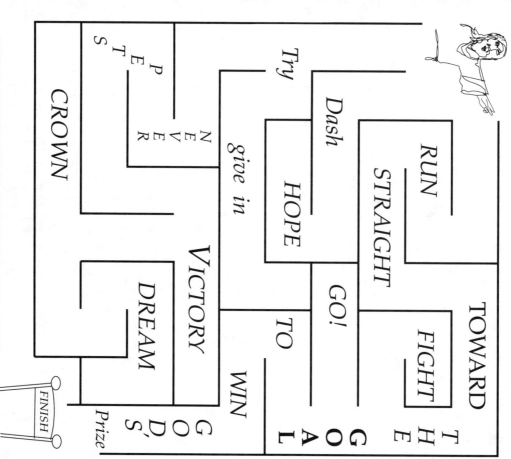

_____ _____ _____ _____ ___ _____ ___ ____ ____ _____.

Answers: Run straight toward the goal to win God's prize.

Proper 22/ © 1992 by Abingdon Press.

PROPER TWENTY-THREE

(Sunday between October 9 and 15 inclusive)

From a Child's Point of View

Old Testament: Exodus 32:1-14. Children today find it hard to believe that anyone would make and seriously worship a golden calf. If they are told that many people in those days worshiped statues of animals, older children try to understand that such actions made sense to people then, and they try to accept the story as a true account of how God's people broke the first two Commandments immediately after agreeing to them. They strongly empathize with God's outrage.

Many adults are offended by God's change of mind. But children, especially those who grow up hearing about the loving God who is always ready to forgive, are confused and offended by Moses' need to talk God out of destroying the calf-worshiping betrayers. It helps to compare God's reaction to our furious urge to hit a best friend who has done something very mean to us. God's problem, and ours, is that we love so much that we are hurt when those we love do not live up to our expectations. The good news of this passage, and the rest of the biblical story, is that God, who loves us so much, will not strike back when hurt by us.

Often when children get into trouble, their excuse is, "I forgot . . . what I was supposed to do, or what the rules were, or who I am." They get so caught up in trying something interesting or in doing what the other kids are doing that they "forget" it is wrong. That was the problem for the calf worshipers. They had forgotten that they were not like their animal-worshiping neighbors. They were the people of the God who had led them out of slavery in Egypt and across the wilderness to a promised home. Thus, one challenge of the text is to remember who we are, so that we will not be led into trouble.

Psalm: 106:1-6, 19-23. If you have been following the Exodus texts, children will understand all the references in this psalm. The Good News Bible offers the clearest translation.

Epistle: Philippians 4:1-9. This passage presents two problems for children: generalities and abstract concepts. Both the generalities ("do not worry," "keep on doing the things you have learned," etc.) and the abstract concepts ("peace of God," "honorable," "pure," etc.) will make sense only when illustrated with everyday examples. Since it is nearly impossible to define all the abstractions without losing the overall message, select one or two of Paul's exhortations for attention today. This warning applies especially to the eight abstractions of verse 8, often thought to be good guides for children to learn.

Gospel: Matthew 22:1-14. Children understand Luke's version of this parable and Luke's point more easily than Matthew's. The mental work required to integrate the vengeful king, the destruction of the Jerusalem Temple, and the exclusion of those who refuse an invitation to the eschatological banquet is beyond the abilities of children. Furthermore, children familiar with parables know that the king in Jesus' parables is meant to be like God, and therefore are confused when this king is so demanding and vengeful. They cannot deduce Matthew's point, but must hear it stated: God invites everyone to be one of God's people and wants everyone to come. But responding to the invitation has important consequences. If you choose to become one of God's people, you must live as God's person every day. If you do not, you miss out on all the joy.

Watch Words

Worshiping the gold calf means *singing and praying* to it. Children cannot identify the pursuit of good grades, popularity, and pretty clothes as the worship of false gods until their ability for abstract thought develops.

Rejoice is used only in worship these days. So paraphrase it as *be happy that* and expound on what real happiness is.

Let the Children Sing

This is a good Sunday for hymns that praise God in the spirit of Paul and provide an alternative to the misguided worship of the Israelites. Some especially good choices are the version of "Rejoice, Ye Pure in Heart" with a chorus made up entirely of Rejoices; "Come, Christians, Join to Sing"; "How Great Thou Art," if it is familiar to children; and "For the Beauty of the Earth."

"I've Got a Joy, Joy, Joy, Joy, Down in My Heart" and "I've Got Peace Like a River" make good anthems for children's classes or choirs.

The Liturgical Child

1. Base a prayer of confession on forgetfulness, such as that of the calf worshipers in the wilderness:

> Lord God of the Universe, we are forgetful people. We forget that you made this world and that we are to care for it and protect it. We forget that you created each of us with wonderful talents and interests to enjoy and to use in serving others. We forget the rules you have given us for good and happy lives. We forget that we are your people, people with jobs to do. Sometimes we "forget on purpose." At other times, we just are so busy or want something so badly that we really do forget. We try to go our own way, do what we want, and make our own plans. Forgive us in Jesus' name. Amen.

Assurance of Pardon: Another thing we forget is that God loves us very much. God loves us enough to forgive us again and again and again. God loves us so much that God lived among us, died, and rose again in Jesus of Nazareth. So whatever you forget, always remember that God loves you and forgives you. Thanks be to God!

2. Recite appropriate verses from the Philippians lection, addressing them to the congregation as the charge and benediction.

3. If you celebrate the Lord's Supper today, stress its connection to the great banquet of God. Do whatever you can to stress the festiveness of that banquet. Invite worshipers to break off chunks of bread from a loaf (rather than pick up tiny pieces) and dip them into a chalice or silver bowl of wine or grape juice. Select happy songs of praise, rather than somber music about sin. Use festive words such as Alleluia! and Rejoice! frequently, and with feeling.

Sermon Resources

1. To make the worship of a calf seem less strange, tell about other animals that have been worshiped as gods:

The Baal worshipers of the Middle East made statues of a bull. According to one of their stories about it, a great bull was killed while fighting a devil that was trying to destroy the earth. The mourning gods cut the bull into pieces and plowed the pieces into the soil of the dying earth. Watered and fertilized by the bull's blood and flesh, the earth grew fertile again and was saved. Baal worshipers sang songs and prayed to the bull in late winter, when it seemed that spring would never come.

The Aztecs of ancient Mexico worshiped the Hummingbird of the South. Their stories told about a hummingbird that had led them south from their old home to a new home and had helped them defeat the people who lived there. Priests wore hummingbird masks when they acted out these stories and sang songs about the Hummingbird of the South.

2. See Sermon Resource 2 of Proper 20 about the things that make us truly happy.

Listen to **Exodus 32: 1-14.** God's people sinned. They worshiped a gold calf. Keep a record of how you worship God today.

▼ I sang these songs:

_____

_____

▼ I prayed for _____

_____

▼ I heard the preacher say, "_____

_____"

▼ I said, "I believe _____

_____

▼ I put _____ in the offering plate.

Paul said,
"REJOICE IN THE LORD !"
Rejoice means to "be happy." Paul was telling us to be happy about what God has done. Write or draw 2 reasons you rejoice.

I AM HAPPY THAT GOD . . .

I AM HAPPY THAT GOD . . .

PROPER TWENTY-FOUR

(Sunday between October 16 and 22 inclusive)

From a Child's Point of View

Old Testament: Exodus 33:12-23. As church children grow up, they absorb the biblical stories about God speaking to people, they sing and pray in public worship about God's presence with us, and they hear adults speak in abstract terms of God's presence with them. Many children wonder why no one today seems to have dramatic experiences of God's presence like those described in the Bible. They wonder why some of their teachers and church leaders speak frequently of God's presence, but others seem uncomfortable with the topic. Many want help in interpreting personal experiences in which they have sensed God's presence.

Moses' dialog with God speaks to these concerns. Verses 12-17 say that God's presence is critically important. Moses was willing to risk an argument with God, in order to talk God into being present with the people as they went into the Promised Land. He got what he wanted, but was reminded that God's presence is demanding as well as supportive, and therefore is dangerous for people who are not willing to respond. Verses 18-23 then reveal that Moses, after years of talking with God and leading the people in God's name, still longed to experience God's presence more fully. If Moses never knew all there is to know about God, certainly we can expect to always be learning more.

Warning: The anthropomorphic language of verse 23 contradicts our efforts to help children envision God in spiritual rather than physical terms. Younger children hear and respond literally to references to God's hand and back, and therefore get the point of the text quickly. Those older children who are attempting to grow beyond visions of God as an old man, perhaps somewhat like Santa Claus, are surprised by the language and need help with it before they can pay attention to the larger point about God's presence with us.

Psalm: 99. Children need help to interpret the references to cherubim, Zion, Jacob, and Samuel. The psalm, however, can be a springboard to discussions about the nature of God. The summary word is *holy*. According to the psalmist, God's holiness is revealed in God's power over all the empires of the world, in God's justice, in God's presence with individuals, and in God's forgiveness.

Epistle: I Thessalonians 1:1-10. Paul begins his letter by listing good things about the people of the church at Thessalonica. They responded to God's word as it was brought to them by Paul. They endured persecution. They put their faith into practice everyday. Their love of one another and their trust in God are obvious to everyone. Paul's list offers children a model, though a rather abstract one, of Christian living.

Gospel: Matthew 22:15-22. The question about the propriety of paying taxes is beyond the experience of most children. Children express simple patriotism based on pride in their country and a sense of belonging to their country. Jesus says to them that these feelings and the usual patriotic activities are fine, as long as they do not usurp God's primary place in our lives. It will be several years before they can identify, with real understanding, the areas in which God and country can conflict.

Watch Words

Though the word *holy* does not appear often in today's texts, it is the key description of God. Use *holy* repeatedly today. Explore what it says about God's power, love, justice, and the fact that God exceeds our imagination. Older children enjoy "playing" with *hole*, *whole*, and *holy*.

Avoid *anthropomorphic*. Describe instead our tendency to describe God as if God were a person.

Let the Children Sing

Even nonreaders can sing the repeated Holys in each verse of "Holy, Holy, Holy!" To help children understand this often-used hymn, read and explain one verse before the congregation sings it.

Praise God with "Now Thank We All Our God."

"Take Time to Be Holy" reminds us to practice God's presence in several very simple, understandable ways.

"Go with Us, Lord," a closing prayer set to the Tallis Canon, could be sung by a children's class or choir, to send the congregation out in God's presence at the benediction.

The Liturgical Child

1. If you are focusing on the presence of God, invite a children's class to memorize and say Psalm 100:1-3a as the call to worship. If the same group concludes the service with the "Go with Us, Lord" canon, their practice time would offer an opportunity to discuss the ways we know of God's presence, both in worship and as we go about our daily lives.

2. Present Exodus 33:12-23 as the dialog that it is. Two readers may take the parts of Moses and God, omitting all the "he saids." Or one reader may read both parts, assuming different positions in the lectern for God and for Moses. Plan carefully the way each phrase will be emphasized. Practice is needed to give this reading feeling. If one reader presents the text, avoid the confusing pronouns of the RSV and the NRSV. The Good News Bible sets the conversation most clearly in its story context and may be the best choice.

3. If you celebrate Communion during this service and generally use a Sanctus, feature it today. Talk about what it says about and to God, and why it is part of the sacrament. If the choir generally sings the Sanctus, ask that it be sung at the time you explore its meaning. Then urge children to listen for it.

4. Invite worshipers to listen to I Thessalonians 1:1-10 as if it were addressed to them. Build the prayers and sermon around ways the text fits, or does not fit, the worshipers, as individuals and as a congregation.

Sermon Resources

1. Point out the word *holy* wherever it is carved, embroidered, or painted in your sanctuary. If there are other symbols for God in your sanctuary, build a sermon around identifying and expounding on them.

2. Identify the ways we sense God's presence with us and compare them with the ways Moses' followers knew of God's presence in the desert. Children often sense God's presence in creation, through their fascination with small animals and insects such as lightning bugs, or through their amazement at the bigness of things such as the ocean. Many children can tell stories about feeling God close to them when they were very frightened (in the dark or during a storm) or when they were alone (especially if they thought they were lost). Children of strong families can sense God's presence in the security and happiness of their family life, if their parents have thus interpreted it to them. Some children carry deep guilt and fear of God's judgment, based on their belief that God has seen them do something of which they are ashamed. These children understand the demand of God's presence and need help to accept God's loving, forgiving presence. Some children sense God's presence in the congregation's worship (particularly in special services such as a candle-lighting service), in work, and in fellowship.

2. Write a letter to your congregation in the spirit of Paul's letter to the Thessalonians. Illustrate general praises with specific examples of congregational strengths and activities. Be sure to cite activities in which children have participated, so they can feel that your letter is for them as well as for the adults.

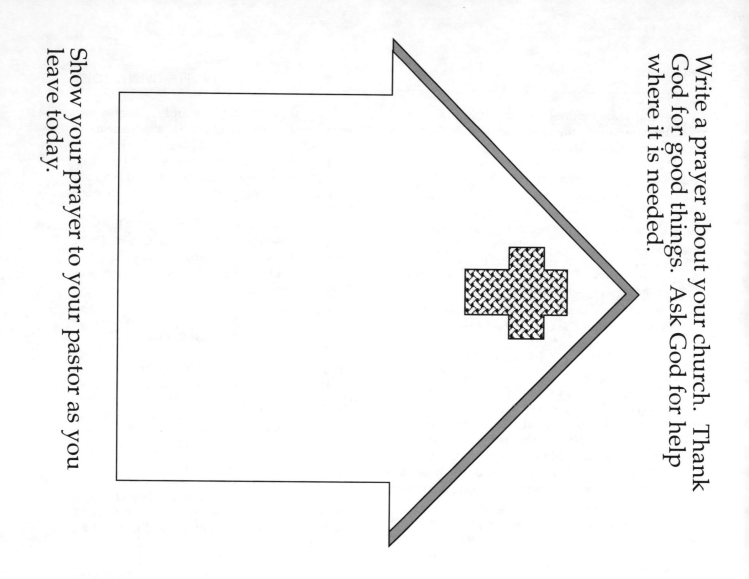

Write a prayer about your church. Thank God for good things. Ask God for help where it is needed.

Show your prayer to your pastor as you leave today.

Listen in worship for words that tell about God. (One word that tells about God is **holy**.) Write the words around the edges of this page when you hear them. Use these words to write a poem about God on the lines below.

GOD

2 "ing" words about God: _____ing, _____ing

3 words that describe God: _____, _____, _____

Another good word for God: HOLY

PROPER TWENTY-FIVE

(Sunday between October 23 and 29 inclusive)

From a Child's Point of View

Old Testament: Deuteronomy 34:1-12. The account of Moses' death and the passing of leadership to Joshua invites children to review the life of Moses. They will, however, need help, even if worship has been focused on the Exodus events for the past weeks. Once they remember how much of Moses' life was devoted to taking the Hebrew slaves to the Promised Land, many will object to the fact that Moses never entered the land. Some will protest that God was not fair to Moses. Older children can appreciate the way God provided continuous leadership—first Moses, then Joshua.

Psalm: 90:1-6, 14-17. When this psalm is paired with the Old Testament lesson, it leads adults to ponder the limits of even the most spectacular lives. But children, for whom the time between Thanksgiving and Christmas seems unending, can only smile indulgently at grown-up exclamations about the brevity of life and the speed with which time passes. They do, however, enjoy pondering the greatness of God, for whom a thousand years is like an evening. And they do find security in the God who was there at the beginning and will be there at the end.

Epistle: I Thessalonians 2:1-8. Paul's description of his work among the Thessalonians can be used to explore the relationship between any pastor and congregation. While adults can consider what any pastor-congregation relationship ought to be, children can only identify aspects of their relationship with the current pastor, and perhaps compare that pastor to one previous pastor, or to a pastor at another church. Because children often carry their parents' feelings about the pastor to an extreme, they may give a respected pastor nearly god-like authority or dismiss a less-respected pastor entirely. They need help to realize that no pastor-congregation relationship is perfectly wonderful or entirely awful. And they need to learn that just as Paul and the Thessalonians needed to work on their relationship, congregations and pastors today need to work on theirs.

Gospel: Matthew 22:34-46. The two great Commandments are familiar to most church children. They enjoy hearing them read and discussed in congregational worship. They benefit from lists of specific ways we can love God. Cite the ways people of all ages can express their love with heart, soul, and strength: singing for God (alone and in the congregation); thanking God for our gifts; using well the talents God created into us; telling God about what we are doing or thinking (as we would tell any friend). Also cite everyday examples of loving neighbors at home, school, and community.

What may be new and interesting for older children is the debate context in which Jesus proclaimed the two commands. Frequently, children are questioned by teachers, who (from the student's point of view) are trying to trip them up. So they empathize with Jesus as he deals with questions designed to make him say something wrong or that will make people angry. And they enjoy Jesus' beating the questioners at their own game.

With some help, they can even understand and appreciate the problem Jesus posed for Jewish leaders: Grandchildren might call their grandparents "my Lord," but grandparents, especially ones like great King David, would never call their grandchildren "my Lord."

Watch Words

Today's texts offer few vocabulary traps.

Let the Children Sing

"O God, Our Help in Ages Past," Psalm 90 set to music, is difficult for children, but if they hear it sung with great feeling, they will pay attention and learn its meaning a phrase at a time. Help them along by explaining why this hymn is often sung at funerals. Suggest that worshipers sing the hymn today for Moses, at the end of his long life.

Choose hymns that reflect the two great Commandments: Sing of our love of God with "For the Beauty of the Earth"; sing about loving neighbors with the new hymn, "Help Us Accept Each Other."

"Blest Be the Tie That Binds" is clearly related to the both commands, but also is filled with words that are unfamiliar to children. If you sing it, take time to point out the words and phrases that refer to each of the commands.

The Liturgical Child

1. Psalm 90 is attributed to Moses. So ask an older male member of the congregation to read the psalm, imagining himself to be Moses as he stood on the mountain, looking toward the Promised Land he would never enter. Children may gather more of the psalm's meaning from the feeling with which it is read than from its words.

2. Present the Gospel as if it were a radio play. Adopt different tones for the different speakers and practice saying their lines with appropriate inflection and passion. Turn slightly in the lectern as you take different roles.

3. Base a responsive Prayer of Confession on the two great commands:

> *Leader:* Jesus told us to love God with all our heart,
> *People:* but we often love our jobs, our homes, and our own possessions more than we love God.
> *Leader:* Jesus told us to love God with all our soul,

> *People:* but we put more soul into our music, our sports, and our hobbies than into expressing our love of God.
> *Leader:* Jesus told us to love God with all our mind,
> *People:* but we seldom study the Bible as much as we study our schoolbooks or bankbooks.
> *Leader:* Jesus also told us to love our neighbors as we love ourselves,
> *People:* but we spend hours meeting our wants and needs and minutes finding excuses for not taking care of others.
> *Leader and People:* Forgive us, Lord. Help us to remember and obey your commands. For we pray in Jesus name. Amen.
> *Leader:* Jesus gave us commands so that we would know how to live. But Jesus also died so that we could be forgiven when we fail to live up to those commands. We are commanded and forgiven because we are loved. Thanks be to God!

4. If you focus on the leadership provided by Moses and Paul, pray for leaders: patrol leaders, class officers, and team captains, as well as elected officials.

Sermon Resources

1. To explain the trap in the question about the greatest Commandment, cite examples of people who would want Jesus to endorse a certain one of the Ten Commandments as the most important (e.g., a store owner might insist that not stealing is most important; a church school superintendent might want keeping the sabbath endorsed). No matter which one Jesus chose, he would make someone angry.

2. In an election year, compare Jesus' debate with the religious leaders to the debates between political candidates. Though children do not follow the content of these debates, they generally are interested in the events and in their purpose—to talk candidates into making public statements that will either make people angry at them or persuade people to vote for them. Fifth- and sixth-graders often stage debates at school at election time.

3. If you preach about the pastor's job, display pictures of the church's former pastors in the sanctuary. Illustrate sermon points with stories from their work with this congregation. Children especially enjoy and benefit from this if portraits of the pastors are permanently displayed somewhere in the church.

There is an extra letter in each word below. Listen when
Matthew 22: 34-46 is read. Then cross out the extra letters.

LOVED   THEY   SLORD   YIOUR
GOLD   WISTH   MALL   YOURN
SHEART,   SOGUL,   SAND   MINED.
GLOVE   YOTUR   SNEIGHBOR
GAS   YOURXSELF.

Write a prayer for your pastor

or

Draw a picture of your pastor at work

Proper 25/ © 1992 by Abingdon Press.

PROPER TWENTY-SIX

(Sunday between October 30 and November 5 inclusive)

From a Child's Point of View

Old Testament: Joshua 3:7-17. If you worshiped around the story of crossing the Reed Sea (Proper 19), even children will recognize the parallels between the crossings. In both, God's people are crossing a border on their trip to the Promised Land. In both, God opened a path through a water barrier so that they could pass. At the Reed Sea, Moses was the leader. At the Jordan River, Moses' successor Joshua was in charge. By opening the Reed Sea, God proved to the people that it was God's power, and not their own, that made their escape from Egypt possible.

At the Jordan River, God reminded the people that God was with them as they claimed the Promised Land. Children are not ready to deal with the possibility of archetypal stories. For them, these are simply two very similar incidents. Rather than raise the issues behind the comparisons, it is advisable to preach on the crossing of either the sea or the river, but not both in such close proximity.

Psalm: 107:33-43. The psalmist recounts a series of surprising turnarounds, in which God acts on behalf of those who are weak and against those who are cruel. The language is difficult for children to follow in any translation, but it's theme is important to them. Children who feel weak and vulnerable appreciate hearing that God takes the side of such people. And successful, strong children need to hear that God punishes those who use their strength and power to hurt others.

Gospel: Matthew 23:1-12. The heart of this text is in verses 11-12. (Consider reading verses 11-12 *before* 1-10, as well as after.) Living up to these verses is as difficult for children as it is for adults. Children are urged by both teachers and parents to be achievers, to become "the best," to be elected to class office, to win awards. Jesus' call to be servants seems to be in opposition to all this pressure for success. The challenge is to help children see the difference between achieving recognition for self and achieving on behalf of others. As an example, compare a coach bent on becoming Number One, with one bent on helping the team members play the best they can and enjoy the sport.

Rather than becoming tangled in the fringes, phylacteries, titles, and seats coveted by the religious leaders in verses 1-10, focus on the summary verses and how they are to be lived out today.

Epistle: I Thessalonians 2:9-13. Paul and his co-workers provide good examples of faithful servants in action. They worked night and day to introduce the Thessalonians to God's love. They were careful to set the very best examples of God's love, and they themselves loved each of the people they worked with. Finally, they were delighted with the good results of all their work.

Watch Words

Before reading the Joshua story, tell worshipers that *Canaanites, Hittites, Hivites, Perizzites, Girgashites, Amorites,* and *Jebusites* were people who lived in the Promised Land.

The *Ark of the Covenant,* unlike Noah's ark, was not a boat. Describe this ark, and what it meant to the Jews, before reading about its role in crossing the river.

In Christian worship, *Jordan River* is used figuratively as the boundary between life and death. Before using it thus with children, explain that the point of today's text—God will go with you—applies to all the big changes in our lives, even to dying.

Let the Children Sing

"Guide Me, O Thou Great Jehovah" is filled with Exodus images which should be familiar if you have been following that story. Explain its use of "the Jordan" and "Canaan" before singing the hymn.

"Lord, I Want to Be a Christian" is the simplest way to commit ourselves to a servanthood like that of Jesus. "I'm Gonna Live So God Can Use Me" is another spiritual that young readers can join in on.

The Liturgical Child

1. Ask a children's class to pantomime the crossing of the Jordan River as it is read. As the reader announces the text, two children (river bearers) take their places at the front of the sanctuary, holding the ends of a long strip of blue fabric, waving it waist high.

The rest of the class enters from the back, with Joshua in the lead, followed by the Ark (a cardboard box painted gold), its carriers, and the rest of God's people. The procession stops when Joshua reaches the river.

Joshua turns around to face the people as verse 7 is read. At the beginning of verse 8, he raises his arms to speak to the people. At verse 14, he drops his arms and steps aside.

As the Ark bearers come to the edge of the river (verse 15), the river bearers drop the blue fabric to the floor for the people to cross the river. The people stand across the front of the sanctuary as the concluding verses are read.

After the reader makes the customary statements to mark the end of the reading, the children respond, "We praise the Lord!" then leave the sanctuary or take their seats.

Practice is essential, and simple costumes (even just head scarfs) make the presentation more effective.

2. To help children identify all the turnarounds God affects in Psalm 107:33-43, read it as follows:

Leader—Introduce the psalm and announce the reading of Scripture in the usual manner.
Reader 1—verses 33-34
Reader 2—verses 35-38
Reader 1—verses 39-40
Reader 2—verse 41
Leader—verses 42-43 (the summary verses)

3. Base a Prayer of Confession on being servants: Lord God of the universe, we confess that we want to be the best, the first, the most, the top. We want to be the one in charge, the one who sets the rules and makes the plans. We want to win all the prizes and always be Number One. We want people to like us, to respect our ideas, and be our friends. We are so full of what we want to do and be that we can think of nothing else. Forgive our self-centeredness. Teach us to look and listen for the needs and wants of others. Remind us that we are called to be servants, not masters. Help us find the happiness that comes when we care for and support others. Amen.

4. Pray for turnarounds such as those in Psalm 107 that are needed today. Give worshipers silence in which to pray for individuals they know who need such a turnaround. Pray for the homeless, for bullies who need an internal turnaround, and for community or national events in which a turnaround is needed.

5. Pray for safety for all who trick-or-treat and enjoy Halloween parties or haunted houses. Pray for the wisdom to remember that behind our masks, we are still God's loving people, and we are to treat people accordingly.

Sermon Resources

1. The stories about Cinderella and her ugly step-sisters, and the fable of the Ugly Duckling, are well-known turnarounds that people of all ages understand.

2. Do a little research on what your children will wear for Halloween. Compare what makes those characters great with what Jesus said makes a person great. Be alert for costumes such as nurses or clowns, which do fit into Jesus' definition of greatness through care of others.

Listen as **Joshua 3: 7-17** is read. Draw a picture of what happened. In your picture draw:

Joshua

a river

travelers wearing shoes

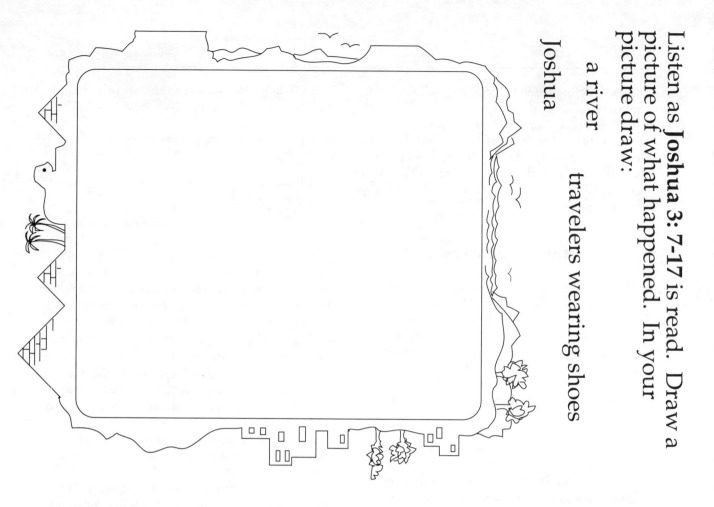

Some of the things Jesus said sounded upside down and backwards. But he meant exactly what he said. The words below are upside down and backwards. Turn each word right to find what Jesus said and meant.

WILL YOU AMONG GREATEST THE

___ ___ _____ _____ ___ ____

(MATTHEW 23: 11) SERVANT YOUR BE

___ __ ____ _____ (_____ __: __)

ALL SAINTS

(November 1 or first Sunday in November)

From a Child's Point of View

John Westerhoff has identified four types of faith: experiential faith, belonging faith, questioning faith, and owned faith. His work indicates that people proceed through these types in the order stated, with lots of repeats. Most elementary-age children are living on belonging faith, which is to say that their faith is based upon their participation in the community of faith. To believe is to worship, study, and serve among God's people. Therefore, All Saints is an important opportunity to review and reenforce their understanding of what it means to be one of the saints. Today's texts are almost an advertisement for the benefits of being one of God's people.

Epistle: I John 3:1-3. This text provides the definition of what it means to be a saint. Though John speaks of "children of God" rather than "saints," he is talking about the same people—those who know that they belong to and are loved by God. God's people not only belong to God; they also belong to one another. Few children appreciate the concern in verse 2 about what we shall become after death (or at the Second Coming), but most easily grasp the point in verse 3 that children of God (saints) try to be like Jesus. Because *purity* is neither familiar to young children nor desired by older children, children respond more readily to calls to make Jesus their hero and example, than to calls to be "pure."

Gospel: Matthew 5:1-12. On All Saints, the Beatitudes are primarily promises of God's blessings for the saints, rather than directions for how to live. This is a good day to explain the Latin base of the word *Beatitudes* and to explore the kind of happiness that is more like having a best friend with whom you can share everything than like the happiness of receiving a new toy. Jesus' promise is that though the saints may lose out on some fleeting happiness, God will give them a longlasting, deep happiness that will mean more. So, to be one of the saints is to be happy.

The content of the Beatitudes is difficult for children to understand. See the commentary for the Fourth Sunday After Epiphany for a children's paraphrase of the Beatitudes.

First Reading: Revelation 7:9-17. On All Saints, this text reminds us of those times when the saints have been in danger. Children need to be told that this was written in code, during a time when a person found with Christian writings could be fed to lions. In the key to the code, the Lamb is Jesus, and the people whose robes are washed white in the blood of the Lamb are Christians (saints). Even with the key, children will need help to decode John's promise that God will stand with the saints and that their suffering finally will end.

Note: See the Sundays of Easter in Year C for further ideas about the use of the Revelation codes with children. This particular text falls on the Fourth Sunday of Easter in Year C.

Psalm: 34:1-10, 22. This is one saint's response to being saved from danger. David was captured but had gained release by pretending to be mad. After he was back with his friends, he celebrated his release, and his sanity, with an acrostic (alphabet poem) about God's watchful care in dangerous times. It is easy to imagine his friends calling out each letter of the Hebrew alphabet, and David replying with a shout of praise that began with that letter. Just as this was David's response to being one of the saints, so it can be ours.

Watch Words

Many words and phrases describe people who belong to God—*Saints, Children of God, Christians,* and *church* are the most obvious ones for today. Using these words interchangeably confuses children, so choose one or two to use exclusively. Or point out that there are many names, then challenge children to write them on their bulletins as they hear them. They may want to share their lists with you as they leave the sanctuary.

If you use *saints*, point out that you are referring to all Christians, not just those who have been declared saints by the Roman Catholic Church.

Blessed means very happy and fortunate.

Let the Children Sing

On All Saints, "I Sing a Song of the Saints of God" and "We Are the Church" are good choices.

Commit yourselves to sainthood with "Lord, I Want to Be a Christian."

Thank God for the blessings of sainthood with "Now Thank We All Our God."

"Blest Be the Tie That Binds" celebrates the communion of the saints in difficult words. Ask worshipers to join hands or put a hand on the shoulder of the person holding the hymnal, to emphasize physically the hymn's message.

The Liturgical Child

1. If your congregation uses paraments, note the change from green to white. Name the other seasons for which white is used and note the significance of white.

2. Decorate the sanctuary with white flowers and palm branches. Recall the fickle branch-wavers of Palm Sunday and compare them with the faithful branch-wavers in Revelation. At the end of worship, give each worshiper a palm branch and urge that they be kept where they can be seen often this week, as a reminder that the worshipers are to be among the saints waving branches in Revelation.

3. Give each person a white paper stole at the beginning of worship. Invite worshipers to write the names or draw pictures on the stoles of saints who have been and are important to them. They may add saints as they think of them during the service. Near the end of the service, instruct worshipers to put on their stoles for a time of prayer for the saints. Offer some public prayers, then provide silence in which worshipers can pray for and about the people whose names or pictures are on their stoles. Worshipers may take their stoles home or drape them over the Communion rail or table as they leave.

Cut stoles about three inches wide and at least one yard long from white chart paper. Newsprint or paper tablecloths are too fragile. Ask a children's class to add church-symbol stickers to the ends.

4. To get into the spirit of David's alphabet poem, invite a children's class, or the whole congregation, to call out the letters of the Hebrew alphabet. The worship leader responds to each letter with the appropriate verse of the psalm. In The New Jerusalem Bible, the Hebrew letter is printed beside each verse.

Sermon Resources

1. To explore the significance of the communion of the saints, tell stories about some of the saints who have been important in your life, being sure to include some from your childhood. Also include children who are saints and have been important to you. If the worshipers have been provided with stoles, suggest that they add names as your stories remind them of saints in their lives.

2. Devote a sermon to designing an advertisement which urges people to become saints. Consider your audience or market. Will you go after successful kids and adults, or failures? Will you invite people who are members of lots of groups, or people who are loners? What would you say to people caught up in drugs, or those who are feeling lonely in a new town? Will you invite, or threaten, or challenge? Then plan your response to those who reply to your ad.

Suggest that children work on the Worship-Worksheet posters as you talk. Comment on their posters as they leave; display them later on a titled bulletin board.

Draw a poster that invites people to become **saints**. Show what saints do. Give reasons for being a saint. Listen to our songs, prayers, and Bible reading for ideas.

Listen to David's ABC psalm about God's care of saints. Then write your own ABC psalm about being a saint. Write one verse for each letter below.

$\mathcal{A}$ _____

$\mathcal{B}$ _____

C _____

$\mathcal{D}$ _____

$\mathcal{E}$ *Even when I feel sad and lonely,* _____

God is with me. _____

PROPER TWENTY-SEVEN

(Sunday between November 6 and 12 inclusive)

From a Child's Point of View

All of today's texts deal with serving God.

Old Testament: Joshua 24:1-3a, 14-25. This is a story appreciated by children who are learning to make choices and live with the consequences. In many ways, they face the same situation the Israelites faced.

The Israelites, after years of wandering in the desert, were settling into houses and taking up farming in the Promised Land. Children today are learning their way into life in a world that is new to them.

It was easy for the Israelites to do what their new neighbors did and to forget what God had taught them in the desert. Children today are tempted to go along with their friends and do what everyone else is doing.

Joshua's warning to the Israelites and to today's children is that they cannot go along with the crowd and still be God's people. They have some choices to make.

Some of the decisions children face today include: whether to try drugs or alcohol; whether to attempt dangerous, forbidden feats; whether to join in cruel pranks or jokes; how to treat the popular and unpopular kids; and what clubs and teams to join.

Psalm: 78:1-7. This psalm parallels Joshua's insistence that the Israelites face a choice because God has acted on their behalf and gave them the Law through the patriarchs. Few children will catch that message as the psalm is read, nor will they particularly understand it if it is explained.

Gospel: Matthew 25:1-13. Because it deals with a wedding, this parable catches the attention of most children. The Middle Eastern focus on the groom's procession, as opposed to the Western focus on the bride's procession, intrigues and amuses them, but it is hard for them to get to the point of the story. Interpreted with apocalyptic literacy, the parable is a call to live as faithful disciples now, because we do not know when the Day of the Lord, Second Coming, or Judgment Day, will occur.

Interpreted in relation to Joshua's call to serve the Lord, the parable insists that serving the Lord is a matter of daily decisions and preparedness. People are to be ready to serve the Lord wherever and whenever God appears. The former threatens children; the latter invites them to bold adventures with God.

Epistle: I Thessalonians 4:13-18. The question of the Thessalonians—whether Christians who died before Jesus returned would be included in Jesus' new kingdom—has been settled and so seems strange to children. But Paul's unspoken assumption that God loves and cares for us, even after we die, is very important to them. They need reassurance that God still loves and cares for the people they love who have died. They need to know that those people are safe in God's love and that God will love and care for us when we die.

Watch Words

Children, who *serve* tennis balls, meet *servers* in restaurants, and read about *servants* in stories, need many specific examples of what it means to *serve* God.

Choose carefully your language about God in action. Children are confused when adults use Day of the Lord, Second Coming, Judgment Day, and "when Jesus returns" interchangeably.

Let the Children Sing

Children enjoy the question/answer format of "'Are Ye Able?' Said the Master," but have trouble with the symbolic language of the chorus. So put the chorus into your own words before the hymn is sung. (The choir might sing the questions in the verses, the congregation answering with the chorus.)

The repeated opening and closing lines of each verse make "Go Forth for God" another commitment hymn children can sing at least part of.

"Lord, I Want to Be a Christian," "I Sing a Song of the Saints of God," and "Take My Life and Let It Be Consecrated" are good commitment hymns.

The Liturgical Child

1. There are at least two attention-grabbing ways to present the Old Testament Lesson:

A. Ask the members of the congregation to imagine themselves among the Israelites who, after wandering in the desert, were settling into new homes in the Promised Land. Recall some of the things they experienced in the desert and describe their new lives and neighbors. Tell them that a meeting has been called, and ask them to stand as the people then did when they gathered. Then read Joshua 24:1-3a and 14-25.

B. Print the text in the bulletin so that it can be read by a narrator (vss. 1-2a, 25); Joshua (vss. 2b-3a, 14-15, 19-20, 22a, 23); and the people/congregation (vss. 16-18, 21, 22b, 24). Omit all the "he saids." "Joshua" should practice his lines using great power to emphasize their meaning.

2. Display an oil lamp (perhaps placed as part of the chancel floral centerpiece) and explain, or even demonstrate, how it works. Point out what happens when the oil is gone. Imagine the inconvenience of carrying both the lamp and an extra jug of oil to an evening wedding. Then read the Gospel text, urging children to listen for mention of some oil lamps and the jugs of extra oil. (Decorative oil lamps are often sold in the candle sections of stores.)

3. Make the charge and benediction responsive:

> Leader—Choose this day who you will serve.
> People—We will serve the Lord!
> Leader—Then go in peace. Serve your Lord faithfully every day. Be ready to do God's work. Be brave and not shy about serving God. And remember that God is with you always, today and every day, even till the end of the world. Amen.

Sermon Resources

1. Not all choices are between good and bad. Many are between two different kinds of good. Children increasingly are making choices between church activities and sports teams or other clubs, practicing or traveling during times that used to be reserved for church. Children (and parents) feel caught between the importance of keeping commitments to a team and serving the Lord through church worship, study, and the serving life. When the team is consistently chosen, we are saying that other commitments are more important than commitments to God.

This true story makes an interesting case study: In the Presbyterian Church, to make a profession of faith and join the church, a person must meet with the Session. After participating in preparation classes, "Chris" did not come to the Session meeting because her softball team had a game at the same time. Others in her class faced similar conflicts, but they chose to be at the meeting. The Session said they would meet "Chris" the following Sunday after church, but she was not able to come to that meeting because her family had made other plans. At that meeting, the Session decided that the choices Chris was making led them to believe she was not ready to make a genuine profession of faith and assume the responsibility of church membership. They suggested that she wait a year. "Chris" and her family were very angry.

2. Tell stories of people who, like the wise bridesmaids, were ready when God called them to serve. Tell about families who welcome refugees into their homes and communities, about youth and adult groups who have gone on mission trips, and children who have undertaken projects they believed God wanted done. If at all possible, tell stories about your congregation's actions, interpreting them in light of today's texts.

193

Like the Israelites, the letters in these words are mixed up. Unscramble them to learn what Joshua told the people they had to do and how the people answered.

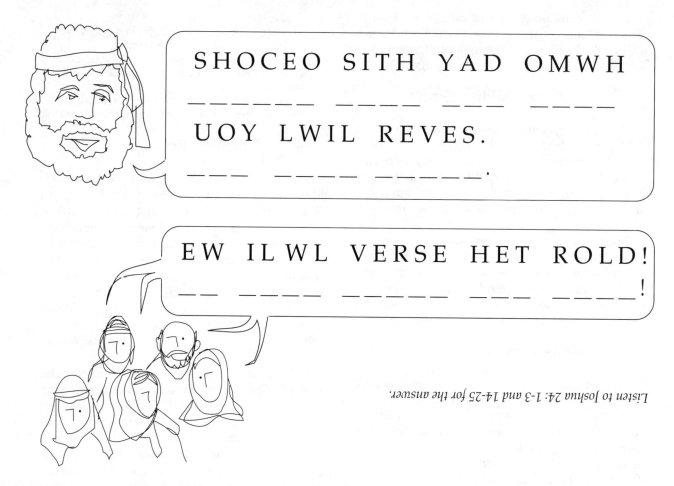

SHOCEO SITH YAD OMWH

_ _ _ _ _ _ _ _ _ _ _ _ _ _ _ _ _

UOY LWIL REVES.

_ _ _ _ _ _ _ _ _ _ _ _.

EW ILWL VERSE HET ROLD!

_ _ _ _ _ _ _ _ _ _ _ _ _ _ _ _ _ _!

Listen to Joshua 24: 1-3 and 14-25 for the answer.

Draw a picture of yourself serving God this week. Talk to God in prayer about what you will do.

God's servant_____at work.

PROPER TWENTY-EIGHT

(Sunday between November 13 and 19 inclusive)

From a Child's Point of View

Old Testament: Judges 4:1-7. This is the only story from Judges included in the Revised Common Lectionary. When only verses 1-7 are read, we learn simply that Deborah spoke for God to call the people to battle against King Jabin, who had oppressed them. Given both these facts, the text is worth expanding.

If you read through verse 16, the point is the point of all Judges stories: When the people sinned, God disciplined them by letting them be conquered. When they were ready to repent, God gave them another chance under a strong God-loving leader.

If you continue through verse 22, the focus is on heroism. War was supposed to be the business of men. But it was a woman (Deborah) who delivered God's call to battle. And it was a wife left behind in her tent (Jael) who won the day. Barak, whom one would have expected to be the hero, on the other hand, hesitated. Heroes and heroines are therefore ordinary people who do what needs to be done where they are.

Some (mainly adults) are offended by the violence of Jael's action. (Strangely, many of those folks find the wholesale slaughter of an army less of a problem than the capture and murder of one general by a woman, who used the only weapon at hand.) Children, especially when hearing the story shortly after Halloween, tend to admire Jael's willingness to do something as gory as pounding a tent peg into an enemy's head. Her name, Jael, which means "Yahweh (or Ya/Ja) is Lord (Elohim or El)" indicates that she killed the general because she felt it was what God wanted.

Psalm: 123. Older children who understand the relationship of slaves and masters can hear this as a prayer the Israelites might have prayed under the cruel rule of King Jabin. It is, however, too removed from today's realities to be of much significance for them.

Epistle: I Thessalonians 5:1-11. This text continues last Sunday's emphasis on preparedness. But last Sunday's parable of the bridesmaids addresses the issue in terms that make more sense to children than does this apocalyptic warning. Images of dark and light, women in labor, armor, and drunkenness lead children to think concretely about those things, rather than move through them to Paul's point.

Gospel: Matthew 25:14-30. Many church children are familiar with this parable. Once they know what a talent is, they easily follow the story and grasp Jesus' point that we are to make good use of the resources entrusted to us. Because they are constantly comparing themselves to others and being compared to others, children appreciate the fact that the first and second servants, though they were working with different amounts, received the same reward for their work. The point for both the five-talent and the two-talent children is that God appreciates those who try.

The third servant's harsh comments about the master, and the master's apparent agreement with that assessment, confuse children who do not yet have the mental facility to interpret allegory. They need to be told simply that the master in the story is *not* like God. The master may

195

have been interested only in the servant's profit, but God is more interested in the servants. If the first two servants of a harsh master were willing to risk losing their master's money by investing it, we, who are servants of a loving God, can surely take risks to invest the resources God has entrusted to us.

Watch Words

Judges in Bible times sometimes settled arguments between people, as judges do in courts today. But most of the time, they acted more like military or government *leaders.*

Talent is an Aramaic word for an amount of money that was equal to about three years' wages. Older children can understand and enjoy the "confusion" that resulted when translators had to leave this old word untranslated in English Bibles. Knowing that a *talent* is money enables children to understand Jesus' financial story and make connections to our use of our other resources, including our abilities (our talents).

If the parable of the talents leads you to talk about being *stewards*, describe the function of a steward. The only steward many children have met is a man who serves drinks on an airplane. Young children who know a person named Stewart are equally baffled.

The word *resources* is not in any of today's texts, but it is worth introducing as a word that stands for all our God-given abilities, money, and advantages (like a good education to prepare one to serve God as a doctor or plumber). After listing such resources, speak of using our resources and being *resourceful* servants.

Let the Children Sing

"I Sing a Song of the Saints of God" is first choice for singing about heroic living. Though the language of "For All the Saints" makes it difficult for children, the stirring music and repeated Alleluias make it an acceptable second choice.

Stewardship hymns children understand are hard to find. "Take My Life and Let It Be Consecrated," in which we dedicate the resources of our bodies, is one of the best.

The Liturgical Child

1. Invite the children to sit with you at the front. Explain that today's Old Testament lesson is a story about heroes who were like Davey Crockett and Paul Bunyan. Then tell selected parts of the story in your own words, using your best storyteller style.

2. The parable of the talents can be pantomimed easily by four young children as it is read. The talents can be represented by grocery bags, stuffed with newspaper to look like big money bags. The ten-talent servant may need a wheelbarrow, and the four-talent servant a big bucket, for their appearances before the master. Simple costumes help.

3. Invite worshipers of all ages to draw or write lists of their resources, including their talents, money, strengths, and so on. Adults (and children) can write in the space provided for that purpose in the bulletins. Younger children can work on their Worship Worksheets. Near the end of the service, pray about these lists. Offer such prayers as:

Creator God, thank you. We thank you for all the abilities and talents you have created in each of us. We thank you for families, and schools, and money to use. Hear all our prayers of thanks. (PAUSE)

Lord of the Universe, it is easy to be selfish with everything you have left in our care . . . .

Sermon Resources

1. Recall some of the costumes the children wore for Halloween. Compare the heroism of Deborah, Jael, and current costume heroes (Ninja Turtles, nurses, etc.) with the timidity of Barak, to explore what makes a person heroic.

2. Tell of the heroism of some children who defended ten Jewish children hidden in their French school during the Nazi occupation. Claire H. Bishop, in *Twenty and Ten* (Penguin, 1978), tells of their brave response to soldiers who came while their teacher was gone.

3. *The Balancing Girl,* by Berniece Rabe (Dutton, 1981) describes how Martha, who happens to be in a wheelchair, makes $101.30 for the school carnival, doing what she can. What she does is set up an enormous maze of domino trails and sell chances. The winner gets to push over the domino that will set off the chain reaction.

God gives us abilities, money, and other resources to use.
Write about or draw some gifts that God has given you.

I, God, turn over to my servant, _____,

I expect these gifts to be used well.

Talk to God about your use of each gift on your list.

PROPER TWENTY-NINE
CHRIST THE KING

(Sunday between November 20 and 26 inclusive)

From a Child's Point of View

Here the church concludes one Christian year and looks forward to Advent-Christmas-Epiphany, with which the next year begins. Christ the King Sunday looks back over the whole story of God's revelation in Christ and looks forward to the consummation of that story. But this is beyond the comprehension of children. For them it is simply a Sunday to think about Jesus as the King, the ultimate power of the universe. Today's texts invite us to praise and serve Jesus, the King who chooses to be a shepherd. See Christ the King Sunday (Year C) for comments on children's view of kings in general.

Epistle: Ephesians 1:15-23. Paul's compound-complex sentences and long abstract words totally overwhelm children. There is no way they can follow the text as it is read. But its proclamation of Christ as King, and of ourselves as power-filled subjects of Christ, is the heart of today's texts.

If verses 20*b* through 22 are read separately, children can hear the proclamation of Jesus as King of the universe. Though they take that proclamation literally, they also grasp the truth that Christ is the absolute power of the universe. No power—not scary storms, not threatening military powers, not monsters that seem to lurk in the closet at night, not even people who make life hard for us—is as powerful as Christ the King.

When it is pointed out to them, children also appreciate God's wish to put that same great power to work in and through us. This means that as servants of this King, we are very powerful people. We have the power to love others as Jesus did, to care enough to heal the sick (using medical as well as prayer power), and to teach people God's ways. We need not be timid about doing the King's work. We can be brave and daring. For children to see themselves as the power-filled servants of Christ the King builds their Christian self-esteem.

Psalm: 100. Though the psalmist does not use the word *king,* the praises of this psalm are addressed to the King of the World. What is added to the Epistle description of the work of this king is his tender care for all people. The king is a shepherd. God, the shepherd king, has great appeal for children.

Gospel: Matthew 25:31-46. Though the text mentions shepherds, this passage describes Christ the King as a judge. To the basic question, How do we serve Christ the King? the answer is, We take care of "the least of these."

For children, "the least of these" includes the youngest child in any multiaged neighborhood group, all younger brothers or sisters (especially bothersome ones), the most ignored kids in the class, the kid who is always chosen last, and so forth. Children, especially idealistic older children, would prefer to care in dramatic ways for the starving, the homeless, the abused. But the King's orders are that we look around us and take care of those close at hand. Children need to hear that until they learn how to care for "the least ones" that they encounter every day, they will not be able to do much about the big problems—like hunger.

Old Testament: Ezekiel 34:11-16, 20-24. The mixture of national and shepherd images make this a difficult passage for children. The text does,

198

however, repeat the promise that God's King will care for the people as a shepherd cares for the sheep; it also offers a promise/warning that is of particular interest to children. That promise/warning is that the King not only will protect the sheep from outside enemies (wolves, fast running water, etc.), but also will protect the weaker sheep from the more aggressive sheep. With help, children can connect the "pushing with shoulder and flank" in verse 21 to their pushy attempts to grab attention or get their own way in their classes and activities. Children therefore learn that Christ the King insists that his subjects treat one another gently.

Watch Words

Watch your *shepherd* vocabulary. It is a foreign language for urban children, to whom *shepherds* are large dogs, and a *staff* is the group of paid people at the church or recreation center.

Let the Children Sing

"Rejoice, the Lord, Is King," "Come, Christians Join to Sing," "When Morning Gilds the Skies," and "From All That Dwell Below the Skies" praise Christ the King in short phrases and simple words. Their repeated choruses or phrases make them easy for nonreaders.

The spiritual "He Is King of Kings" can be sung by the congregation or by a children's class or choir.

As Thanksgiving approaches, children are studying about the pilgrims. "All People Who on Earth Do Dwell" sets Psalm 100 to music, in the style the pilgrims sang. So sing this hymn to recall that people in other times have also worshiped God the King.

Avoid the complex theological language of most shepherd hymns. If you focus on the shepherd King, sing the most familiar hymn version of Psalm 23.

The Liturgical Child

1. Read Ephesians 1:21-22 as the Call to Worship. Conclude the reading by saying, or by inviting the congregation to respond, "*Let us worship the King!*" The Good News Bible offers the clearest translation for children.

2. The short phrases and simple vocabulary of Psalm 100 invite responsive readings. Fifth- and sixth-graders can usually read along in the New Revised Standard or Good News translations. Third- and fourth-graders can read several lines with practice. The psalm can be read responsively by halves of the congregation, by congregation and choir, or by two children's classes.

3. Turn a section about Jesus from a familiar creed into a responsive affirmation of faith by asking the congregation to respond after each phrase: *Christ is King!* For example, in the Apostles' Creed:

> I believe in Jesus Christ, [God's] only Son our Lord,
> *Christ is King!*
> who was conceived by the Holy Ghost (Spirit)
> *Christ is King!*
> [who was] born of the Virgin Mary,
> *Christ is King!*
> [and so forth.]

4. See Christ the King Sunday (Year C) for a way to repeat the Lord's Prayer with emphasis on the last phrase.

Sermon Resources

1. Talk about the various symbols of several countries (e.g., an eagle for USA, a dragon for China). Describe the characteristics of the creature being claimed by each country. Then examine what we can learn about a king who chooses as his symbol not a fierce, strong animal, but a gentle shepherd who works hard and risks his life for his sheep. Talk about how such a king would act and what the subjects of that king would do.

2. Paraphrase Matthew 25:35-36. For example:

> I sat alone in the cafeteria, with little to eat,
> and you sat with me and shared your lunch.
> Kids laughed at my old clothes,
> but you treated me as if they were brand new.
> I was never chosen for any team,
> but when it was your turn to choose, you chose me.
> Everyone laughed at my mistakes,
> but you said kind words to make me feel better.
> When I stayed home, I thought no one would miss me,
> but you called me and asked when I would be back.

199

Listen carefully when **Matthew 25 : 31-46** is read.

Draw or list some of "the least of these" you meet every day. They may be children who are teased or ignored.

Write prayer-promises to God about each of them.

_____

_____

_____

_____

_____

_____

Keep your promises this week.

Draw a flag for Christ the King. Put a shepherd or a shepherd's tool on the flag.

Proper 29/ © 1992 by Abingdon Press.

THANKSGIVING

From a Child's Point of View

Running through all of today's texts is the understanding that both life and the world in which we live are gifts. For many adults and most children, this is not an easy concept to grasp. Adults tend to give thanks as the father did in the movie *Shenandoah*:

> Lord, we cleared this land, we plowed it, sowed it, and harvested it. We cooked the harvest. It wouldn't be here, and we wouldn't be eatin' if we hadn't done it all ourselves. We worked dog-bone hard for every crumb and morsel, but we thank you just the same, anyway, Lord, for this food we're about to eat. Amen.

Children whose basic needs are met tend to view that fact simply as the way things are. So the task at Thanksgiving is not to urge people to say, Thank you, but to help them see the world in a way that leads them to *be* thankful.

Old Testament: Deuteronomy 8:7-18. This passage must be understood from the perspective of the Israelites as they stood on the edge of the Promised Land. It assumes knowledge of what happened during the Exodus. If you have been preaching on these texts, children are prepared to hear Moses' reminder about what the world is like, and his warning about remembering that worldview. If you have not focused on Exodus this fall, children will need the message translated into more familiar situations. Native American declarations about our relationship to the earth can be particularly helpful.

Psalm: 65. This psalm, as a whole, is too complex and rich for children to follow. They will hear only occasional phrases that describe God's involvement with the world as they know it.

Epistle: II Corinthians 9:6-15. Paul's point here is that if we see our lives and the world as gifts from God and trust God to care for us, then we are free to be generous. We know that it is God, not ourselves, that ensures our security. Since few children worry about their ability to provide for themselves now or in the future, this point means little to them.

Children do, however, appreciate the reference to what we sow and reap. Older children can understand that just as people who diligently practice a sport or instrument will excel and therefore receive more enjoyment from the game or music, so people who practice sharing will find they have plenty to share and that sharing is a happy way to live.

Gospel: Luke 17:11-19. The story of the ten lepers is often told to children to remind them to say, Thank you. The story is not, however, about manners. The tenth leper expressed his thanks and praised God because he was not too busy thinking about what being healed meant for him personally to notice that Jesus had just done something marvelous. He simply had to stop to say, "Wow, God! You are incredible! Neat job! We are lucky that you are in charge of the world!" While the other nine knew only that they were cured, the tenth leper knew that God loves and cares for us and is at work in the world. This difference is not easy for children, who are naturally egocentric, to grasp. But if they will accept the challenge to be detectives, looking for signs of God's loving care in nature and in everyday events, they will develop the alert attitude of the tenth leper.

(See Proper 23, Year C, for further comments and suggestions.)

Watch Words

Do not assume that children know about the pain and isolation experienced by *lepers*.

It is easier for children to express *gratitude* than to talk about such feelings as *gratitude* or *being thankful*.

Let the Children Sing

"For the Beauty of the Earth," with its repeated chorus in which even nonreaders can join, is the best general Thanksgiving hymn for children. "Now Thank We All Our God" is second.

The simpler agricultural terms in "We Plow the Fields and Scatter" make it preferable to "Come, Ye Thankful People, Come."

Older children can read and enjoy the simple scientific language of "Thank You, God, for Water, Soil, and Air."

Remember that we no longer can count on schoolteachers to explain the obsolete vocabulary of such traditional Thanksgiving hymns as "We Gather Together to Ask the Lord's Blessing" and "Come, Ye Thankful People, Come."

The Liturgical Child

1. Link God's abundant gifts with our sharing: Spread a bountiful cornucopia of fruits and vegetables on a table at the center of the chancel, and surround the table with canned goods gathered for the food bank. Point out and ponder this connection during the sermon.

2. Set the Deuteronomy passage in context by inviting worshipers to imagine that they are among the Israelites, preparing to enter the Promised Land. Briefly remind them of some of the things that happened during the forty-year Exodus. Tell them that Moses has called them together for final instructions before they go into the new land. Then take on Moses' role and read the text with all the power Moses would have used in addressing the crowd.

3. After singing the Doxology at the usual time, interrupt to explain what we are saying when we sing it at that particular point during worship. Then invite the congregation to sing it again.

4. In your prayers, include children's Thanksgiving excitement about seeing grandparents or other relatives. Pray for safe trips, and for the patience and wisdom to avoid bickering in crowded backseats.

5. Check the Thanksgiving suggestions in other years of the lectionary cycle.

Sermon Resources

1. Paraphrase Moses' warning in a warning to your congregation in their current situation. When naming the blessings of "the Land," mention the blessings which children especially appreciate, as well as those adults value: Mention sports, specific foods (like pizza), even computer games that are interesting and fun. Describe how such things are God's gifts and remind people that these blessings are to be enjoyed according to God's guidelines. Describe the disasters that follow when people abuse their blessings (e.g., vacation trips that turn into feuds; fights that erupt over hoarded games and food).

2. To explore Paul's message, tell about Chris and Lee, two boys who went trick or treating together, but whose attitudes made their experiences very different.

a. After Halloween, Chris spread all his candy on his bed and counted every piece. There didn't seem to be much. It always looked as if the other kids ended up with more than he did. He ate a few pieces every day. He ate every piece all by himself. He could hardly believe that the candy did not even last until Thanksgiving.

b. After Halloween, Lee spread all his candy on his bed. It was a wonderful haul. He traded with his friends so that they all had more of their favorites. His pockets were full for a while. He gave some to his friends and they gave him some of theirs. He even gave a piece or two to his sister. He could hardly believe that it lasted until almost Thanksgiving.

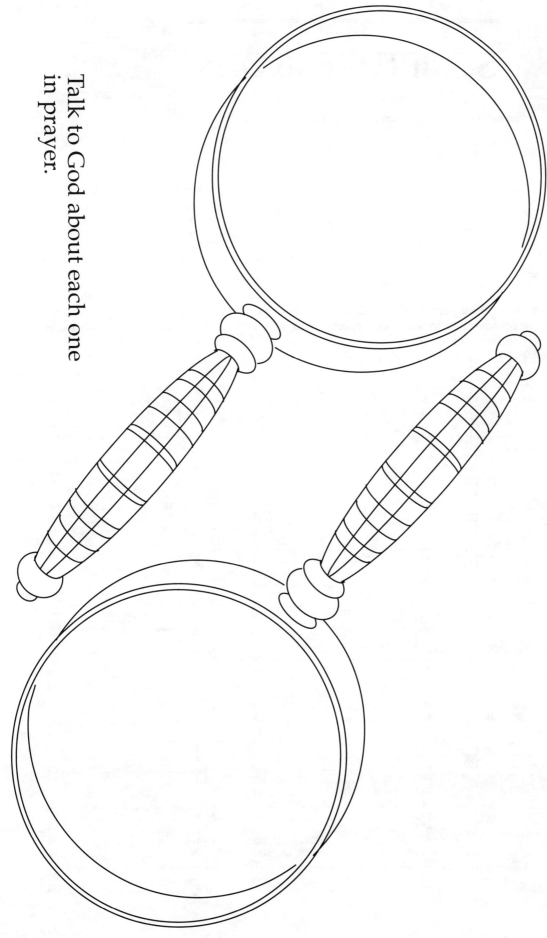

Be a Thanksgiving detective!

Draw or write in each detective's glass one clue that tells us
God loves us and takes care of us.

Talk to God about each one
in prayer.

Thanksgiving Day/ © 1992 by Abingdon Press.

SCRIPTURE INDEX

This index is provided especially for those who do not use the lectionary every week. The page numbers are those on which the commentary for each text appears. Read all the suggestions for the Sunday a text is featured to find the related worship suggestions.

TABLE OF LITURGICAL DATES
1992–1995

Year A, 1992–1993

Nov. 29	1st Sunday of Advent	May 20	Ascension Day
Dec. 6	2nd Sunday of Advent		*(Note: May 23 may be observed as Ascension Sunday.)*
Dec. 13	3rd Sunday of Advent	May 23	7th Sunday of Easter
Dec. 20	4th Sunday of Advent	May 30	Day of Pentecost
Dec. 24/25	Christmas Eve/Day	June 6	Trinity Sunday
Dec. 27	1st Sunday After Christmas	June 13	2nd Sunday After Pentecost
Jan. 1	New Year's Eve/Day	June 20	3rd Sunday After Pentecost
Jan. 3	2nd Sunday After Christmas	June 27	4th Sunday After Pentecost
Jan. 6	Epiphany	July 4	5th Sunday After Pentecost
	(Note: January 3 may be observed as Epiphany Sunday.)	July 11	6th Sunday After Pentecost
Jan. 10	Baptism of the Lord	July 18	7th Sunday After Pentecost
Jan. 17	2nd Sunday After the Epiphany	July 25	8th Sunday After Pentecost
Jan. 24	3rd Sunday After the Epiphany	Aug. 1	9th Sunday After Pentecost
Jan. 31	4th Sunday After the Epiphany	Aug. 8	10th Sunday After Pentecost
Feb. 7	5th Sunday After the Epiphany	Aug. 15	11th Sunday After Pentecost
Feb. 14	6th Sunday After the Epiphany	Aug. 22	12th Sunday After Pentecost
Feb. 21	Transfiguration	Aug. 29	13th Sunday After Pentecost
Feb. 24	Ash Wednesday	Sept. 5	14th Sunday After Pentecost
Feb. 28	1st Sunday in Lent	Sept. 12	15th Sunday After Pentecost
March 7	2nd Sunday in Lent	Sept. 19	16th Sunday After Pentecost
March 14	3rd Sunday in Lent	Sept. 26	17th Sunday After Pentecost
March 21	4th Sunday in Lent	Oct. 3	18th Sunday After Pentecost
March 28	5th Sunday in Lent	Oct. 10	19th Sunday After Pentecost
April 4	Passion/Palm Sunday	Oct. 17	20th Sunday After Pentecost
April 8	Holy Thursday	Oct. 24	21st Sunday After Pentecost
April 9	Good Friday	Oct. 31	22nd Sunday After Pentecost
April 11	Easter	Nov. 1	All Saints
April 18	2nd Sunday of Easter		*(Note: November 7 may be observed as All Saints Sunday.)*
April 25	3rd Sunday of Easter	Nov. 7	23rd Sunday After Pentecost
May 2	4th Sunday of Easter	Nov. 14	24th Sunday After Pentecost
May 9	5th Sunday of Easter	Nov. 21	Christ the King
May 16	6th Sunday of Easter	Nov. 25	Thanksgiving

Year B, 1993–1994

Nov. 28	1st Sunday of Advent		*(Note: May 15 may be observed as Ascension Sunday.)*
Dec. 5	2nd Sunday of Advent	May 15	7th Sunday of Easter
Dec. 12	3rd Sunday of Advent	May 22	Day of Pentecost
Dec. 19	4th Sunday of Advent	May 29	Trinity Sunday
Dec. 24/25	Christmas Eve/Day	June 5	2nd Sunday After Pentecost
Dec. 26	1st Sunday After Christmas	June 12	3rd Sunday After Pentecost
Jan. 1	New Year's Eve/Day	June 19	4th Sunday After Pentecost
Jan. 2	2nd Sunday After the Christmas	June 26	5th Sunday After Pentecost
Jan. 6	Epiphany	July 3	6th Sunday After Pentecost
(Note: January 2 may be observed as Epiphany Sunday.)		July 10	7th Sunday After Pentecost
Jan. 9	Baptism of the Lord	July 17	8th Sunday After Pentecost
Jan. 16	2nd Sunday After the Epiphany	July 24	9th Sunday After Pentecost
Jan. 23	3rd Sunday After the Epiphany	July 31	10th Sunday After Pentecost
Jan. 30	4th Sunday After the Epiphany	Aug. 7	11th Sunday After Pentecost
Feb. 6	5th Sunday After the Epiphany	Aug. 14	12th Sunday After Pentecost
Feb. 13	Transfiguration	Aug. 21	13th Sunday After Pentecost
Feb. 16	Ash Wednesday	Aug. 28	14th Sunday After Pentecost
Feb. 20	1st Sunday in Lent	Sept. 4	15th Sunday After Pentecost
Feb. 27	2nd Sunday in Lent	Sept. 11	16th Sunday After Pentecost
March 6	3rd Sunday in Lent	Sept. 18	17th Sunday After Pentecost
March 13	4th Sunday in Lent	Sept. 25	18th Sunday After Pentecost
March 20	5th Sunday in Lent	Oct. 2	19th Sunday After Pentecost
March 27	Passion/Palm Sunday	Oct. 9	20th Sunday After Pentecost
March 31	Holy Thursday	Oct. 16	21st Sunday After Pentecost
April 1	Good Friday	Oct. 23	22nd Sunday After Pentecost
April 3	Easter	Oct. 30	23rd Sunday After Pentecost
April 10	2nd Sunday of Easter	Nov. 1	All Saints
April 17	3rd Sunday of Easter	*(Note: November 6 may be observed as All Saints Sunday.)*	
April 24	4th Sunday of Easter	Nov. 6	24th Sunday After Pentecost
May 1	5th Sunday of Easter	Nov. 13	25th Sunday After Pentecost
May 8	6th sunday of Easter	Nov. 20	Christ the King
May 12	Ascension Day	Nov. 24	Thanksgiving

207

Year C, 1994–1995

Nov. 27	1st Sunday of Advent		May 25	Ascension Day
Dec. 4	2nd Sunday of Advent			*(Note: May 28 may be observed as Ascension Sunday.)*
Dec. 11	3rd Sunday of Advent		May 28	7th Sunday of Easter
Dec. 18	4th Sunday of Advent		June 4	Day of Pentecost
Dec. 24/25	Christmas Eve/Day		June 11	Trinity Sunday
Jan. 1	New Year's Eve/Day		June 18	2nd Sunday After Pentecost
	1st Sunday After Christmas		June 25	3rd Sunday After Pentecost
Jan. 6	Epiphany		July 2	4th Sunday After Pentecost
(Note: January 1 may be observed as Epiphany Sunday.)			July 9	5th Sunday After Pentecost
Jan. 8	Baptism of the Lord		July 16	6th Sunday After Pentecost
Jan. 15	2nd Sunday After the Epiphany		July 23	7th Sunday After Pentecost
Jan. 22	3rd Sunday After the Epiphany		July 30	8th Sunday After Pentecost
Jan. 29	4th Sunday After the Epiphany		Aug. 6	9th Sunday After Pentecost
Feb. 5	5th Sunday After the Epiphany		Aug. 13	10th Sunday After Pentecost
Feb. 12	6th Sunday After the Epiphany		Aug. 20	11th Sunday After Pentecost
Feb. 19	7th Sunday After the Epiphany		Aug. 27	12th Sunday After Pentecost
Feb. 26	Transfiguration		Sept. 3	13th Sunday After Pentecost
March 1	Ash Wednesday		Sept. 10	14th Sunday After Pentecost
March 5	1st Sunday in Lent		Sept. 17	15th Sunday After Pentecost
March 12	2nd Sunday in Lent		Sept. 24	16th Sunday After Pentecost
March 19	3rd Sunday in Lent		Oct. 1	17th Sunday After Pentecost
March 26	4th Sunday in Lent		Oct. 8	18th Sunday After Pentecost
April 2	5th Sunday in Lent		Oct. 15	19th Sunday After Pentecost
April 9	Passion/Palm Sunday		Oct. 22	20th Sunday After Pentecost
April 13	Holy Thursday		Oct. 29	21st Sunday After Pentecost
April 14	Good Friday		Nov. 1	All Saints
April 16	Easter		*(Note: Nov. 5 may be observed as All Saints Sunday.)*	
April 23	2nd Sunday of Easter		Nov. 5	22nd Sunday After Pentecost
April 30	3rd Sunday of Easter		Nov. 12	23rd Sunday After Pentecost
May 7	4th Sunday of Easter		Nov. 19	Christ the King
May 14	5th Sunday of Easter		Nov. 23	Thanksgiving
May 21	6th Sunday of Easter			